Illicit Enrichment

A Guide to
Laws Targeting
Unexplained
Wealth

This work was funded by the core donor group of the International Centre for Asset Recovery in 2020–2021: the Government of Jersey, Principality of Liechtenstein, Norwegian Agency for Development Cooperation (Norad), Swiss Agency for Development and Cooperation (SDC) and UK Foreign, Commonwealth & Development Office (FCDO).

Contents

Acknowledgements

I owe a significant amount of gratitude to the NYU School of Law's LLM Pro Bono Research Program administered by Miriam Eckenfels-Garcia and Shirley Wu, and in particular, the hours of research put in by my extraordinary research team, consisting of Aastha Bajaj, Alejandro Jose Cervantes Enamorado, Anna Trine Raudsepp, Apoorva Ahuja, Di Zhao, Doris Matu, Filippo Ciani, Guilherme Donega, Lu Zhang, Lucas Siyang Lim, Mario Cistaro, Minchi Huang, Qiuling Huang, Shiwen Li and Weili Chi. Without this incredible amount of support, this book would not have been possible.

I also owe special thanks to my colleagues at the Basel Institute on Governance for the support they've provided over the entire process, including Jonathan Spicer and Stephen Ratcliffe (for the time they put into reviewing and editing drafts), Chantal Weigert (for her many hours of assistance in researching, reviewing, editing and translating), Monica Guy (for her thorough review and finalisation of the advanced drafts), Shane McLean (for her creative efforts regarding the design and layout of the publication) and Peter Huppertz (for his assistance in creating the database of illicit enrichment laws on LEARN). I also very much appreciate the support I received from Iman Alwan, Oscar Solórzano, Diana Cordero, and Phyllis Atkinson.

My sincere thanks also go to the practitioners who agreed to provide contributions for the book, including Phillip G. Kagucia, Preeya Raghoonundun, Dr. Alcides Chinchay, Francis H. Cassidy, and Jonathan Spicer (again).

I must also sincerely thank Jason Sharman, J.C. Weliamuna, and Martin Polaine for agreeing to peer review my work, and for providing constructive comments on how it could be improved.

And last but not least I'd like to thank my partner Leïla for her support (and tolerance) of my overabundant illicit enrichment-related conversation starters during the last year and a half.

Andrew Dornbierer

Acronyms and abbreviations

ACECA	Anti-Corruption and Economic Crimes Act 2003 (Kenya)
ACHPR	African Charter on Human and Peoples' Rights
ACHR	American Convention on Human Rights
AUCPCC	African Union Convention on Preventing and Combating Corruption
EACC	Ethics and Anti-Corruption Commission (Kenya)
ECHR	European Convention on Human Rights
ECtHR	European Court of Human Rights
GGIR	Good Governance and Integrity Reporting Act 2015 (Mauritius)
IACAC	Inter-American Convention Against Corruption
MLA	Mutual Legal Assistance
ICCPR	International Covenant on Civil and Political Rights
NCB	non-conviction based (confiscation/forfeiture)
UDHR	Universal Declaration of Human Rights
UK	United Kingdom
UNCAC	United Nations Convention Against Corruption
US	United States of America
UWO	Unexplained Wealth Order

Introduction

It is notoriously challenging for law enforcement agencies to identify and recover proceeds of crime. In the modern and globalised economy, criminal proceeds can be laundered almost instantly, through a variety of different forms, and across borders with ease. In cash-heavy economies, hard currencies can be easily converted and transferred quickly between parties without leaving any significant or lasting record.

This challenge of recovering proceeds of crime is exacerbated in the context of corruption. Corruption offences are a difficult category of crime to identify and investigate – in most cases they occur as part of a conspiracy between two or more willing parties and therefore there is no immediate and obvious victim who can make a complaint. Thus, a significant amount of corruption remains undetected, and the criminal parties are able to enjoy and benefit from the proceeds of their corruption.

Dozens of jurisdictions around the world have sought to specifically target these challenges by introducing illicit enrichment legislation that focuses on the obvious and demonstrable results of corruption and criminality, rather than the original criminal action itself. These laws allow investigators and prosecutors to instead recover assets that have clearly not come from lawful sources without having to prove, to either a criminal or civil standard of proof, the initial criminal action that gave rise to these proceeds.

As noted below, and as will be noted several times throughout this publication, illicit enrichment is a controversial area of law. Nonetheless, as demonstrated by the existing jurisprudence, this does not automatically mean that the introduction and application of illicit enrichment laws are incompatible with established legal principles. On the contrary, if introduced and applied in a reasonable way, illicit enrichment laws have been deemed by courts in many countries as fair and effective tools for the combating of corruption and the recovery of proceeds of crime.

In this vein, this publication offers a thorough overview and examination of the concept of illicit enrichment with the objective of providing policy guidance to potential drafters of illicit enrichment laws, and technical guidance to law enforcement practitioners and courts charged with applying these laws.

A controversial legal concept

Illicit enrichment invokes an extremely varied array of opinions. While some view it as a critical tool in the combating of corruption and other crimes and the recovery of assets, others view it as a violation of common legal principles. Any attempt to introduce illicit enrichment laws in a country often results in a heavily polarised legislative debate.

The reason for this is as follows: Illicit enrichment laws allow courts to sanction a person for acquiring or enjoying an amount of wealth which has not, or cannot, be explained by reference to lawful sources of income – and this can be done without the court being satisfied, to either a civil or criminal standard, that a separate or underlying criminal action has taken place.

These laws deviate somewhat from traditional legal thinking, and it is therefore not surprising that any efforts to introduce these types of laws will often spark fierce debate.

An illustrative and symbolic example of the polarising effect that this legal concept has is contained in the *Travaux Préparatoires*[1] of the United Nations Convention Against Corruption (UNCAC), which outlines the negotiation process behind the inclusion of Article 20 on 'Illicit Enrichment'. When options for a proposed Article on illicit enrichment were introduced to the negotiating committee, a number of delegations quickly expressed substantial concerns, with Russia and the member states of the European Union even going so far as to state their 'strong wish' to delete the proposed Article from the treaty altogether. At the other end of the spectrum, other delegations adamantly supported the Article. Consequently, following several sessions of negotiation, an agreement was made: Article 20 would be adopted, but only in a non-mandatory form.

The divergent attitudes towards this legal concept have also been clearly reflected in the different approaches taken by jurisdictions in response to this non-mandatory recommendation. On the one hand, dozens of States Parties to the UNCAC have implemented the Article and introduced illicit enrichment legislation. On the other hand, other States Parties have stood resolute in their objection to the legal concept, and their courts have even refused to provide international cooperation in asset recovery efforts that have been launched on the basis of illicit enrichment laws in other countries.

Even amongst countries that have adopted illicit enrichment laws, there is disagreement on the actual form that such laws should take. Consequently, legislation on the concept has been drafted in remarkably varied and diverse designs throughout the world. For example, while some countries consider illicit enrichment as an act that should be dealt with criminally, others have instead legislated that it should be dealt with under civil procedures. Moreover, while some countries believe that illicit enrichment laws should only target public officials and corruption, other countries believe that these types of laws are valuable in the combating of other crimes, such as drug-related offences. Even the basic terminology surrounding the concept is a point of disagreement, with many countries using alternative terms to describe and define it in their legislation, such as 'unexplained wealth' or 'unjust enrichment'.

The differing attitudes and opinions are also amplified by the fact that to date, illicit enrichment largely remains an untested and underdeveloped area of law. While some states had already introduced illicit enrichment laws in the 1950s and 1960s, only a very limited number of countries had an illicit enrichment law on their statute books up until the turn of the century.

---

1   United Nations Office of Drugs and Crime, *Travaux Préparatoires of the negotiations for the elaboration of the United Nations Convention against Corruption*, United Nations, New York, 2010, pp.195-200.

Dozens of additional countries have introduced illicit enrichment legislation in the past two decades, yet there still exists a significant amount of uncertainty amongst practitioners surrounding how these laws should be applied. Consequently, many countries have been tentative in using them. For example, while an illicit enrichment law has existed in Tanzania since 2007, the first court proceedings concerning these provisions were only commenced in 2019.

As a result of this tentative utilisation of illicit enrichment laws as a whole, there is a general shortage of jurisprudence and legal experience on this issue. Consequently the continued debate surrounding the effectiveness of illicit enrichment laws and their overall compatibility with established legal norms is understandable.

In light of the overall underdeveloped nature of illicit enrichment legislation, this publication falls short of recommending these laws as a 'silver bullet' solution in the fight against corruption and other crimes. There are many intricacies regarding the concept that are yet to be properly tested in courts and it is still important to approach the area of illicit enrichment law with some caution. Nonetheless, there is also no doubt that illicit enrichment laws have remarkable potential in the field of asset recovery. Following the successful application of these types of laws in a number of jurisdictions, it is no surprise that an increasing number of countries are turning to these mechanisms to target corruption and criminality in general, and recover proceeds of crime.

Structure of this book

This publication is made up of five parts. **Part 1** draws from international treaties and legislation from around the world to provide a basic definition of the core concept of illicit enrichment, as well as an overview of what constitutes an 'illicit enrichment law'. It outlines the difference between criminal law-based and civil law-based illicit enrichment laws. It also explains the difference between regular illicit enrichment laws and qualified illicit enrichment laws, which require a state to prove a threshold of reasonable 'suspicion' or 'belief' before they can be applied. This part also discusses the characteristics that distinguish an illicit enrichment law from other common types of asset recovery legislation, such as extended confiscation laws and non-conviction based confiscation laws.

Part 2 provides an in-depth overview of the various approaches taken by legislative bodies in different jurisdictions to address illicit enrichment. It covers the key similarities and differences between illicit enrichment laws from different jurisdictions, outlining how legislators from different countries have drafted their laws to target different categories of wealth and people. It explores how some jurisdictions have included different evidential thresholds regarding such things as the value of the alleged enrichment. This Part also outlines the types of safeguards that have been introduced by countries with illicit enrichment laws to ensure that these laws are applied fairly, are not abused, and are reviewed on a regular basis. This Part should be read in conjunction with Annex 1, which is a compilation of 98 illicit enrichment laws and a number of other legislative instruments similar to these types of laws.

Part 3 provides guidance to investigators and prosecutors on how illicit enrichment can be, and has been, proven or disproven. It includes a summary of the fundamental facts of illicit enrichment that need to be established by the concerned parties in either criminal or civil courts. It also examines the common methodologies that have been accepted and adopted by courts around the world to determine whether illicit enrichment has occurred. Furthermore, drawing on jurisprudence from different jurisdictions, this Part outlines the common types of evidence that have been used by investigators and prosecutors to effectively prove that a person or entity has benefited from illicit enrichment.

Part 4 provides guidance to legal practitioners on the common legal challenges that arise regarding the adoption and use of illicit enrichment legislation. Specifically, this section examines common legal challenges that have been lodged throughout the world, particularly with reference to established rights such as the presumption of innocence, the right to remain silent, the privilege against self-incrimination and the principle against the retroactive application of laws.

Finally, **Part 5** consists of external contributions. Three of these overviews provide practitioner insights into the illicit enrichment mechanisms in Mauritius, Kenya and Peru, from the point of view of local practitioners. Another contribution provides a brief overview of the unique proceeds of crime-focused mechanism currently operating in Ireland. The final contribution analyses the challenges that may arise during the investigation and prosecution of illicit enrichment cases with an international element, and specifically the problems practitioners may need to anticipate when seeking mutual legal assistance in this context.

The publication is also accompanied by two annexes:

Annex 1, 'A Compilation of Illicit Enrichment Legislation and Other Relevant Legislation', contains excerpts of text from all the illicit enrichment laws that were identified in the research process behind this publication. It also includes excerpts from text of the other asset recovery legislative instruments that are mentioned in this publication for comparative purposes.

Annex 2, 'Proving Illicit Enrichment Using Financial Investigations and Source and Application of Funds Analysis' is a technical guide for practitioners. It provides an overview of one method that can be used to clearly demonstrate that a person has enjoyed wealth that could not possibly have been derived from lawful sources, namely the Source and Application of Funds Analysis method. It includes a step-by-step guide to the financial investigation that should be used to inform this analysis process.

A note on definitions and research methodology

Research for this publication was conducted by the author, additional staff from the Basel Institute on Governance and a team of fifteen New York University law masters students through the NYU LLM Pro Bono Research Program. Using a wide range of sources (including government websites and databases, legal databases, academic publications, NGO and international organisation reports and media sources) researchers sought to identify each and every jurisdiction in which an illicit enrichment law or a similar type of law has been enacted. Researchers also sought to identify reported judicial decisions regarding these laws to provide further clarity on how they are applied in practice.

The initial parameters for research were broad, and researchers focused on all types of laws that enabled a court to potentially impose sanctions where the legal sources for a person's wealth were not established. These parameters obviously meant that a number of other types of asset recovery laws fell within the scope of the research, including traditional civil recovery laws and extended confiscation laws. This was intentional however, as it facilitated the analysis of a wide range of relevant legislative material, so as to:

- Identify potential universal features that distinguish 'illicit enrichment laws' from other existing asset recovery focused mechanisms; and

- Guide the creation of a definition of 'illicit enrichment' and an 'illicit enrichment law' that would enable a much more universal understanding of the concept.

Following the analysis of the material collected during this research process, the act of illicit enrichment has been defined in this publication as **the enjoyment of an amount of wealth that is not justified through reference to lawful income**. A further explanation and justification of this definition is contained in Section 1.2.

The purpose of creating a universal definition for the act of 'illicit enrichment' was to provide clarity to a topic where there are multiple definitions and phrases that are being used to refer to the same concept. For instance, terms such as 'illicit enrichment', 'unexplained wealth' and 'unjust enrichment' are currently being used interchangeably to refer to the exact same, or an incredibly similar, set of circumstances. Consequently, this publication has sought to reduce existing ambiguities and add an element of consistency by outlining a basic universal definition of the concept that encompasses the widest possible number of interpretations present in international treaties, domestic legislation and academic publications.

In addition to guiding the drafting of a definition for the act of illicit enrichment, the analysis of the collated material also facilitated the formulation of a definition for the concept of an 'illicit enrichment law'. Within this publication, 'illicit enrichment laws' are laws that fall within the following parameters:

- They **empower a court to impose a criminal or civil sanction if they are satisfied that the act of illicit enrichment has taken place** (in accordance with the above definition of illicit enrichment).

- They **do not specify that a separate or underlying criminal activity needs to be established before the sanction can be imposed.**

As will be demonstrated in this text, the form of illicit enrichment laws varies enormously throughout the world. Despite these variations, these laws all share key commonalities, and permit the imposition of final legal consequences if the exact same, or an incredibly similar, set of facts is demonstrated to a court. This is regardless of whether the law itself is based in criminal or civil procedure.

The creation of the above parameters is based on the thorough analysis of legislation and judicial decisions from over 100 countries and facilitated in the assessment of exactly which laws should be included in a broad discussion regarding illicit enrichment. The parameters are based on a universal set of features that exist in identified 'illicit enrichment laws' that, crucially, distinguish them from other existing types of 'proceeds of crime' focused legislation.

Admittedly, this is a wider set of parameters than those that have been used in previous publications – which usually limit the phrase 'illicit enrichment law' to those laws that take the form of a criminal offence. However, as both the criminal and civil forms of laws discussed in this publication permit a court to impose sanctions if the broad definition of the act of illicit enrichment is established, then for the sake of ensuring that all relevant laws are taken into account in the discussion of this concept, this publication has set these wider parameters.

To provide consistency and clarity throughout the publication however, further sub-categories of illicit enrichment laws have also been outlined and relevant laws have additionally been classified as either 'criminal illicit enrichment laws' or 'civil illicit enrichment laws' depending on whether they are based in criminal or civil procedure.[2] Additionally, other laws have been classified as 'qualified illicit enrichment laws' if they contain particular thresholds relating to a reasonable suspicion or reasonable belief that criminality of some sort has occurred.[3] The creation of these sub-categories seeks to further highlight the key similarities and differences that exist within laws that fall under the broad term of 'illicit enrichment law' and to further reduce any ambiguities that may arise in future discussions on this topic.

As a final note it is also important to highlight that the classification of some countries' laws as 'illicit enrichment laws' or 'qualified illicit enrichment laws' in this publication has been

---

2   A further justification for the selection of the term 'civil illicit enrichment laws' rather than 'unexplained wealth laws' is contained in Section 1.3.

3   A detailed explanation of the term 'qualified illicit enrichment laws' is contained in Section 1.4.2.

made as accurately as possible based on the wording of identified legislative instruments as well as any information contained in identified judicial decisions. Of course, the actual application of laws will often depend on how certain legal regulations further clarify different elements of a law, or how a state's judiciary interprets certain phrases within the law itself. Every effort has been made to locate existing regulations and judicial interpretations of the laws included in this publication. However, it is also possible that some relevant regulations or critical elements of interpretation have not been taken into account, particularly if such material was not available through online sources. If new information comes to light following publication, every effort will be made to correct any inaccuracies.

Part 1

Defining an illicit enrichment law

Part 1 Summary

It is important to note from the outset that the definition of 'illicit enrichment' varies significantly from jurisdiction to jurisdiction.

The name 'illicit enrichment' isn't even a universal term, and depending on the country the concept may be referred to as such things as 'illegal enrichment', 'illicit gain', 'unjust enrichment', or the acquisition of 'unexplained wealth' or 'unexplained property'.

Similarly, the scope of what constitutes the act of 'illicit enrichment' can vary significantly between jurisdictions depending on different characteristics that an individual jurisdiction may have included in their law. Unsurprisingly, there is a general lack of consistency in publications and discussions on the topic, and consequently there is a significant amount of confusion amongst practitioners as to what 'illicit enrichment' actually refers to.

To address this, this Part:

- Explains the historical context behind the concept of illicit enrichment;

- Provides a basic, and universally applicable, definition for the act of 'illicit enrichment';

- Outlines what constitutes an 'illicit enrichment law' and explains the difference between 'criminal illicit enrichment laws' and 'civil illicit enrichment laws', as well as regular illicit enrichment laws and 'qualified illicit enrichment laws'; and

- Demonstrates the difference between illicit enrichment laws and other common asset recovery mechanisms.

Summary of definitions of key concepts (further explanations contained in Part 1)

Illicit Enrichment	The enjoyment of an amount of wealth that is not justified through reference to lawful income.
'Enjoyment of an amount of wealth'	The acquisition, receipt or use of something of pecuniary value.
'Not justified through reference to lawful income'	An absence of evidence that demonstrates the legitimate or non-criminal sources from which the enjoyed wealth was derived.
Illicit enrichment law	Any provision in a statutory instrument that empowers a court to impose a criminal or civil sanction if they are satisfied that illicit enrichment has taken place (in accordance with the definition above) and that does not specify a need to establish a separate or underlying criminal activity before this sanction can be imposed.
Criminal illicit enrichment law	Any illicit enrichment law that constitutes a criminal offence, is applied according to criminal procedures, and attracts criminal punishments.
Civil illicit enrichment law	Any illicit enrichment law that takes the form of a civil order process, is applied according to civil procedures, and may result in a compensatory-type order against a person.
Qualified illicit enrichment law	Laws that would fall within the definition of an illicit enrichment law above, but for the fact that they require a state to provide evidence to a court of a 'reasonable suspicion' or a 'reasonable belief' that some sort of underlying or separate criminality has taken place.

1.1   Historical context

As explained anecdotally in *On the Take – Criminalizing Illicit Enrichment to Fight Corruption*, one of the first attempts to pass a bill on the concept of 'illicit enrichment' was made by a 1930s Argentinian congressman, Rodolfo Corominas Segura, after being inspired by an encounter he had with a public official who openly displayed an amount of wealth that could not possibly have come from his official salary.[4] While this initial attempt failed in Argentina, successful efforts to legislate against illicit enrichment slowly appeared in a number of countries around the world over the following decades.

In the early 1950s, Hong Kong introduced a regulation that outlined disciplinary offences for public officials that could not explain how they managed to own assets or maintain a standard of living that was disproportionate to their official salaries.[5] This law would be the precursor to Hong Kong's actual illicit enrichment law, which came into force in 1971. In 1955, the Philippines introduced their first version of an illicit enrichment law, under which property held by a public official that was 'manifestly out of proportion' to their lawful income was 'presumed prima facie to have been unlawfully acquired' unless the person explained, to the 'satisfaction of the court' how the property in question had been derived from lawful sources.[6] In 1960, Pakistan inserted an illicit enrichment criminal offence into their Prevention of Corruption Act, under which the 'possession of property disproportionate to known sources of income' could result in imprisonment, fines and the confiscation of property.[7] Meanwhile in 1964, India enacted a law of their own, as did Argentina, which finally managed to introduce the concept of illicit enrichment onto their statutory books more than twenty years after Rodolfo Corominas Segura's first attempt.[8]

Building upon this slow and steady momentum, a number of additional countries brought in legislation over the following two decades. Egypt introduced a law in 1975 which described 'any increase in wealth' by a public official that is 'not proportional with [their] resources' as an 'illegal gain'.[9] Sénégal passed a law in 1981 which specified illicit enrichment as a situation where a public official 'is unable to prove the lawful origin of the resources that enable him to be in

---

4   L. Muzila et al., *On the Take: Criminalizing Illicit Enrichment to Fight Corruption*, The World Bank, Washington, 2012, p.7.

5   I. McWalters SC et al., *Bribery and Corruption Law in Hong Kong*, LexisNexis, Hong Kong, 2015, pp. 381–382.

6   Republic Act No. 1379, An Act Declaring Forfeiture in Favor of the State Any Property Found to have been Unlawfully Acquired by any Public Officer or Employee and Providing for the Proceedings Therefor (18 June 1955) (Philippines).

7   The Prevention Of Corruption (West Pakistan Amendment) Ordinance 1960 (W.P. Ordinance XVII of 1960), Section 2; This Section inserted Section 5C into the Prevention of Corruption Act 1947 (Pakistan).

8   L. Muzila et al., *On the Take: Criminalizing Illicit Enrichment to Fight Corruption*, The World Bank, Washington, 2012, p.8.

9   Law no. 62 of 1975, Regarding Illegal Gains (Egypt), Article 2.

possession of property or to lead a lifestyle unrelated to his lawful income'.[10] Brunei Darussalam passed a law in 1982, reflecting the model introduced in neighbouring Hong Kong and outlining an offence for the 'possession of unexplained property', whereby a public official that controls property or maintains a standard of living that is disproportionate to their lawful income could face potential criminal sanctions.[11] Laws were also drafted and passed in countries such as Cuba,[12] Turkey[13] and Niger.[14]

In 1996, international recognition for the concept of illicit enrichment took a substantial step forward when the Inter-American Convention Against Corruption (IACAC) became the first convention to include illicit enrichment under Article IX, describing the concept as 'a significant increase in the assets of a government official that he cannot reasonably explain in relation to his lawful earnings during the performance of his functions...'.[15]

In 2003, the African Union Convention on Preventing and Combating Corruption (AUCPCC) became the second convention to include a provision on illicit enrichment. It similarly described the concept under Article 1 as: '...the significant increase in the assets of a public official or any other person which he or she cannot reasonably explain in relation to his or her income'.[16]

Finally, in the same year, the UNCAC also included a provision on illicit enrichment in 2003, outlining in Article 20 that:

> *Subject to its constitution and the fundamental principles of its legal system, each State Party shall consider adopting such legislative and other measures as may be necessary to establish as a criminal offence, when committed intentionally, illicit enrichment, that is, a significant increase in the assets of a public official that he or she cannot reasonably explain in relation to his or her lawful income.*[17]

---

10   [Unofficial translation] Code Pénal, Loi No 1965-60 (Sénégal), Article 163 bis (Original text: 'De l'enrichissement illicite: L'enrichissement illicite de tout titulaire d'un mandat public électif ou d'une fonction gouvernementale, de tout magistrat, agent civil ou militaire de l'Etat, ou d'une collectivité publique, d'une personne revêtue d'un mandat public, d'un dépositaire public ou d'un officier public ou ministériel, d'un dirigeant ou d'un agent de toute nature des établissements publics, des sociétés nationales, des sociétés d'économie mixte soumises de plein droit au contrôle de l'Etat, des personnes morales de droit privé bénéficiant du concours financier de la puissance publique, des ordres professionnels, des organismes privés chargés de l'exécution d'un service public, des associations ou fondations reconnues d'utilité publique, est puni d'un emprisonnement de cinq à dix ans et d'une amende au moins égale au montant de l'enrichissement et pouvant être portée au double de ce montant. Le délit d'enrichissement illicite est constitué lorsque, sur simple mise en demeure, une des personnes désignées ci-dessus, se trouve dans l'impossibilité de justifier de l'origine licite des ressources qui lui permettent d'être en possession d'un patrimoine ou de mener un train de vie sans rapport avec ses revenus légaux.').

11   Prevention of Corruption Act 1982 (Brunei Darussalam), Section 12.

12   Ley no. 62, Código Penal de la República de Cuba, de 29.12.1987.

13   Law on Declaration of Assets and Combat against Bribery, Law No. 3628 (Acceptance date 19.4.1990) (Turkey).

14   Ordonnance no. 92-024 du 18 Juin 1992 portant répression de l'enrichissement illicite (Niger).

15   Inter-American Convention Against Corruption, Article IX.

16   African Union Convention on Preventing and Combating Corruption, Article 1.

17   United Nations Convention Against Corruption, Article 20.

While the IACAC was the only international convention to use mandatory language when outlining illicit enrichment,[18] the inclusion of illicit enrichment in these three conventions still sparked an exponential increase in the prevalence of illicit enrichment laws throughout the world.

As more jurisdictions introduced these types of laws, they did so in progressively more varied ways. Notably, while illicit enrichment laws were predominantly drafted in the form of criminal offences up until the turn of the century,[19] an increased number of countries started to implement illicit enrichment laws based in civil procedure – under which the act of illicit enrichment was no longer viewed as an offence but as grounds for a civil compensatory-type order against a person for the value of the proven enrichment. For instance in 2000, one of Australia's state-level jurisdictions,[20] Western Australia, introduced 'unexplained wealth declarations', under which the court can now order that the value of a person's wealth in excess of their 'lawfully acquired wealth' be paid to the state.[21] This law was a significant deviation from the norm for two reasons. Firstly, because it is based in civil procedure, and secondly, because it can be used to target not only public officials for corruption-related proceeds, but 'any person' that possessed unexplainable wealth. In fact, the primary intention of the law was to target proceeds of crime held by drug traffickers.[22]

Amongst the dozens of other countries that have brought in illicit enrichment laws to date are Kenya (which introduced a civil-based order targeting 'unexplained assets' in 2007 into their anti-corruption legislation),[23] Cambodia (which legislated to target increases in wealth of public officials that could not be explained 'in comparison to his or her legal income'),[24] Djibouti (where 'the fact that a public official cannot reasonably justify the substantial increase of his assets in relation to his legitimate income is now punishable by fifteen years'

---

18   While mandatory language is used in Article IX – which states that each State Party 'shall take the necessary measures to establish under its laws' an offence of illicit enrichment – Article IX also includes a limitation whereby such actions may be '[s]ubject to its Constitution and the fundamental principles of its legal system' – arguably nullifying the mandatory nature of the language used.

19   With the notable exception of the Republic Act No. 1379, An Act Declaring Forfeiture in Favor of the State Any Property Found to have been Unlawfully Acquired by any Public Officer or Employee and Providing for the Proceedings Therefor (18 June 1955) (Philippines).

20   Australia is a federal-type legal system and is made up of nine separate legal jurisdictions that exist in parallel with one another: one federal jurisdiction and eight state/territory jurisdictions.

21   Criminal Property Confiscation Act 2000 (Australia - Western Australia), Section 12.

22   Western Australia, *Parliamentary Debates*, Legislative Assembly, 29 June 2000, 8611 (Mr Baron Sullivan - Parliamentary Secretary); See for example the following excerpt from the second reading speech: 'The drug trade has flourished under the deficiencies within the current system. The heads of drug rings continue to operate while the authorities lack evidence to tie their retained wealth to criminal activities. Furthermore, as the burden of proof lies with the authorities, it has been difficult to prove a relationship between unexplained wealth and criminal conduct. Without an effective confiscation system the profit has remained in the drug trade. This new era of organised crime requires a more effective and better targeted approach, underpinned by a strong statutory framework, to confiscation of proceeds of criminal activity and property used in criminal activity.'.

23   Anti-Corruption and Economic Crimes Act 2003 (Kenya), Section 55.

24   Anti-Corruption Law 2010 (Cambodia), Article 36.

imprisonment'),[25] Ecuador (where someone who has 'obtained for themselves or for third parties an unjustified increase in wealth' may be punishable under the Criminal Code),[26] Moldova (where public officials may be criminally punished if they are found to hold assets of a value that 'substantially exceeds the acquired income' and which 'could not have been legally obtained'),[27] and eight other Australian jurisdictions, which have each introduced their own version of civil orders targeting 'unexplained' wealth.[28]

In total, 98 illicit enrichment laws were identified during research for this publication that are currently in force around the world.[29]

---

25   [Unofficial translation] Loi N° 111/AN/11/6ème L relative à la lutte contre le terrorisme et autres infractions graves (25.05.2011) (Djibouti), Article 11 (Original text: 'Le fait pour un agent public de ne pouvoir raisonnablement justifier l'augmentation substantielle de son patrimoine par rapport à ses revenus légitimes, est puni de 15 ans d'emprisonnement de 5.000.000 FD d'amende.').

26   [Unofficial translation] Código Orgánico Integral Penal de la República de Ecuador, de 10.02.2014, Artículo 279 (Original text: 'Las o los servidores públicos y las personas que actúen en virtud de una potestad estatal en alguna de las instituciones del Estado, determinadas en la Constitución de la República, que hayan obtenido para sí o para terceros un incremento patrimonial injustificado a su nombre o mediante persona interpuesta, producto de su cargo o función, superior a cuatrocientos salarios básicos unificados del trabajador en general, serán sancionados con pena privativa de libertad de siete a diez años.').

27   Criminal Code 2002 (as amended by the Criminal Law 326 as of 23.12.13) (Moldova), Article 330/2.

28   Proceeds of Crime Act 2002 (Australia - Federal), Part 2-6; Confiscation of Criminal Assets Act 2003 (as amended by the Confiscation of Criminal Assets (Unexplained Wealth) Amendment Act 2020) (Australia - Australian Capital Territory), Part 7A; Criminal Assets Recovery Act 1990 No 23 (Australia - New South Wales), Part 3, Division 2; Criminal Property Forfeiture Act 2002 (Australia - Northern Territory), Part 6, Division 1; Criminal Proceeds Confiscation Act 2002 (as amended by the Criminal Proceeds Confiscation (Unexplained Wealth and Serious Drug Offender Confiscation Order) Amendment Act 2013) (Australia - Queensland), Part 5A; Serious and Organised Crime (Unexplained Wealth) Act 2009 (Australia - South Australia), Part 2; Crime (Confiscation of Profits) Act 1993 (as amended 2014)(Australia - Tasmania), Part 9; Confiscation Act 1997 (as amended 2014)(Australia - Victoria), Part 4A.

29   Including 'qualified illicit enrichment laws' (which are explained in Section 1.4.2).

1.2   Defining the act of 'illicit enrichment'

Despite the fact that illicit enrichment has now become a widely adopted legal concept, there is still a significant amount of uncertainty amongst practitioners over what the concept actually refers to. This is understandable, as there is no unanimously applied definition of illicit enrichment and the actual form, wording and practical operation of illicit enrichment laws around the world vary significantly from jurisdiction to jurisdiction.

While UNCAC does provide some guidance in this regard, even the wording of Article 20 cannot be considered a universal definition of illicit enrichment, as many countries with illicit enrichment laws have taken markedly different approaches to UNCAC when defining the concept in their own jurisdictions. For instance, while UNCAC classifies illicit enrichment as the 'intentional' and 'significant' increase of the assets of a 'public official' that cannot be explained in relation to his or her lawful income, many jurisdictions take a much broader interpretation of the concept and do not necessarily specify that the enrichment needs to be 'intentional' or 'significant', or that it can only be committed by public officials.

In light of the significant variance in legislative wording around the world, a universal definition of illicit enrichment (or 'unjust enrichment' or the 'acquisition of unexplained wealth', etc.) should be much wider to accommodate these broader approaches.

Based on the examination of definitions provided by 98 laws, it can be argued that the act of illicit enrichment can be stripped down to two broad fundamental components that are present in some form in all legislative interpretations, regardless of jurisdiction. Specifically, at its most basic level, the act of illicit enrichment can be broadly defined as **the enjoyment of an amount of wealth that is not justified through reference to lawful income**.

Of course, how these two underlined phrases are specifically legislated for and applied will often vary substantially depending on the individual interpretation of a jurisdiction and the scope of the definitions of 'wealth' and 'income' outlined in its laws. Moreover, the type of 'person' that may be liable for an act of illicit enrichment will of course vary depending on whether a particular law targets all people or a limited category of persons, such as public officials.

1.2.1   What is meant by "the enjoyment of an amount of wealth"?

In the context of illicit enrichment 'the enjoyment of an amount of wealth' refers to the acquisition, receipt or use of something of **pecuniary value**.

The specific things that a person can acquire, receive or use which may contribute to a person's illicit enrichment change significantly from one jurisdiction to the next. Many jurisdictions only legislate for a limited definition of illicit enrichment, and only take into account situations in which someone has acquired traditional tangible and/or intangible assets that cannot be justified in reference to their lawful income (for instance when a person inexplicably acquires a number of houses or enjoys a significant increase in their bank balance).

The definitions in other jurisdictions also take into account situations where someone has benefited from a broader, but still limited, list of intangible items of value such as a reduction of pecuniary liabilities (for instance, the repayment of a mortgage) or the receipt of services.

At the widest end of the spectrum, however, many jurisdictions define illicit enrichment to include the unjustifiable enjoyment of anything of pecuniary value that can be considered to contribute to someone's 'standard of living'.

1.2.2   What is meant by "not justified through reference to lawful income"?

While also interpreted in various ways according to the jurisdiction, the phrase 'not justified through reference to lawful income' refers to an absence of evidence that demonstrates the legitimate or non-criminal sources from which the enjoyed wealth was derived (such as salaries, profits from legitimate businesses, pension payments, inheritances, gifts or even loans from banks).

1.3   What is an 'illicit enrichment law'?

For the sake of clarity, this section outlines the two key features that must exist in a particular legislative provision before it has been classified as an 'illicit enrichment law' within this publication.

This publication considers an 'illicit enrichment law' to include any provision in a statutory instrument that **empowers a court to impose a criminal or civil sanction if they are satisfied that illicit enrichment has taken place** (e.g. if the court is satisfied that a person has enjoyed an amount of wealth that has not been justified through reference to lawful income). Furthermore, to qualify as an illicit enrichment law, the provision must **not specify that a separate or underlying criminal activity needs to be established before the sanction can be imposed.**

Of course these are not always the only features of a specific illicit enrichment law. Many laws include a variety of other elements that may need to be satisfied before a sanction can be imposed (e.g. a state may also need to prove someone is a public official). These two features however are the two key features that are present in all illicit enrichment laws.

An important note on terminology

This publication uses the broad term 'illicit enrichment law' to cover all criminal and civil procedure-based laws that target people who have enjoyed an amount of wealth that is not justified through reference to their lawful income, without including a requirement to demonstrate any separate criminal activity before a sanction can be imposed. This is important to highlight, as there are many laws covered by this publication which do not include the phrase 'illicit enrichment' but instead favour the phrases 'unexplained wealth' or 'unexplained property'. For instance, the criminal law in Hong Kong refers to the 'possession of unexplained property' while the civil law in Mauritius outlines an application process for 'unexplained wealth orders'. Other laws again use additional phrases such as 'unjust enrichment'. Consequently, for the sake of clarity and consistency, this publication includes all these types of laws in the broad category of 'illicit enrichment laws' as long as they empower a court to impose a sanction if a person is deemed to have illicitly enriched themselves, within the broad definition provided above. Further clarifying terms such as 'criminal illicit enrichment laws' and 'civil illicit enrichment laws' are also used to specify the type of procedure within which a particular law is based.

1.3.1   Feature 1: The imposition of a criminal or civil sanction if illicit enrichment has taken place

This feature distinguishes illicit enrichment laws from other laws that may contain references to 'illicit enrichment' or 'unexplained wealth', but which do not empower a court to impose any sanctions if they are satisfied that illicit enrichment has been established.

For instance, the jurisdiction of Mauritius has two laws that refer to 'unexplained wealth'. Only one of these laws, however, is categorised as an illicit enrichment law within this publication.

The Prevention of Corruption Act[30] contains a provision titled 'possession of unexplained wealth' which gives authority to the Independent Commission Against Corruption to investigate whether a person 'owns or is in control of, property to an extent which is disproportionate to his emoluments or other income' and is unable 'to give a satisfactory account' as to how they came into control of this property.[31]

If such an investigation establishes that the person does in fact control a disproportionate amount of property, and that they are unable to account for it, then this provision only specifies that evidence establishing these facts 'shall be admissible to corroborate other evidence relating to the commission of [a separate] offence.'[32] Consequently, as this provision does not outline a criminal or civil sanction that can be imposed as a direct consequence of the proven 'possession of unexplained wealth', but instead only provides for a mechanism to acquire and use evidence of illicit enrichment as part of a separate legal procedure, then this law is not considered an 'illicit enrichment law' within this publication.

In contrast, Mauritius has another law, the Good Governance and Integrity Reporting Act,[33] which authorises the Integrity Reporting Services Agency to apply for an 'unexplained wealth order' against a person who appears to own property 'which is disproportionate to his emoluments and other income' and which 'cannot be satisfactorily accounted for'.[34] Under this Act, if a judge is satisfied that the person has illicitly enriched themselves (or is benefiting from 'unexplained wealth') then they may issue an order for the payment of the 'monetary equivalent' of the value of this wealth. As this law clearly imposes a civil sanction against a person who is proven to control unexplained and disproportionate wealth, then the law is considered an 'illicit enrichment law' in this publication.

Another example of a law that references 'unexplained wealth' but doesn't directly impose a legal sanction for the acquisition of the unexplained wealth is the Proceeds of Crime Act currently in force in the United Kingdom (UK).[35] While this law provides a mechanism to issue an 'Unexplained Wealth Order' against a person, this order only requires a person to provide financial information relating to the source of their wealth and does not obligate a person to repay the value of any unexplained wealth that they control.[36] Instead, once the information has been provided (or not provided) this can be subsequently used as evidence in a separate

---

30   Prevention of Corruption Act 2002 (Mauritius).

31   ibid., Section 84.

32   ibid.

33   The Good Governance and Integrity Reporting Act 2015 (Mauritius).

34   ibid., Section 2.

35   Proceeds of Crime Act 2002 (United Kingdom).

36   ibid., Sections 362A-362T.

non-conviction based (NCB) recovery proceeding under which a 'recovery' order can be made if it is proven, on the balance of probabilities, that the assets in question were obtained unlawfully. Consequently, in the context of this publication, this law is not categorised as an illicit enrichment law.[37]

1.3.2 Feature 2: The absence of a requirement to prove underlying or separate criminal activity

Illicit enrichment laws do not require the state to demonstrate that a person has already been convicted of a criminal offence, that any underlying or separate criminal activity has even taken place, or that any wealth was provably derived from crime.

Instead, under an illicit enrichment law, a civil or criminal sanction may be imposed by a court solely on the basis that the acquisition, receipt or use of a certain amount of wealth by a person cannot be, or has not been, justified through reference to their lawful income.

This characteristic specifically distinguishes illicit enrichment laws from similar categories of asset recovery laws, such as extended confiscation laws, NCB confiscation laws or even money laundering-based legislation. Unlike illicit enrichment laws, these laws generally require the state to either achieve a previous criminal conviction, or to prove the existence of underlying or separate criminal activity and/or the criminal origin of assets, to a requisite court standard.

A simple example

If an individual worked as a public tax assessor from 2010 to 2020 and earned a cumulative total salary of \$400,000 during this period, but instead was found to possess \$4,000,000 in his bank account at the end of this period, then the \$3,600,000 difference between his total lawful income and his actual income may spark an investigation and court proceeding in line with an existing illicit enrichment law. If during legal proceedings it is not possible for the individual to demonstrate that the additional \$3,600,000 was derived from other existing sources of legitimate income during this time (such as a loan from a bank, earnings from a side business, or the receipt of inheritance) then under an illicit enrichment law, the court may presume that this unjustifiable increase in wealth has not been derived from lawful sources and will impose a relevant sanction, even if no evidence of underlying or separate criminal activity is presented to the court.

Understandably, the fact that illicit enrichment laws do not require the state to prove a specific crime or an illicit source of funds has resulted in numerous judicial challenges on the compatibility of illicit enrichment laws with established legal rights, such as the right to be presumed innocent and the right to remain silent. Nonetheless, the majority of courts that have considered such challenges have deemed illicit enrichment laws to be a proportional

---

37 An examination of the mechanism contained in this law is nonetheless outlined in Section 2.6.1.

mechanism to recover proceeds of crime, and particularly the benefits derived by public officials through corruption offences. These issues are discussed in greater detail in Part 4 of this publication.

1.3.3 Three demonstrative examples of different illicit enrichment laws

Illicit enrichment laws do not have a set model, and can vary significantly in form and wording while still containing the two key features listed above. A quick comparison of the legislative provisions from Hong Kong, Argentina and Western Australia provide a good example of how illicit enrichment laws with markedly different forms can still contain these two features and be utilised to target the same action.

The criminal illicit enrichment law of Hong Kong, contained in Section 10 of the Prevention of Bribery Ordinance,[38] reads as follows:

10. Possession of unexplained property

(1) Any person who, being or having been the Chief Executive or a prescribed officer –

(a) maintains a standard of living above that which is commensurate with his present or past official emoluments; or

(b) is in control of pecuniary resources or property disproportionate to his present or past official emoluments,

shall, unless he gives a satisfactory explanation to the court as to how he was able to maintain such a standard of living or how such pecuniary resources or property came under his control, be guilty of an offence.

12. Penalty for offences

(1) Any person guilty of an offence under this Part, other than an offence under Section 3, shall be liable –

(a) on conviction on indictment –

(i) for an offence under section 10, to a fine of HK$1,000,000 and to imprisonment for 10 years;

...

(b) on summary conviction –

(i) for an offence under section 10, to a fine of HK$500,000 and to imprisonment for 3 years;

---

38   Cap.201 Prevention of Bribery Ordinance 1971 (China - Hong Kong), Section 10.

> ...
>
> (3) In addition to any penalty imposed under Subsection 1, the court may order a person convicted of an offence under Section 10(1)(b) to pay to the Government –
>
> (a) a sum not exceeding the amount of the pecuniary resources; or
>
> (b) a sum not exceeding the value of the property,
>
> the acquisition of which by him was not explained to the satisfaction of the court.

This legislative provision above clearly contains the first feature of an illicit enrichment law in that it empowers a court to issue a sanction, namely imprisonment and a fine (as well as an additional forfeiture penalty) against a person who is proven to have illicitly enriched themselves, in this case by maintaining an incommensurate standard of living or by controlling disproportionate property that they can't justify through reference to legal sources of income.

Moreover, the legislation also has the second feature of an illicit enrichment law, in that it does not require the state to prove the existence of any underlying or separate criminal activity. The fact that the wealth (represented by the person's standard of living or property) is disproportionate and cannot be justified by the person's total lawful income is enough in itself to trigger the criminal sanction against the person and recover the value of this disproportionate wealth.

In comparison, Argentina's criminal illicit enrichment law, outlined in Article 268 of the Argentine Criminal Code,[39] reads as follows:

> [Unofficial translation]
>
> **Article 268(2) Unlawful enrichment of officials and employees**
>
> Any person who, upon being duly requested, does not justify the origin of appreciable enrichment of his or her own wealth or that of a third party seeking to conceal it, which occurs after assuming a public office or employment and up to two (2) years after having ceased to perform his or her duties, shall be punished by imprisonment of two (2) to six (6) years, a fine of two (2) to five (5) times the value of the enrichment, and absolute disqualification for life.

Despite its very different form (and a number of additional conditions) this law also includes

---

39 [Unofficial translation] Código Penal de la Nación Argentina Ley 11.179 (T.O. 1984 actualizado), Artículo 268(2) (Original text: 'Será reprimido con prisión de dos (2) a seis (6) años, multa de dos (2) a cinco (5) veces del valor del enriquecimiento, e inhabilitación absoluta perpetua, el que al ser debidamente requerido, no justificare la procedencia de un enriquecimiento patrimonial apreciable suyo o de persona interpuesta para disimularlo, ocurrido con posterioridad a la asunción de un cargo o empleo público y hasta dos (2) años después de haber cesado en su desempeño.').

the same two key features of an illicit enrichment law. Specifically, judicial sanctions (imprisonment and a fine) may be imposed on someone who has illicitly enriched themselves – or someone who is not able to justify the lawful 'origin' of wealth (or 'property') that has come into their possession. Moreover, criminal sanctions may be enforced without the need to bring evidence of any sort of underlying or separate criminal activity.

As a final example, the civil illicit enrichment law in the jurisdiction of Western Australia demonstrates a different approach again, with an illicit enrichment provision that exists in the form of a civil order. The Western Australian law (which refers to illicit enrichment as the control of 'unexplained wealth') is contained in the Criminal Property Confiscation Act,[40] with excerpts reading as follows:

---

11. Unexplained wealth declarations, applying for

(1) The DPP [Director of Public Prosecutions] or the CCC [the Corruption and Crime Commission] may apply to the court for an unexplained wealth declaration against a person.

...

12. Unexplained wealth declarations, making

(1) On hearing an application under section 11(1), the court must declare that the respondent has unexplained wealth if it is more likely than not that the total value of the respondent's wealth is greater than the value of the respondent's lawfully acquired wealth.

(2) Any property, service, advantage or benefit that is a constituent of the respondent's wealth is presumed not to have been lawfully acquired unless the respondent establishes the contrary.

(3) Without limiting the matters to which the court may have regard, for the purpose of deciding whether the respondent has unexplained wealth, the court may have regard to the amount of the respondent's income and expenditure at any time or at all times.

...

13. Unexplained wealth, assessing value of

(1) The value of the respondent's unexplained wealth is the amount equal to the difference between –

(a) the total value of the respondent's wealth; and

(b) the value of the respondent's lawfully acquired wealth.

...

---

40   Criminal Property Confiscation Act 2000 (Australia - Western Australia).

---

14. Unexplained wealth declaration, effect of

When the court makes an unexplained wealth declaration, the respondent is liable to pay to the State an amount equal to the amount specified in the declaration as the assessed value of the respondent's unexplained wealth.

While this particular piece of legislation is quite different from the previous two examples, it still clearly contains the two key features of an illicit enrichment law. Specifically, it outlines a judicial sanction (namely a civil order entitled an 'unexplained wealth declaration') that can be made and enforced against a person who has illicitly enriched themselves, or more specifically, who has acquired wealth that is not justified through reference to their lawful income (or their 'lawfully acquired' wealth).

Moreover, there is no need under this provision to demonstrate any underlying or separate criminal activity. Instead, if the person is unable to demonstrate adequate lawful sources to justify the acquisition of certain wealth, then the court will rule that the wealth was derived from illicit origins and a judicial sanction will be ordered.

1.4 Categories of illicit enrichment laws

To provide additional clarity when defining and discussing illicit enrichment laws, it is possible to further classify these laws into certain categories, based on whether they are rooted in criminal or civil procedures.

Furthermore, there are some laws (both criminally and civilly based) that operate almost exactly like illicit enrichment laws, but which need to be qualified on the basis that they contain an additional minor threshold of proof regarding suspicion of criminal activity.

1.4.1 Criminal vs. civil illicit enrichment laws

Illicit enrichment laws that constitute a criminal offence, are applied according to criminal procedures, and attract criminal punishments have been categorised within this publication as criminal illicit enrichment laws. For instance, both the previously mentioned Argentinian and Hong Kong laws are examples of criminal illicit enrichment laws.

Illicit enrichment laws that take the form of a civil order process, are applied according to civil procedures, and which may result in a compensatory-type order against a person have been categorised within this publication as civil illicit enrichment laws. The previously mentioned Western Australian law is an example of this category of illicit enrichment law.

The distinction between criminal-based laws and civil-based laws is an important one, as there are different issues arising in the application of one category which may not exist in the application of the other – such as the effect such laws may have on common legal rights including the presumption of innocence.

Criminal illicit enrichment laws	Civil illicit enrichment laws

SIMILARITIES

Person can be targeted if they enjoy wealth that is not justified through reference to their lawful income	Person can be targeted if they enjoy wealth that is not justified through reference to their lawful income
No need to prove underlying or separate criminal activity took place	No need to prove underlying or separate criminal activity took place

DIFFERENCES

Determined by criminal prosecution, conducted in accordance with criminal procedure rules	Determined by application hearing, conducted in accordance with civil procedure rules
Criminal standard of proof is applicable (e.g. beyond reasonable doubt)	Civil standard of proof is applicable (e.g. the balance of probabilities)
May result in criminal punishment (imprisonment/fine/confiscation)	May only result in a civil compensatory-type order (requiring person to forfeit/ repay the amount of illicit enrichment)

Despite these key differences, this publication includes both criminal and civil illicit enrichment laws within the same broad category of laws, as courts adjudicating both these types of laws must be satisfied of the same fundamental facts in order to impose a sanction, namely:

1. That a person has enjoyed an amount of wealth; and

2. That this amount of wealth has not been justified by reference to lawful income.

Furthermore, neither criminal nor civil illicit enrichment laws require proof of separate or underlying criminal activity. Consequently in practice, the approach to investigating and proving both these categories of law is fundamentally the same.

1.4.2 Qualified illicit enrichment laws: The additional requirement to establish a 'reasonable suspicion' or 'reasonable belief'

It is important to note that a number of jurisdictions have criminal or civil based legislative instruments that operate almost identically to illicit enrichment laws, but for a minor deviation from the above-listed requirements – namely, they require a state to provide evidence to a court of a 'reasonable suspicion' or a 'reasonable belief' that some sort of underlying or separate criminality has taken place. These laws are referred to in this publication as **qualified illicit enrichment laws**, and can be either civilly or criminally based like regular illicit enrichment laws.

For instance, Kenya's Anti-Corruption and Economic Crimes Act[41] empowers a court to make a civil forfeiture order against a person if they are deemed to hold 'unexplained assets', or assets that are 'disproportionate' to the person's 'known sources of income' and for which they do not have an explanation.[42] In addition to this, however, for these assets to be considered 'unexplained', the person must have acquired them 'at or around the time' that they were 'reasonably suspected of corruption or economic crime'.[43]

Similarly, in the Australian jurisdiction of Queensland, the Supreme Court may issue a civil order under the Criminal Proceeds Confiscation Act[44] for unexplained wealth, which is assessed under this Act as the amount of a person's wealth that is in excess of their lawfully acquired wealth.[45] Such an order however, may only be issued if the court 'is satisfied there is a reasonable suspicion that... the person has engaged in one or more serious crime related activities' or 'has acquired, without giving sufficient consideration, serious crime derived property from a serious crime related activity of someone else, whether or not the person knew or suspected the property was derived from illegal activity'.[46]

Of course, while the definition of a 'reasonable suspicion' or 'reasonable belief' will depend on the jurisdiction, thresholds contained in qualified illicit enrichment laws requiring the demonstration of a reasonable suspicion or belief of underlying criminality are arguably lower than those contained in other asset recovery laws such as NCB confiscation laws – which require the state to demonstrate to a civil standard (e.g. on the balance of probabilities) that some sort of underlying criminality actually occurred, or more specifically, that an asset is either the proceeds of crime or was used in the commission of an offence. For instance, while general case law in Australia suggests that a reasonable suspicion is 'not arbitrary', and that 'some factual basis for the suspicion must be shown' to justify it, it also describes a reasonable

---

41   Anti-Corruption and Economic Crimes Act 2003 (Kenya).

42   ibid., Sections 2, 55.

43   ibid., Section 2.

44   Criminal Proceeds Confiscation Act 2002 (as amended by the Criminal Proceeds Confiscation (Unexplained Wealth and Serious Drug Offender Confiscation Order) Amendment Act 2013) (Australia - Queensland).

45   ibid., Section 89L.

46   ibid., Section 89G.

suspicion as 'less than a reasonable belief, but more than a possibility'[47] and suggests that the requirement to demonstrate such a suspicion does not necessarily imply that it needs to be well-founded or that all the grounds for suspicion must be factually correct.[48] Moreover in Australia, the establishment of such a suspicion may rely on hearsay material or other material that may normally be inadmissible as evidence.[49]

Consequently, as 'reasonable suspicion' or 'reasonable belief' thresholds are substantially lower than a requirement to prove separate or underlying criminality to a civil or criminal standard of proof, qualified illicit enrichment laws can be distinguished from other asset recovery mechanisms such as NCB confiscation laws and extended confiscation laws. Accordingly, this publication's analysis surrounding the application of illicit enrichment laws has also included the judicial interpretation of qualified illicit enrichment laws, where appropriate.

---

47   R v Rondo [2001] NSWCCA 540 at [53] per Smart JA (full text of quote: '(a) A reasonable suspicion involves less than a reasonable belief but more than a possibility. There must be something which would create in the mind of a reasonable person an apprehension or fear of one of the state of affairs covered by s.357E [of the Crimes Act 1900]. A reason to suspect that a fact exists is more than a reason to consider or look into the possibility of its existence. (b) Reasonable suspicion is not arbitrary. Some factual basis for the suspicion must be shown. A suspicion may be based on hearsay material or materials which may be inadmissible in evidence. The materials must have some probative value. (c) What is important is the information in the mind of the police officer stopping the person or the vehicle or making the arrest at the time he did so. Having ascertained that information the question is whether that information afforded reasonable grounds for the suspicion which the police officer formed. In answering that question regard must be had to the source of the information and its content, seen in the light of the whole of the surrounding circumstances.'). The idea that a reasonable suspicion must have a 'factual basis' was again more recently confirmed by the Australian High Court in Lordianto v Commissioner of the Australian Federal Police, Kalimuthu v Commissioner of the Australian Federal Police [2019] HCA 39. The issue is also covered in R v Chan (1992) 28 NSWLR 421 and George v Rockett (1990) 170 CLR 104, though it is important to note that these cases did not relate to the relevant illicit enrichment laws in Australia, so there remains some uncertainty as to whether the same definition would also be applied under the context of these laws.

48   Tucs v Manly (1985) 62 ALR 460.

49   R v Rondo [2001] NSWCCA 540 at [53].

Illicit enrichment law or qualified illicit enrichment law?

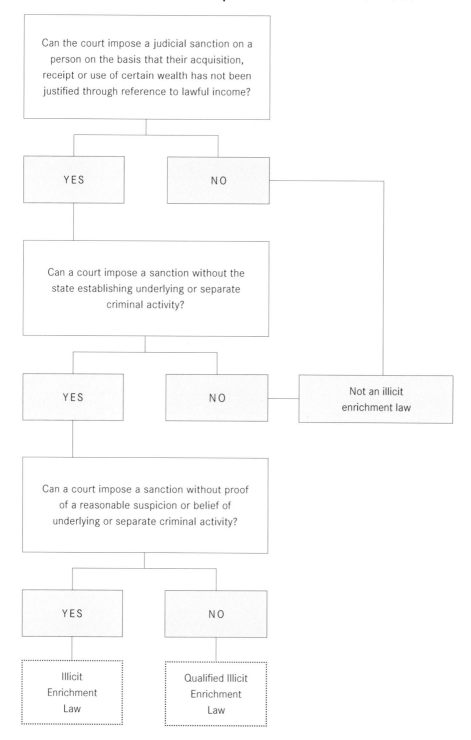

1.5 Difference between illicit enrichment laws and other similar asset recovery-focused laws

The specific features of illicit enrichment laws differentiate them from other asset recovery-focused laws such as NCB confiscation laws and extended confiscation laws. These differences are explained below.

1.5.1 Difference between illicit enrichment laws and broader NCB confiscation legislation

Traditional non-conviction based (NCB) confiscation (otherwise known as NCB forfeiture or civil recovery) is an asset recovery tool that can be used to target assets that are the proceeds or instrumentalities of crime. NCB confiscation is a judicial proceeding against the asset itself, not an individual. It generally requires a state to establish, on the balance of probabilities, that the asset is either the proceeds of crime or was used in the commission of an offence. As the name suggests, NCB confiscation is not dependent on the existence of a criminal conviction. Consequently, it can be used when the owner of an asset is no longer able to face trial, or when the available evidence is only strong enough to establish, to a civil standard of proof, that a certain offence took place or that certain proceeds were connected to criminal activity.

Illicit enrichment provisions are less strict than NCB confiscation provisions. They do not require the state to establish that certain assets have stemmed from, or were used in, criminal activity. Instead, sanctions in an illicit enrichment proceeding can be imposed solely on the basis that a person has enjoyed an amount of wealth that has not been justified by reference to legal sources of income.

Furthermore, while NCB confiscation is generally focused on actual assets, illicit enrichment legislation is often much wider, and may also take into account anything of pecuniary value that contributed to a person's lifestyle, based on the amounts they have spent or services that they have received. For instance, unlike many NCB confiscation laws, illicit enrichment legislation can often be used to target non-tangible items that contribute to a person's standard of living, such as the reduction of a debt.

1.5.2 Difference between illicit enrichment legislation and extended confiscation legislation

Extended confiscation mechanisms are asset recovery mechanisms that can be used after a conviction has been reached to potentially target assets controlled by the convicted person. Following the conviction of a person for a particular type of offence (such as a money laundering or an organised crime-related offence) extended confiscation mechanisms allow the courts to presume that all assets controlled by the convicted person over a certain period of time were derived from criminal activity unless proven otherwise.[50] Like with illicit enrichment measures, this presumption is triggered without the need to demonstrate the criminal activity from which the assets were derived.[51] However, unlike with illicit enrichment, extended confiscation measures can only be triggered after the state proves that the person has committed a criminal offence. The presumption cannot be triggered simply by establishing the disproportionality between a person's assets and their lawful income.

1.5.3 Difference between illicit enrichment laws and the concept of 'unjust enrichment' as a private claim for civil restitution

The term 'illicit enrichment' is used interchangeably with the term 'unjust enrichment' in some jurisdictions. It should be noted, however, that 'unjust enrichment' is also a label given to a private claim for restitution based in civil law, where one party seeks to restore for themselves the gains that another party has unduly made at their expense.[52] These types of claims are often utilised when one party has arguably paid money to a second party as a result of a mistake. Private claims of 'unjust enrichment' in this sense are not related to the subject of this publication.

---

50   For an example, see the Proceeds of Crime Act 2002 (United Kingdom), Sections 6, 10, and 75.

51   For example, refer to the Directive 2014/42/EU Of the European Parliament and of the Council, 3 April 2014, on The Freezing And Confiscation Of Instrumentalities And Proceeds Of Crime In The European Union, Article 5.

52   LexisNexis, 'Restitution for unjust enrichment – elements of the claim', LexisNexis, https://www.lexisnexis.co.uk/legal/guidance/restitution-for-unjust-enrichment-elements-of-the-claim, accessed 26 March 2021.

Differing characteristic of illicit enrichment laws and other confiscation laws targeting proceeds of crime

	Sanctions applied solely on the basis that a person has enjoyed wealth that is not justified by reference to lawful income	Requirement to establish a reasonable suspicion or belief that criminal activity took place, or that the assets were criminally derived	Requirement to establish to a civil standard that an actual criminal activity took place, or that assets were criminally derived	Requirement for a criminal conviction
Illicit enrichment laws	✓	✗	✗	✗
Qualified illicit enrichment laws	✗	✓	✗	✗
Non-conviction based confiscation	✗	→	✓	✗
Extended confiscation	✗	→	→	✓

Part 2

Different approaches to drafting illicit enrichment laws

A comparative overview of illicit enrichment legislation

Part 2 Summary

The wording and form of illicit enrichment laws around the world are remarkably diverse. This Part of the publication provides an in-depth overview of the varied approaches taken by legislative bodies in different jurisdictions to address illicit enrichment. In doing so, this Part:

- Provides a list of countries in which illicit enrichment laws have been passed and an overview of the regional adoption of these types of laws;

- Explains the key points on which legislators have taken divergent approaches, including:

  - The legal nature of the law (whether the law is civil or criminal in nature);

  - The scope of application of the law (who the law targets, what types of wealth are considered, whether there are any value thresholds that must be reached, or whether any time limitations are applied);

  - Burdens of proof (whether the law has outlined which party needs to prove certain issues);

  - The inclusion of powers to obligate the disclosure of information; and

  - Sanctions.

- Outlines the types of safeguards that have been introduced by countries with illicit enrichment laws to ensure that these laws are applied fairly and are reviewed on a regular basis;

- Outlines the more common "models" of illicit enrichment law that exist around the world;

- Describes laws that exist around the world that contain similar features to illicit enrichment laws, including legislation from the UK, Ireland, Switzerland and France.

This Part should be read in conjunction with Annex 1, which is a comprehensive table of the text of all the illicit enrichment laws identified by this publication. Annex 1 also includes the text of laws similar to illicit enrichment laws mentioned in this Part.

2.1   General overview of illicit enrichment laws

In total, 98 laws have been identified in this publication as illicit enrichment laws or qualified illicit enrichment laws, within the definitions provided in Part 1.

These laws exist throughout the world: 36 are from jurisdictions in the Asia-Pacific region, 35 are from African jurisdictions, 25 are from jurisdictions in the Americas and 2 are from European jurisdictions.

Laws by region

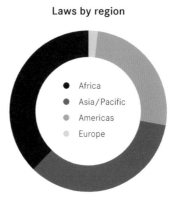

These laws are also spread over both common law and civil law systems: 47 are from jurisdictions with predominantly civil law-based legal systems, 35 are from jurisdictions with predominantly common law legal systems and 16 are from jurisdictions with mixed legal systems.

The vast majority of these laws are based in criminal law, with 78 classified as either criminal or qualified criminal illicit enrichment laws, and 18 classified as civil or qualified civil illicit enrichment laws. A further 2 laws are classified as administrative laws.

Criminal I.E. Laws

Afghanistan	Congo (Republic of the)	Jordan	Pakistan
Algeria	Côte D'Ivoire	Kuwait	Palestine
Antigua and Barbuda	Cuba	Kyrgyz Republic	Panama
Argentina	Djibouti	Lebanon	Paraguay
Armenia	Dominican Republic	Libya	Peru
Benin	Ecuador	Lithuania	Rwanda
Bhutan	Egypt	Madagascar	Saint Lucia
Bolivia	El Salvador	Malawi	São Tomé and Príncipe
Botswana	Eswatini	Mali	Sénégal
Brunei Darussalam	Ethiopia	Marshall Islands	Seychelles
Burkina Faso	Fiji	Mauritania	Sierra Leone
Cambodia	Guatemala	Mexico	Sudan
Chile	Guinea	Moldova	Tanzania
China	Guyana	Mongolia	Togo
China - Hong Kong	Haiti	Mozambique	Tunisia
China - Macau	Honduras	Nepal	Turkey
Colombia	India	Nicaragua	Uganda
Congo (DRC)	Jamaica	Niger	Venezuela

Qualified Criminal I.E. Laws		Administrative I.E. Laws	
Bangladesh	Malaysia	Angola	Brazil
China - Taiwan	Singapore		
Lesotho	Zambia		

Qualified Civil I.E. Laws		Civil I.E. Laws	
AUS - Australian Capital Territory		AUS - Federal Jurisdiction	Fiji
AUS - New South Wales		AUS - Northern Territory	Mauritius
AUS - Queensland	Kenya	AUS - South Australia	Philippines
AUS - Victoria	Peru	AUS - Tasmania	Tanzania - Zanzibar
Bahamas	Trinidad and Tobago	AUS - Western Australia	Thailand

2.2 The key distinguishing characteristics of illicit enrichment laws

Despite the fact that articles on illicit enrichment exist in three international treaties, there is certainly no set model for illicit enrichment laws around the world. Consequently, the following sections seek to provide an overview of a number of the key points on which legislators around the world have taken divergent approaches to design illicit enrichment laws that are tailored to their own priorities and requirements.

2.2.1 Legal nature

Is the illicit enrichment law criminal or civil in nature?

This particular characteristic has already been explained to some extent in Part 1, however it is important to highlight it again as it is a key differentiating factor between certain illicit enrichment laws.

Illicit enrichment laws will either constitute a criminal offence, or will take the form of a civil order procedure (though it should be noted that two Lusophone countries have also categorised illicit enrichment as an act of public or administrative 'improbity').[53]

The vast majority of illicit enrichment laws identified in this publication take the form of a criminal offence.

Peculiarly, the jurisdiction of Fiji has both a criminal illicit enrichment law and separate civil illicit enrichment law and serves as an illustrative example of how such laws can take both forms. Section 10 of Fiji's Prevention of Bribery Act creates an offence of 'Possession of unexplained property' under which a prescribed officer (public official) may face up to ten years' imprisonment, a fine and a pecuniary order if they are found to maintain a standard of living or control property that is disproportionate to their income.[54] Alongside this, under Section 71F of Fiji's Proceeds of Crime Act, if any person (not just a public official) is found to maintain a standard of living or control property that is disproportionate to their income, they may be subjected to an 'unexplained wealth declaration', requiring them to pay the value of their established illicit enrichment to the state.[55] An application for an 'unexplained wealth declaration' is made according to civil procedures.

---

53   This classification is not as serious as a criminal offence classification, but penalties (fines, administrative sanctions, confiscation etc.) will still be imposed on a person found to have committed an act of illicit enrichment under the laws in Angola (see the Lei da Probidade Pública 2010, Artigo 25, 31) and Brazil (Lei Nº 8.429, De 2 De Junho De 1992 Artículo 9, 12); In Mozambique, Article 40 of the Lei de Probidade Pública (Lei no. 16/2012)) classifies illicit enrichment as a 'public improbity', but does not include any sanctions – and therefore is not classified as an illicit enrichment law within this publication. Mozambique does however list illicit enrichment as an offence under Article 428 of the newly revised Código Penal (Lei no. 24/2019).

54   Prevention of Bribery Act (Promulgation No. 12 of 2007) (Fiji), Section 10.

55   Proceeds of Crime Act 1997 (as amended by the Proceeds of Crime Amendment Act No. 7 of 2005 and by the Proceeds of Crime (Amendment) Decree 2012 (Decree No. 61 of 2012)) (Fiji), Section 71F.

Notably, there are stricter consequences for a person subjected to Fiji's criminal illicit enrichment law, including an incarceration period, a substantial fine and a requirement to pay back the amount of illicit enrichment. However, in line with this, the standard of proof that the state must reach in proceedings under this law is also much higher – namely the state is required to prove illicit enrichment has taken place beyond reasonable doubt. On the other hand, if the state is only able to prove illicit enrichment to a civil standard (or if the targeted person is not a public official) the state may instead apply for a purely monetary-focused sanction under civil proceedings, namely an 'unexplained wealth declaration' under which they can at least recover the value of the unjustified wealth found to have been enjoyed by the person.

The differences in the characteristics of the criminal and civil laws in Fiji are in fact quite reflective of the general differences between criminal and civil illicit enrichment laws world-wide. Specifically, while criminal illicit enrichment laws often include stronger sanctions, they are often also more limited in scope. In contrast, civil illicit enrichment laws generally only require the repayment of the proven value of illicit enrichment, but can be applied to a much wider scope of persons with a lower threshold of proof required. Of course, this is not a universal rule.

2.2.2   Scopes of application

Illicit enrichment laws can target different categories of people, can include narrow or wide interpretations of the concept of 'wealth', and can include specific conditions relating to the amount of wealth or time periods that need to be met before the law can be applied.

2.2.2.1 Personal scope

Who does the illicit enrichment law target?

Another major differentiating characteristic amongst illicit enrichment laws is the categories of persons that are targeted by the legislation. While some laws are drafted to specifically target public officials, or those directly connected to public officials, other laws can be applied to all private citizens.

The narrow approach: Laws only applicable to people who are (or have been) public officials
The majority of the laws identified in this publication do not target private citizens, but are instead drafted to target public officials that may have illicitly enriched themselves through corruption.

Of course, while the definition of 'public officials'[56] varies between jurisdictions, most laws outline a relatively wide definition of the concept. For example in Tanzania, a public official includes 'any person holding a legislative, executive, judicial, administrative, political, military, security, law enforcement and local government authority or any other statutory office'

---

56   Also sometimes referred to as other labels, such as 'civil servants', 'public servants' and 'public officers'.

including 'any person performing a public function or providing a public service'.[57] The illicit enrichment law in Mali even expressly includes any 'agent' or 'employee' of 'cooperative bodies', 'unions' and 'bodies of an industrial or commercial nature in which the State or a public authority holds a fraction of the share capital'.[58]

It is important to note that in many jurisdictions, public officials that have left office may still be considered the same as serving public officials despite the fact that they have become private citizens. This consideration will often apply for a certain number of years after leaving office, with the person still potentially liable for any enrichment that occurs within this period. For instance, in Guatemala, if a public official is proven to have illicitly enriched themselves during the first five years after leaving office, then they will have committed an illicit enrichment offence regardless of the fact that they were a private citizen during this time.[59] A similar situation exists in São Tomé and Príncipe, where an illicit enrichment charge can be made against a public official who acquires disproportionate wealth within the first 'three years following termination' from their position.[60] This legislative approach may be used to cover situations where a public official delays the receipt of illicit payments until after they have left office – a tactic commonly used by corrupt officials to avoid the higher level of financial scrutiny that may apply during their employment.

The wide approach: Laws applicable to "any person"

Rather than merely targeting public officials, a significant number of both criminal and civil-based illicit enrichment laws identified can be applied to a much broader category of persons. At the widest end of the spectrum, such laws can be applied to any private citizen. For example, under the civil illicit enrichment law in Western Australia, an 'unexplained wealth order' can be made against 'a person' – and to date this law has mainly been used to target private citizens suspected of drug offences and organised crime (which was one of the original

---

57   Prevention and Combating of Corruption Act 2007 (Tanzania), Section 3.

58   [Unofficial translation] Loi N°2014-015/ Du 27 mai 2014 portant prévention et répression de l'enrichissement illicite, Article 3 (Original text: 'Sont assujettis à la présente loi, toute personne physique civile ou militaire, dépositaire de l'autorité publique, chargée de service public, même occasionnellement, ou investie d'un mandat électif ; tout agent ou employé de l'Etat, des collectivités publiques, des sociétés et entreprises d'Etat, des établissements publics, des organismes coopératifs, unions, associations ou fédérations desdits organismes, des associations reconnues d'utilité publique, des ordres professionnels, des organismes à caractère industriel ou commercial dont l'Etat ou une collectivité publique détient une fraction du capital social, et de manière générale, toute personne agissant au nom ou pour le compte de la puissance publique et/ou avec les moyens ou les ressources de celle-ci.').

59   Código Penal, Decreto Número 17-73 (modificado por Ley Contra La Corrupción, Decreto Número 31-2012) (Guatemala), Artículo 448 (Original text: 'Comete el delito de enriquecimiento ilícito de particulares, quien sin ser funcionario o empleado público, administre, ejecute o maneje recursos públicos o bienes del Estado, hasta cinco años después de haber cesado en dicha función, que obtenga para sí mismo o para cualquier persona un beneficio patrimonial, incremento en su nivel de gastos, o cancelación de deudas u obligaciones que no correspondan al que haya podido obtener derivado de su administración, ejecución o manejo u otros ingresos lícitos.').

60   [Unofficial translation] Código Penal, Aprovado pela Lei 6/2012 (São Tomé and Príncipe), Artigo 455 (Original text: 'O funcionário que, durante o período do exercício de funções públicas ou nos três anos seguintes a cessação dessas funções, adquirir um património ou um modo de vida que seja manifestamente desproporcionais ao seu rendimento e que não resultem de outro meio de aquisição lícito, com perigo de aquele património ou modo de vida provir de vantagens obtidas pela prática de crimes cometidos no exercício de funções públicas, é punível com pena de prisão até 5 anos.').

intentions of this law).[61] Similarly, the criminal illicit enrichment law of Lithuania can also be applied against all private citizens.[62]

While not limiting themselves to public officials, other jurisdictions have taken a more tempered approach than that in Western Australia and have attached some limitations regarding the application of their illicit enrichment law to private persons. For example, while the illicit enrichment law in Bolivia has separate provisions to target the illicit enrichment of public officials as well as 'any natural person', a charge of illicit enrichment against the latter requires a prosecutor to additionally show that the illicit enrichment 'affected' the assets of the state.[63]

In some illicit enrichment laws, the personal scope of the law itself is a little more ambiguous. For instance, while the laws in Uganda,[64] Pakistan[65] and Rwanda[66] can be applied to 'any person', the provisions themselves are specifically contained in anti-corruption statutes rather than more general criminal codes or proceeds of crime statutes. This begs the question as to whether or not these provisions could be applied outside of an anti-corruption context.

Additional option 1: Criminal illicit enrichment laws applicable to "legal persons"

Some criminal illicit enrichment laws are also expressly applicable to legal entities. Most notably, a legal entity can also be held liable for the offence of 'unjust enrichment' under Lithuania's Criminal Code,[67] while legal entities in Madagascar may be forced to cease commercial operations for up to twenty years if they are found to have knowingly received wealth originating from someone who had illicitly enriched themselves.[68] Furthermore, in Sénégal, the illicit enrichment law may also be applied to a legal entity, governed by private law, if they have received 'financial assistance from public authorities'.[69]

Additional option 2: Criminal illicit enrichment laws also applicable to aiders and abettors

---

61 Western Australian Parliament, Legislative Assembly, Hansard, 29 June 2000.

62 Law on the Approval and Entry into Force of the Criminal Code 26 September 2000 No VIII-1968 (as amended 21 November 2017 No XIII-791) (Lithuania), Article 189(1).

63 [Unofficial translation] Ley De Lucha Contra La Corrupción, Enriquecimiento Ilícito e Investigación De Fortunas "Marcelo Quiroga Santa Cruz" (Ley No 004 from 31.03.2010 (Bolivia), Artículo 28 (Original text: 'La persona natural que mediante actividad privada hubiere incrementado desproporcionadamente su patrimonio respecto de sus ingresos legítimos afectando el patrimonio del Estado, no logrando desvirtuar tal situación, será sancionada con la privación de libertad de tres a ocho años, multa de cien a trescientos días y el decomiso de los bienes obtenidos ilegalmente. Incurrirán en el mismo delito y la misma pena, los representantes o ex representantes legales de las personas jurídicas que mediante actividad privada hubieren incrementado el patrimonio de la persona jurídica, afectando el patrimonio del Estado y que no pueda demostrar que provienen de una actividad lícita; adicionalmente, la persona jurídica restituirá al Estado los bienes que le hubiesen sido afectados además de los obtenidos como producto del delito y será sancionada con una multa del 25% de su patrimonio.').

64 Anti Corruption Act 2009 (Uganda), Section 31.

65 National Accountability Ordinance (XVIII of 1999) (Pakistan), Section 3.

66 Law N° 54/2018 of 13.08.2018 on Fighting Against Corruption (Rwanda), Article 9.

67 Law on the Approval and Entry into Force of the Criminal Code 26 September 2000 No VIII-1968 (as amended 21 November 2017 No XIII-791) (Lithuania), Article 189(1).

68 Code pénal Malagasy (modifié par Loi No 2016-020 du 22 août 2016 sur la lutte contre la corruption), Article 183.1.

69 Code Pénal, Loi No 1965-60 (Sénégal), Article 163 bis.

In addition to targeting the public official, person, or entity that has illicitly enriched themselves, some illicit enrichment laws cast an even wider net and also expressly target individuals or entities that assisted or abetted in the illicit enrichment of someone else.

For example, the illicit enrichment offence in Mauritania can apply not just to the person who enriched themselves, but equally to any person who has 'knowingly contributed by any means whatsoever to concealing the illicit origin of the property', with the same punishment applied to the contributing individual as to the person who has actually illicitly enriched themselves.[70] Similar express provisions also exist in Algeria,[71] Argentina,[72] El Salvador,[73] Mali[74] and Tunisia.[75]

Finally, it should be noted that many illicit enrichment laws can also be used to indirectly target people who are holding property on 'trust' or on 'behalf' of the person that is actually being targeted by the law. In such contexts, while these separate parties may not be directly sanctioned by a particular illicit enrichment law (e.g. face criminal charges for illicit enrichment) they may nonetheless be indirectly affected by efforts to confiscate the proceeds of the person targeted by the illicit enrichment law. This is discussed in greater detail under Sections 2.2.2.2 and 3.3.3.1.

> Author's note: Assessing the options
>
> Each of the options above have their own advantages and disadvantages and the decision of a jurisdiction to take one approach over another is often dependent on the legislative purpose behind the introduction of the illicit enrichment law.
>
> For countries actively seeking to specifically target corruption (or merely seeking to meet obligations outlined in International anti-corruption treaties) limiting the application of an illicit enrichment law to public officials is a sufficient approach. This choice can further be justified by the argument that public officials should be subjected to stricter oversight mechanisms, and exposed to stronger deterrent measures, based on the fact that they hold a position of responsibility over public funds.
>
> For countries seeking to recover wider criminal assets, not just those stolen through corruption, the application of illicit enrichment laws to 'any person' is the more logical

---

70 [Unofficial translation] Loi n° 2016.014 relative à la lutte contre la corruption (Mauritania), Article 16 (Original text: 'Encourt la même peine, toute personne qui aura sciemment contribué par quelque moyen que ce soit à occulter l'origine illicite des biens visés à l'alinéa précédent.').

71 Loi n°06 - 01 du 20 février 2006 relative à la prévention et à la lutte contre la corruption (Algeria), Article 37.

72 Código Penal de la Nación Argentina Ley 11.179 (T.O. 1984 actualizado), Artículo 268(2).

73 Código Penal de la República de El Salvador, 26.04.1997 (29.01.2020), Artículo 333.

74 Loi N°2014-015/ Du 27 mai 2014 portant prévention et répression de l'enrichissement illicite (Mali) Article 4.

75 Law No. 46 of 2018, dated August 1, 2018, relating to the declaration of gains and interests and the fight against illicit enrichment and conflicts of interest (Tunisia), Article 45.

choice. For instance, as noted above, the parliament of Western Australia did not limit their unexplained wealth declaration laws to public officials, but instead designed them to apply to everyone, as the primary intention for introducing the law in the first place was to target perpetrators of organised crime and drug offences.

Otherwise, countries can of course opt to introduce laws that cover both public officials and private persons differently, requiring different standards of proof and resulting in different levels of punishment. For instance, Fiji introduced both a criminal illicit enrichment law to target public officials and a civil illicit enrichment law that could be applied to all persons.

2.2.2.2 Scope of 'wealth' applicable under the law

What type of 'wealth' does the law take into consideration?

Illicit enrichment laws target the enjoyment of an amount of 'wealth' that is not justified through reference to lawful income. These laws however differ significantly on the types of 'wealth' that can be included in the overall assessment of whether or not someone has committed the act of illicit enrichment. Some laws take a narrow approach and only target traditional assets capable of being 'acquired' or 'controlled', while other laws take into account a much wider approach and will also consider any pecuniary-based item (including all services received or general expenditures made) that contributes to a person's 'standard of living'.

Narrow approach: Calculating wealth through reference to property, assets and pecuniary resources that can be acquired or controlled

Some criminal illicit enrichment laws take a narrow approach regarding the types of items or benefits that can be considered when determining if a person has illicitly enriched themselves. These laws only take into account the actual assets, property or pecuniary resources that have been acquired or controlled by a person.

For example in Bangladesh, a person will only be deemed to have illicitly enriched themselves under the Anti-Corruption Commission Act if they have 'obtained ownership of moveable or immoveable property' not consistent with their known sources of income.[76] Similarly, the Togolese Penal Code also limits its offence of illicit enrichment to the acquisition of unjustifiable 'moveable or immoveable property'.[77]

Other countries simply take into account an increase in 'assets', such as the Jamaican Corruption (Prevention) Act, which focuses solely on situations where someone 'owns assets

---

76 The Anti-Corruption Commission Act 2004 (Bangladesh), Section 27.

77 [Unofficial translation] Loi N°2015-10 du 24.11.2015 portant nouveau code pénal (Togo), Article 620 (modifiée par la loi N°2016-027 du 10 octobre 2016) (Original text: 'acquisition de biens mobilier ou immobilier').

disproportionate to his lawful earnings',[78] or the Malagasy Penal Code, under which an illicit enrichment offence can be applied to someone who 'cannot reasonably justify a substantial increase in his assets'.[79]

Civil-type laws rarely apply a narrow interpretation when defining the types of wealth to which the law can apply - though there are some exceptions (eg. Kenya and the jurisdiction of Zanzibar in Tanzania).

Wider approach: Calculating wealth through reference to a standard of living or other specific items

Most illicit enrichment laws (both criminal and civil) apply to a much wider category of 'wealth'. Not only do these laws take into account any assets, property or pecuniary resources that may have come under the control of a person, but they also take into consideration whether or not a person has benefited from anything else that may have contributed towards their 'lifestyle' or 'standard of living'.

For instance, while the criminal illicit enrichment law in Hong Kong targets a person that has 'control of pecuniary resources or property' that is 'disproportionate to their official emoluments', the law also targets those who have maintained 'a standard of living above that which is commensurate with his present or past official emoluments'.[80] This exact or similar phrasing is also included in the criminal illicit enrichment laws of countries such as Antigua and Barbuda,[81] Bhutan,[82] Botswana,[83] Brunei Darussalam,[84] Eswatini,[85] Ethiopia,[86] Fiji,[87] Lesotho,[88] Malawi,[89] the Marshall Islands,[90] Pakistan,[91] Sierra Leone,[92] Tanzania,[93] and

---

78   The Corruption (Prevention) Act 2000 (Jamaica), Section 14.

79   [Unofficial translation] Code pénal Malagasy (modifié par Loi No 2016-020 du 22 août 2016 sur la lutte contre la corruption), Article 183.1 (Original text: 'qui ne peut raisonnablement justifier une augmentation substantielle de son patrimoine par rapport à ses revenus légitimes.').

80   Cap.201 Prevention of Bribery Ordinance 1971 (China - Hong Kong), Section 10.

81   The Prevention of Corruption Act (Law No.21 of 2004) (Antigua and Barbuda), Article 7.

82   Anti-Corruption Act of Bhutan 2011, Section 60.

83   Corruption and Economic Crime Act 1994 (Botswana), Section 34.

84   Prevention of Corruption Act 1982 (Brunei Darussalam), Section 12.

85   The Prevention of Corruption Act 2006 (Eswatini), Section 34.

86   The Criminal Code of the Federal Democratic Republic of Ethiopia Proclamation no.414/2004, Article 419.

87   Prevention of Bribery Act (Promulgation No.12 of 2007) (Fiji), Section 10.

88   Prevention of Corruption and Economic Offences Act 1999 (as amended by the Prevention of Corruption and Economic Offences (Amendment) Act of 2006) (Lesotho), Section 31.

89   Corrupt Practices Act 1995 (as amended in 2004) (Malawi), Section 32.

90   Criminal Code 2011 (Marshall Islands), Section 240.8.

91   National Accountability Ordinance (XVIII of 1999) (Pakistan), Section 9.

92   Anti-Corruption Act 2008 (Sierra Leone), Section 27.

93   Prevention and Combating of Corruption Act 2007 (Tanzania), Section 27.

Uganda.[94] Fiji's civil illicit enrichment law also includes this style of wording.[95]

Similarly, a person may be convicted under the criminal illicit enrichment laws of Benin,[96] Burkina Faso,[97] Guinea,[98] Mali,[99] Niger,[100] São Tomé and Príncipe,[101] and Sénégal[102] if they are unable to justify the sources of funds used for their 'train de vie' or 'modo de vida' ('way of life') and in Nepal,[103] a person may have committed an offence if they have led an 'an incompatible or unsuitable lifestyle'.

Peculiarly, most of these laws do not include a definition of what a 'standard of living' or 'way of life' actually entails. An exception is the law in São Tomé and Príncipe, which states that a 'way of life' refers to 'all expenditure on consumer goods or donations made at home or abroad'.[104] In the absence of legislative definitions, however, some courts have taken it upon themselves to interpret the phrase and assess the types of items or benefits that can be construed as contributing to a person's lifestyle. For instance, in the Hong Kong case of *Ernest Percival Max Hunt v the Queen*,[105] the court surmised that '...the maintenance of a standard of living involves the acquisition of goods and services...' and that a 'standard of living, during a particular period, includes the amenities of life enjoyed during that period'.[106] In the case of *Uganda v Geoffrey Kazinda*,[107] the High Court of Uganda referred to the *Cambridge International Dictionary of English* and defined a standard of living as the level of 'wealth, comfort, material goods and necessities' available to a person.[108]

In line with these descriptions, laws that reference a 'standard of living' or 'lifestyle' arguably allow for a much broader approach to the measurement of a person's wealth. These laws not only take into account the acquisition of traditional assets but also consider the enjoyment of

---

94   Anti Corruption Act 2009 (Uganda), Section 31.

95   Proceeds of Crime Act 1997 (as amended by the Proceeds of Crime Amendment Act No. 7 of 2005 and by the Proceeds of Crime (Amendment) Decree 2012 (Decree No. 61 of 2012)) (Fiji), Section 71F.

96   Loi N° 2011-20 du 12 Octobre 2011 portant lutte contre la corruption et autres infractions connexes en République du Bénin, Article 55.

97   Loi N° 004-2015/CNT Portant prévention et répression de la corruption au Burkina Faso, Article 63.

98   Code Pénal (Guinea), Loi 59/2016, Article 776.

99   Loi N°2014-015/ Du 27 mai 2014 portant prévention et répression de l'enrichissement illicite (Mali), Article 2.

100 Ordonnance no. 92-024 du 18 Juin 1992 portant répression de l'enrichissement illicite (Niger), Article 1.

101 Código Penal, Aprovado pela Lei 6/2012 (São Tomé and Príncipe), Article 455.

102 Code Pénal, Loi No 1965-60 (Sénégal), Article 163 bis.

103 The Prevention of Corruption Act, 2059 (2002 AD) (Nepal), Section 20.

104 [Unofficial translation] Código Penal, Aprovado pela Lei 6/2012 (São Tomé and Príncipe), Article 455(3) (Original text: 'Para efeitos do n.º1 entende-se por modo de vida todos os gastos com bens de consumo ou com liberalidades realizados no país ou no estrangeiro.').

105 Ernest Percival Max Hunt v the Queen [1974] HKCA 111.

106 ibid.

107 Uganda v Geoffrey Kazinda Session Case No. HCT-AC/CO No. 004/2016 (Judgement delivered 28 October 2020).

108 ibid.

any item at all (of a measurable financial value) when assessing whether or not a person may have benefited from more wealth than can be justified through their lawful sources of income.

It should also be noted that a number of countries do not specifically include the all-encompassing phrase 'standard of living' or 'way of life' in their criminal illicit enrichment laws, but nonetheless still allow for a broad interpretation when measuring a person's total wealth. These laws instead outline specific actions or items beyond the acquisition of traditional assets which can contribute to a person's financial standing or lifestyle. For instance, in addition to targeting the acquisition of traditional property, the criminal illicit enrichment laws in China,[109] Cuba,[110] Guatemala,[111] and Peru[112] also specify that a person's 'expenditure' or 'expenses' should be taken into account when determining whether illicit enrichment has occurred. The law in the Philippines[113] can also be used to target any 'ostentatious displays of wealth'. Moreover, the criminal illicit enrichment laws in Argentina,[114] Ecuador,[115] Guatemala,[116] Kuwait,[117] Panama,[118] and Paraguay[119] also specifically take into consideration any 'debts', 'obligations' or 'liabilities' that have been reduced or cancelled, while those in Malawi[120] and Paraguay[121] also specify the receipt of services as a means through which someone could be illicitly enriched.

---

109 Criminal Law of the People's Republic of China (as amended 2017), Section 395.

110 [Unofficial translation] Ley no. 62, Código Penal de la República de Cuba, de 29.12.1987, Artículo 150 (Original text: 'gastos').

111 [Unofficial translation] Código Penal, Decreto Número 17-73 (modificado por Ley Contra La Corrupción, Decreto Número 31-2012) (Guatemala), Artículo 448 (Original text: 'gastos').

112 [Unofficial translation] Código Penal del Estado Peruano, Decreto Legislativo N°635, Artículo 401 (Original text: 'gasto económico personal').

113 Republic Act No. 3019, Anti-Graft and Corrupt Practices Act (17 August 1960) (Philippines), Section 8.

114 [Unofficial translation] Código Penal de la Nación Argentina Ley 11.179 (T.O. 1984 actualizado), Artículo 268(2) (Original text: '...sino también cuando se hubiesen cancelado deudas o extinguido obligaciones que lo afectaban.').

115 [Unofficial translation] Código Orgánico Integral Penal de la República de Ecuador, de 10.02.2014, Artículo 279 (Original text: 'Se entenderá que hubo enriquecimiento ilícito no solo cuando el patrimonio se ha incrementado con dinero, cosas o bienes, sino también cuando se han cancelado deudas o extinguido obligaciones.').

116 [Unofficial translation] Código Penal, Decreto Número 17-73 (modificado por Ley Contra La Corrupción, Decreto Número 31-2012) (Guatemala), Artículo 448 (Original text: 'cancelación de deudas u obligaciones').

117 Law No. 2 of 2016 On Establishing Kuwait Anti-Corruption Authority and the Provisions on Disclosure of Assets and Liabilities, Article 1.

118 Código Penal de la República De Panamá, Ley 14 de 2007 (con las modificaciones y adiciones introducidas por la Ley 26 de 2008), Artículo 351.

119 [Unofficial translation] Ley No. 2523 Que previene, tipifica y sanciona el enriquecimiento illcito en la función pública y el tráfico de influencias (de 13.12.2004) (Paraguay), Artículo 3 (Original text: 'Haya cancelado, luego de su ingreso a la función pública, deudas o extinguido obligaciones que afectaban su patrimonio, el de su cónyuge o su conviviente, y sus parientes hasta el segundo grado de consanguinidad y de afinidad, en condiciones que sobrepasen sus legítimas posibilidades económicas.').

120 Corrupt Practices Act 1995 (as amended in 2004) (Malawi), Section 32.

121 Ley No. 2523 Que previene, tipifica y sanciona el enriquecimiento illcito en la función pública y el tráfico de influencias (de 13.12.2004) (Paraguay), Artículo 3 (Original text: 'Haya obtenido la propiedad, la posesión, o el usufructo de bienes, derechos o servicios, cuyo valor de adquisición, posesión o usufructo sobrepase sus legítimas posibilidades económicas, y los de su cónyuge o conviviente.').

In general, civil illicit enrichment laws apply to an extremely wide interpretation of wealth.[122] These laws will often include an in-depth description of the categories of items that can be considered as contributing to a person's 'wealth' that usually includes all 'property' that can be owned, acquired or disposed of, as well as any services, advantages or benefits that a person may have received. An example of this approach is the Criminal Property Forfeiture Act 2002 of the Australian jurisdiction of the Northern Territory, which can expressly be applied to all property, services, advantages and benefits that a person may have enjoyed (see below).

Example: The extensive legislative definition of "wealth" contained in the civil illicit enrichment law of Northern Territory (Australia)

Criminal Property Forfeiture Act 2002

70. The constituents of a person's wealth

The following property, services, advantages and benefits constitute a person's wealth:

(a) all property that the person owns, whether the property was acquired before or after the commencement of this Act;

(b) all property that the person effectively controls, whether the person acquired effective control of the property before or after the commencement of this Act;

(c) all property that the person has given away at any time, whether before or after the commencement of this Act;

(d) all other property acquired by the person at any time, whether before or after the commencement of this Act, including consumer goods and consumer durables that have been consumed or discarded (but not including necessary food, clothing and other items reasonably necessary for ordinary daily requirements of life);

(e) all services, advantages and benefits that the person has acquired at any time, whether before or after the commencement of this Act;

(f) all property, services, advantages and benefits acquired, at the request or direction of the person, by another person at any time, whether before or after the commencement of this Act, including consumer goods and consumer durables that have been consumed or discarded (but not including necessary food, clothing and other items reasonably necessary for ordinary daily requirements of life);

---

122 Exceptions include qualified civil illicit enrichment law in Kenya (Anti-Corruption and Economic Crimes Act 2003) and the civil illicit enrichment laws in Zanzibar, Tanzania (The Zanzibar Anti-Corruption and Economic Crimes Act 2012) and Mauritius (The Good Governance and Integrity Reporting Act 2015) which only apply to 'assets'.

(g) anything of monetary value acquired by the person or another person, in Australia or elsewhere, from the commercial exploitation of any product or any broadcast, telecast or other publication, where the commercial value of the product, broadcast, telecast or other publication depends on or is derived from the person's involvement in the commission of a forfeiture offence, whether or not the thing was lawfully acquired and whether or not the person has been charged with or convicted of the offence.

Treatment of third-party assets and benefits

A number of civil and criminal illicit enrichment laws specifically take into account wealth held or received by people closely connected to the accused/respondent if it can be proven that the person is holding the wealth on behalf of the accused/respondent, or did not pay adequate consideration for it. This ensures that the law can still apply in situations where a person has attempted to disguise the true owner or beneficiary of certain items of wealth.

For example, the laws in a number of jurisdictions, such as Bhutan,[123] Botswana,[124] Eswatini,[125] Fiji,[126] Hong Kong (China),[127] Lesotho,[128] the Marshall Islands,[129] Tanzania,[130] Zanzibar (Tanzania),[131] Sierra Leone,[132] and Uganda[133] specifically target any assets deemed to be held by another party 'in trust for or otherwise' on behalf of the person subjected to illicit enrichment proceedings. The jurisdictions of the Northern Territory (Australia)[134] and Tasmania (Australia)[135] also take into account property that the person in question may have simply 'given away'.

Moreover, the illicit enrichment law in Mexico[136] allows the court to take into consideration assets obtained by a 'spouse' or 'dependants' when calculating the total amount of illicit enrichment that has taken place (unless the accused person can prove that these assets were

---

123   Anti-Corruption Act of Bhutan 2011, Section 60.

124   Corruption and Economic Crime Act 1994 (Botswana), Section 34.

125   The Prevention of Corruption Act 2006 (Eswatini), Section 34.

126   Prevention of Bribery Act (Promulgation No.12 of 2007) (Fiji), Section 10.

127   Cap.201 Prevention of Bribery Ordinance 1971 (China - Hong Kong), Section 10(2).

128   Prevention of Corruption and Economic Offences Act 1999 (as amended by the Prevention of Corruption and Economic Offences (Amendment) Act of 2006) (Lesotho), Section 31.

129   Criminal Code 2011 (Marshall Islands), Section 240.8.

130   Prevention and Combating of Corruption Act 2007 (Tanzania), Section 27.

131   The Zanzibar Anti-Corruption and Economic Crimes Act 2012 (Tanzania - Zanzibar), Section 66.

132   Anti-Corruption Act 2008 (Sierra Leone), Section 27.

133   Anti Corruption Act 2009 (Uganda), Section 31.

134   Criminal Property Forfeiture Act 2002 (Australia - Northern Territory), Article 70.

135   Crime (Confiscation of Profits) Act 1993 (Australia - Tasmania), Section 138.

136   Código Penal Federal (Mexico), Artículo 224.

obtained independently by them). The law in Paraguay[137] also specifically takes into account any cancelled debts or obligations of an accused person's spouse or other relatives in similar calculations.

2.2.2.3 Value thresholds restricting the scope of application

Does the state need to prove a minimum value of wealth, or an increase in overall wealth, or an increase in disproportionate wealth before the law can be applied?

While the vast majority of jurisdictions do not impose a value limitation in their illicit enrichment laws, many laws require the state to establish either a minimum value of:

- the overall wealth of the targeted person;
- the increase in the overall wealth of a person over a certain period of time; or
- the increase in the wealth of a person over and above their lawful income.

For example, with regards to the first option, the qualified civil illicit enrichment law of Trinidad and Tobago[138] will only impose an 'unexplained wealth order' on a person with a provable total wealth over 500,000 Trinidad and Tobago Dollars, while with regards to the second option, the criminal illicit enrichment law in Afghanistan[139] is only applicable if a person has increased their assets by over 500,000 Afghanis in a single year. Finally, with regards to the third option, the criminal illicit enrichment law of Honduras[140] can only be applied if it can be proven that the targeted person has increased their assets by more than 500,000 Lempiras above their legitimate income.

In parallel with the wording included in Article 20 of UNCAC, some criminal illicit enrichment laws impose an indefinite value threshold and outline instead that an unjustifiable increase in assets needs to be 'significant' or 'substantial' before the law can be applied. For example, the law in the Republic of the Congo[141] outlines that the illicit enrichment offence will apply to a person 'who cannot reasonably justify a substantial increase of his assets in comparison

---

137 Ley No. 2523 Que previene, tipifica y sanciona el enriquecimiento ilícito en la función pública y el tráfico de influencias (de 13.12.2004) (Paraguay), Artículo 3(1)(b).

138 Civil Asset Recovery and Management and Unexplained Wealth Act, 2019 (Trinidad and Tobago), Section 58.

139 Penal Code (Afghanistan), Article 419(2).

140 Código Penal (Decreto No. 130-2017)(Honduras), Artículo 484.

141 [Unofficial translation] Loi n° 5-2009 sur la corruption, la concussion, la fraude et les infractions assimilées (Republic of the Congo), Article 20 (Original text: 'Sera reconnu coupable du crime d'enrichissement illicite et puni de la réclusion pour une durée allant de cinq ans à dix ans au plus sans possibilité de bénéficier du produit des travaux effectués, tout agent public, personne chargée d'une mission de service public, personne investie d'un mandat public électif, tout dirigeant, mandataire ou salarié d'entreprise publique ou toute autre personne qui ne peut raisonnablement justifier l'augmentation substantielle de son patrimoine par rapport à ses revenus légitimes.').

with his legitimate income' while the law in Nicaragua[142] outlines that illicit enrichment occurs when a public official 'obtains an increase in his or her wealth that is significantly in excess of his or her legitimate income'. Similar thresholds are also included in the laws of Algeria,[143] Argentina,[144] Armenia,[145] Chile,[146] Côte d'Ivoire,[147] the Democratic Republic of the Congo,[148] Djibouti,[149] Haiti,[150] Madagascar, [151] Mali,[152] and Moldova.[153]

2.2.2.4 Limitation periods for application (criminal illicit enrichment laws)

Are there any time limitations in which the illicit enrichment law needs to be applied?

A number of criminal illicit enrichment laws take contrary approaches regarding the inclusion of limitation periods. While the laws in a number of jurisdictions explicitly outline that there is no limitation period that can be applied to the enforcement of illicit enrichment offences, laws in other jurisdictions outline strict time limits in which criminal proceedings can be commenced.

For instance, the law in a number of countries explicitly states that illicit enrichment is, by nature, a continuous offence, due to the fact that the accused person is perpetually enjoying a direct or indirect benefit from the act of enrichment. For example the laws in Algeria,[154]

---

142 [Unofficial translation] Código Penal, Ley N°. 641, Aprobado el 13 de Noviembre de 2007 (Nicaragua), Artículo 448 (Original text: 'La autoridad, funcionario o empleado público, que sin incurrir en un delito más severamente penado, obtenga un incremento de su patrimonio con significativo exceso, respecto de sus ingresos legítimos, durante el ejercicio de sus funciones y que no pueda justificar razonablemente su procedencia, al ser requerido por el órgano competente señalado en la ley, será sancionado de tres a seis años de prisión e inhabilitación por el mismo período para ejercer cargo o empleo público.').

143 Loi n°06 - 01 du 20 février 2006 relative à la prévention et à la lutte contre la corruption (Algeria) Article 37.

144 Código Penal de la Nación Argentina Ley 11.179 (T.O. 1984 actualizado), Artículo 268(2).

145 Criminal Code of The Republic of Armenia of April 29, 2003, No. ZR-528 (as amended on 13-11-2019), Article 310(1).

146 Código Penal de noviembre 12 de 1874 (enmendada por la Ley 20088 de 2006) (Chile), Artículo 241 bis.

147 Ordonnance n° 2013-660 relative à la prévention et à la lutte contre la corruption et les infractions assimilées (20.09.2013) (Côte d'Ivoire), Article 56.

148 Code Pénal Congolais, Décret du 30 janvier 1940 (tel que modifié par la loi N° 05/006 du 29.03.2005) (Democratic Republic of the Congo), Article 6.

149 Loi N° 111/AN/11/6ème L relative à la lutte contre le terrorisme et autres infractions graves (25.05.2011) (Djibouti), Article 11.

150 1987 Constitution de la République d'Haiti, Article 242 (though Haiti's actual offence of illicit enrichment does not mention this type of threshold, see loi portant prévention et répression de la corruption (Loi No. CI-2014-008), Article 5.2).

151 Code pénal Malagasy (modifié par Loi No 2016-020 du 22 août 2016 sur la lutte contre la corruption), Article 183.1.

152 Loi N°2014-015/ Du 27 mai 2014 portant prévention et répression de l'enrichissement illicite, (Mali) Article 2.

153 Criminal Code 2002 (as amended by the Criminal Law 326 as of 23.12.13) (Moldova), Article 330/2.

154 [Unofficial translation] Loi n°06 - 01 du 20 février 2006 relative à la prévention et à la lutte contre la corruption (Algeria), Article 37 (Original text: 'L'enrichissement illicite, visé à l'alinéa 1er du présent article, est une infraction continue caractérisée par la détention des biens illicites ou leur emploi d'une manière directe ou indirecte.').

Burkina Faso[155] and Mauritania[156] outline that illicit enrichment 'is a continuous offence characterised by the possession of illicit property or its use in a direct or indirect manner'. Similar phrasing is also used in the illicit enrichment law of Madagascar,[157] while in Niger,[158] the law specifies that illicit enrichment 'constitutes a continuous offence which is deemed to be committed by the mere perpetuation of its criminal effects'. Other countries such as Tanzania do not expressly state that the illicit enrichment offence is continuous, but indirectly grant the offence a continuous status by not applying an explicit limitation period to its enforcement.[159]

The laws in other countries take a contrary stance, and apply time limitations on the enforcement of illicit enrichment provisions. For example, in Haiti,[160] the Constitution imposes a limitation period of twenty years.

Interestingly, Mali takes a different approach again and classifies the illicit enrichment offence as continuous, but then imposes a limitation period from the date on which the elements of the offence are discovered.[161]

2.2.3   Explicit reverse onus provisions

Does the illicit enrichment law specifically include a provision requiring a targeted person to produce evidence regarding the lawful sources of their wealth?

A number of illicit enrichment laws include an explicit mechanism that may be triggered to

---

155 [Unofficial translation] Loi N° 004-2015/CNT Portant prévention et répression de la corruption au Burkina Faso, Article 63 (Original text: 'Le délit d'apparence, ainsi visé, est une infraction continue caractérisée par la détention des biens illicites ou leur emploi d'une manière directe ou indirecte.').

156 [Unofficial translation] Loi n° 2016.014 relative à la lutte contre la corruption (Mauritania), Article 16 (Original text: 'L'enrichissement illicite, visé à l'alinéa premier du présent article, est une infraction continue caractérisée par la détention des biens illicites ou leur emploi d'une manière directe ou indirecte.').

157 Code pénal Malagasy (modifié par Loi No 2016-020 du 22 août 2016 sur la lutte contre la corruption), Article 183.1 (Original text: 'L'enrichissement illicite constitue une infraction continue caractérisée par la détention du patrimoine ou l'emploi des ressources illicites.').

158 [Unofficial translation] Ordonnance no. 92-024 du 18 Juin 1992 portant répression de l'enrichissement illicite (Niger), Article 2 (Original text: 'L'enrichissement illicite constitue une infraction permanente qui est réputée consommée par la seule perpétuation de ses effets délictueux La prescription de l'action publique frappant éventuellement les faits à l'origine de l'enrichissement illicite ne peut lui être opposée dès lors que les éléments constitutifs de l'enrichissement illicite en tant que délit spécifique, tel que défini à l'article 1er, sont réunis.').

159 In Tanzania there is no statute on limitations for corruption offences contained in the Prevention and Combating of Corruption Act 2007 – Conference of State Parties to the United Nations Convention Against Corruption, *Review of the Implementation of the United Nations Convention Against Corruption (United Republic of Tanzania) CAC/COSP/IRG/I/3/1/Add.9*, United Nations, Vienna, 2014, p.5.

160 1987 Constitution de la République d'Haiti, Article 243 (Original text: 'Le Fonctionnaire coupable des délits sus-désignés ne peut bénéficier que de la prescription vicennale. Cette prescription ne commence à courir qu'à partir de la cessation de ses fonctions ou des causes qui auraient empêché toute poursuite.'). It is unclear if this limitation applies to the offence of illicit enrichment contained in the loi portant prévention et répression de la corruption (Loi No. CI-2014-008).

161 Loi N°2014-015/ Du 27 mai 2014 portant prévention et répression de l'enrichissement illicite (Mali), Article 5 (Original text: 'L'enrichissement illicite est une infraction continue. Le délai de prescription ne court qu'à compter du jour de la découverte des éléments constitutifs de l'enrichissement illicite. L'enrichissement illicite est une infraction réputée consommée par la seule continuation de ses effets.').

obligate a person to produce evidence regarding the lawful sources of their wealth. While some laws require a person to explain the lawful sources of 'all' the wealth that they have enjoyed, other laws are less onerous and only require a person to explain the value of wealth that is established by the state to be disproportionate to their known sources of income.

The inclusion of such specifically outlined obligations is not universal, and many laws do not include them. There are even some illicit enrichment laws that take an opposing approach and instead specify that the state holds the responsibility of bringing evidence to prove the alleged illicit enrichment at all times.

Note that throughout this publication, the phrase reverse 'onus' and reverse 'burden' are used interchangeably as both these terms are used in illicit enrichment legislation.

2.2.3.1   An obligation on a person to prove the lawfulness of all their wealth

Many civil illicit enrichment laws contain a specifically drafted provision that clearly places a burden on the person targeted by the law to prove the legitimate sources of all their established wealth. For example, in proceedings under the civil illicit enrichment law of Western Australia, '[a]ny property, service, advantage or benefit that is a constituent of the respondent's wealth is presumed not to have been lawfully acquired unless the respondent establishes the contrary'.[162] Under the civil illicit enrichment law of Mauritius 'the onus shall lie on the respondent to establish, on a balance of probabilities, that any property is not unexplained wealth'.[163] Similarly in the qualified civil illicit enrichment law in another Australian jurisdiction, New South Wales, '[t]he burden of proof in proceedings against a person for an unexplained wealth order is on the person to prove that the person's current or previous wealth is not or was not illegally acquired property or the proceeds of an illegal activity'.[164] Finally, in the qualified civil illicit enrichment law of Trinidad and Tobago, it is also specifically outlined that 'the burden of proving the wealth of the respondent is lawfully acquired lies on the respondent.'[165]

Such direct and unambiguous mechanisms are undoubtedly quite controversial, particularly as the initiator of the legal action, the state, will only be required to establish that a person controls or enjoys wealth before the reverse onus mechanism is triggered and the person is required to establish the legality of this wealth. There is no obligation under such mechanisms for the state to establish that the wealth in question is in any way disproportionate to a person's known legal income before it is presumed to have been unlawfully sourced. Instead, once the state has established that a person has benefited from certain wealth then it is

---

162   Criminal Property Confiscation Act 2000 (Australia - Western Australia), Section 12(2).

163   The Good Governance and Integrity Reporting Act (Mauritius), Section 3(5).

164   Criminal Assets Recovery Act 1990 (Australia - New South Wales), Section 28B(3).

165   Civil Asset Recovery and Management and Unexplained Wealth Act, 2019 (Trinidad and Tobago), Section 65(4).

completely the responsibility of the targeted person to prove that the established wealth has come from lawful sources.

In light of this, however, it is important to note that these laws also include specific safeguards to prevent against their abuse. These are discussed in more detail in Section 2.3.

2.2.3.2 An obligation on a person to prove the lawfulness of an amount of wealth determined to be disproportionate to their known lawful income

Many criminal illicit enrichment laws take a more tempered approach and specify that a person may be convicted of an illicit enrichment offence if they are unable to provide a 'satisfactory' or 'reasonable' explanation for an amount of enjoyed wealth that is established to be over and above their known sources of legal income.

For example, in Tanzania if the state establishes that a public official has maintained a standard of living incommensurate with their present or past lawful income, or owns property disproportionate to their present or past lawful income, then they will be guilty of an offence 'unless [they] give a satisfactory explanation to the court as to how [they were] able to maintain such a standard of living or how such property came under [their] ownership'.[166] Similarly, in India, a public official will be presumed to have illicitly enriched themselves if it is established that they are in possession of pecuniary resources or property disproportionate to their known sources of income that they 'cannot satisfactorily account for'[167] while in Nicaragua, an official who obtains an increase in their assets that is significantly in excess of their legitimate income may be guilty of an illicit enrichment offence if they 'cannot reasonably justify its origin'.[168]

As can be seen from the phrasing used above, these laws differ from the civil examples mentioned in the previous approach as the state must first establish that a person has benefited from a certain amount of disproportionate wealth before an obligation to provide evidence of lawful income is placed on the person.

While this style of statutory obligation is somewhat less controversial, arguments have still been raised about the overall compatibility of such obligations with established criminal law rights such as the presumption of innocence, the right to silence and the privilege against self-incrimination. To date, however, the prevailing judicial view is that these mechanisms are

---

166 Prevention and Combating of Corruption Act 2007 (Tanzania), Section 27.

167 Prevention of Corruption Act 1988 (as amended by the Prevention of Corruption (Amendment) Act 2018) (India), Section 13(1).

168 [Unofficial translation] Código Penal, Ley N°. 641, Aprobado el 13 de Noviembre de 2007 (Nicaragua), Artículo 448 (Original text: 'La autoridad, funcionario o empleado público, que sin incurrir en un delito más severamente penado, obtenga un incremento de su patrimonio con significativo exceso, respecto de sus ingresos legítimos, durante el ejercicio de sus funciones y que no pueda justificar razonablemente su procedencia, al ser requerido por el órgano competente señalado en la ley, será sancionado de tres a seis años de prisión e inhabilitación por el mismo período para ejercer cargo o empleo público.').

compatible with such rights, as they are viewed as a proportional and necessary mechanism to combat certain crimes, such as corruption. This is discussed in detail in Part 4.

2.2.3.3 An alternative approach – laws in which the entire burden of proof is explicitly placed on the state

There are examples of criminal illicit enrichment laws that take a completely different approach to the laws above, expressly stating that the burden of establishing the existence of illicit enrichment rests solely with the state. For example, the criminal illicit enrichment law of Chile expressly states that '[t]he proof of unjustified enrichment…shall always be the responsibility of the Public Prosecutor's Office.'[169] The inclusion of such clarifications may serve to alleviate concerns that the particular law violates rights such as the presumption of innocence.

2.2.3.4 Beyond the legislation – judicial interpretations of obligations contained in illicit enrichment laws

It is important to highlight that some courts with criminal illicit enrichment laws have nullified both express and implied obligations that exist in these laws by ruling that the laws under no circumstances impose a requirement on an accused person to produce evidence or prove their innocence. In doing so, courts have sought to negate concerns that these laws contravene established legal principles, such as the presumption of innocence and the right to silence. For instance, while Argentina's law targets 'any person who, upon being duly requested, does not justify the origin of appreciable enrichment of his or her own property',[170] the Supreme Court has subsequently clarified that this wording does not require a person to 'justify' their assets, but instead merely gives them 'the possibility of justifying the origin of [their] enrichment as well as the power to refuse to testify'.[171]

---

169 [Unofficial translation] Código Penal de noviembre 12 de 1874 (enmendada por la Ley 20088 de 2006) (Chile), Article 241 bis (Original text: 'La prueba del enriquecimiento injustificado a que se refiere este artículo será siempre de cargo del Ministerio Público.').

170 [Unofficial translation] Código Penal de la Nación Argentina Ley 11.179 (T.O. 1984 actualizado) (Original text: 'Será reprimido con prisión de dos (2) a seis (6) años, multa de dos (2) a cinco (5) veces del valor del enriquecimiento, e inhabilitación absoluta perpetua, el que al ser debidamente requerido, no justificare la procedencia de un enriquecimiento patrimonial apreciable suyo o de persona interpuesta para disimularlo, ocurrido con posterioridad a la asunción de un cargo o empleo público y hasta dos (2) años después de haber cesado en su desempeño.').

171 [Unofficial translation] Poder Judicial de la Nación, Juzgado Criminal y Correccional Federal 3, 'César Santos Gerardo del Corazón de Jesús Milani', CFP 6734/2013 (2017/09) (Original text: 'De esta forma, con el llamamiento efectuado, no se invirtió la carga de la prueba ni fue violatorio de la prohibición de declarar en contra de uno mismo, sino que, con dicha convocatoria, se le brindó a Milani la posibilidad de justificar el origen de su enriquecimiento como así también la facultad de negarse a declarar (cfr. C.N.C.P., in re: 'Alsogaray', ya citado).'). It is also important to note that despite the continued upholding of this view in the court, the issue of whether or not Argentina's illicit enrichment law includes a reversal of the burden of proof continues to be debated amongst Argentinian legal commentators – see for example: G. Marnich, *Análisis Constitucional del Artículo 268(2) del Código Penal a la Luz del Caso 'Alsogaray'*, Secretaría General de Capacitación y Jurisprudencia, 2018 and E. Aguirre et al., Constituciona Lidad del Art 268(2) C.P, Universidad Nacional de La Pampa (tesis), Santa Rosa, 2010.

The operation of reverse burden mechanisms within illicit enrichment laws, as well as subsequent judicial interpretations regarding these mechanisms are further examined in detail in Part 3.

2.2.4 A legal power to obligate the disclosure of information

Does the illicit enrichment law or its overarching legislative instrument include a provision that allows the state to obligate a person to reveal financial information?

Illicit enrichment laws (or the overarching legislative instrument under which the illicit enrichment law is contained) sometimes also include a mechanism that grants a legal power to the state to obligate a person to provide financial information surrounding their wealth and the sources of income used to acquire or enjoy this wealth.

This legal power is similar, but unconnected to, commonly existing asset declaration mechanisms that require public officials to regularly declare their assets as a condition of holding a public position. This separate power can instead be utilised during an illicit enrichment investigation to require a person to make a sworn statement outlining details surrounding their wealth, such as a complete list of the assets that they own and the sources of income used to acquire these assets.

The form and extent of this disclosure power will generally differ between criminal illicit enrichment laws and civil illicit enrichment laws. In criminal illicit enrichment laws, this disclosure power is often granted directly to the relevant law enforcement agency by the legislation itself, empowering the relevant law enforcement officers to request this information from a person during the course of an investigation. For example, under the Prevention of Corruption Act of Brunei Darussalam (the overarching legislative instrument containing the country's illicit enrichment law) a public prosecutor has the power to issue a written notice to a person suspected of an illicit enrichment offence requiring them to:

> ...furnish a statutory declaration or, as the Public Prosecutor sees fit, a statement in writing enumerating all movable or immovable property belonging to or possessed by such person and by the spouse, parents, or sons and daughters of such person, and specifying the date on which each of the properties enumerated was acquired whether by way of purchase, gift, bequest, inheritance or otherwise...[172]

A failure to comply with such an order is an offence in itself, and may result in a fine and imprisonment for a year.[173]

This point in particular is quite controversial, as a compulsory requirement to disclose information for the purposes of a criminal investigation is arguably contrary to the privilege against self-incrimination.

---

172 Prevention of Corruption Act 1982 (Brunei Darussalam), Section 23A(1)(a).

173 Prevention of Corruption Act 1982 (Brunei Darussalam), Section 23A(2).

In Niger, parts of the illicit enrichment law have even been ruled unconstitutional on this point. Under the Ordonnance no. 92-024 du 18 Juin 1992 portant répression de l'enrichissement illicite, as soon as a formal investigation into illicit enrichment was opened against a person, the Public Prosecutor's Office was previously empowered to send a request to this person for information relating to their assets and income.[174] A response to this request was compulsory, and an absence of a reply would result in an automatic presumption against the person that they have illicitly enriched themselves.[175] While the rest of the law was deemed to be valid, these specific powers (and the resulting presumption in the absence of a reply) were deemed to be unconstitutional.[176]

In contrast to the examples above, civil illicit enrichment laws that include disclosure powers will often take a more tempered approach. Rather than granting the power to obligate disclosure directly to the relevant law enforcement agency, the law will instead require the law enforcement agency to seek an independently issued court order that can be used to obligate a person to reveal their financial information. When applicable, this information will then be used as evidence during an application hearing for a subsequent final court order to establish the existence of illicit enrichment.

For example, under the qualified illicit enrichment law of the Bahamas, before the state applies for a final 'unexplained wealth order' against a person, it first applies for an 'unexplained wealth order *nisi*' under which the targeted person may be required to file declarations or answer questions as required in relation to their assets.[177] The state will then be able to use this information in its application for an 'unexplained wealth order *absolute*'. Interestingly, while the information contained in such a statement can be used for the purpose of the subsequent civil application for a final order, 'anything disclosed in any statement and any information, document, or thing obtained as a direct or indirect consequence of the statement shall not be admissible against the person in any criminal proceeding except a proceeding in respect of the falsity of the statement.'[178] This is an important point as it arguably counters any claims that the above disclosure obligations contravene the right to silence and the privilege against self-incrimination.

Similarly, under the civil illicit enrichment law of Mauritius, if the Integrity Reporting Services Agency suspects that someone may have illicitly enriched themselves, it has the statutory power to issue a non-compulsory written request to a person to explain 'the source of any funds which the person owns, possesses, has custody or control of, or which are believed

---

174   Ordonnance no. 92-024 du 18 Juin 1992 portant répression de l'enrichissement illicite (Niger), Article 4.

175   Ordonnance no. 92-024 du 18 Juin 1992 portant répression de l'enrichissement illicite (Niger), Article 5.

176   Arrêt n° 07/08/CC/MC du 20 novembre 2008 (Cour Constitutionnelle) (Niger).

177   The Proceeds of Crime Act 2018 (Bahamas), Section 75(4).

178   The Proceeds of Crime Act 2018 (Bahamas), Section 75(3).

to have been used in the acquisition of any property'.[179] In the event that the person fails to reply to the request, the Agency is then empowered to apply for a court-mandated disclosure order for 'information on property held by a person or by any other person on his behalf' or the 'sources of funds used to acquire, possess or control any property.'[180] The information obtained from either the request or the order may subsequently be used to apply for a final 'unexplained wealth order' against the person.

2.2.5 Requirement to establish a 'reasonable suspicion or 'reasonable belief'

Does the state need to establish a 'reasonable suspicion' that criminal activity has taken place or that the wealth was derived from crime?

As discussed in Part 1, some illicit enrichment laws (classified within this publication as 'qualified illicit enrichment laws') contain an extra characteristic that sets them apart from regular illicit enrichment laws, namely that they require a state to provide evidence to a court of a 'reasonable suspicion' or 'reasonable belief' that criminality of some sort has taken place or that the wealth in question has been derived from an offence. This is a much easier threshold to meet than that contained in traditional non-conviction based confiscation laws (which instead require criminality to be established to a civil standard) and consequently these laws should still be considered within the category of illicit enrichment laws, albeit under their own classification. Nonetheless, this qualification adds an extra evidential threshold to the law that does not exist in other illicit enrichment laws.

While this 'reasonable suspicion' characteristic is quite common in civil illicit enrichment laws around the world, it can also exist in criminal illicit enrichment laws. For example in 2018, Singapore introduced Section 47AA of the Corruption, Drug Trafficking and Other Serious Crimes (Confiscation of Benefits) Act[181] in an effort to target 'money mules' for criminal syndicates.[182] Under this provision, any person who 'possesses or uses any property that may be reasonably suspected of being... directly or indirectly, representing, any benefits of drug dealing or benefits from criminal conduct' shall be guilty of an offence if they cannot account for how they acquired the property.

---

179 The Good Governance and Integrity Reporting Act 2015 (Mauritius), Section 5(1).

180 The Good Governance and Integrity Reporting Act 2015 (Mauritius), Sections 5(2), 13.

181 The Corruption, Drug Trafficking and Other Serious Crimes (Confiscation of Benefits) Act 1992 (Singapore) Section 47AA (introduced by the the Serious Crimes and Counter-Terrorism (Miscellaneous Amendments) Act 2018 (Singapore)).

182 Singapore, Parliamentary Debates (Second Reading of the Serious Crimes and Counter Terrorism (Miscellaneous Amendments) Bill 2018), Parliament of Singapore, 19 November 2018 (Josephine Teo, Minister for Manpower and Second Minister for Home Affairs).

2.2.6   Sanctions

What legal measures are imposed if illicit enrichment is proven?

Like with any laws, the sanctions outlined by illicit enrichment laws differ enormously from jurisdiction to jurisdiction. Of course, an obvious distinction exists between civil illicit enrichment laws, where sanctions are purely monetary-based, and criminal illicit enrichment laws, which may outline further criminal punishments such as imprisonment and additional fines.

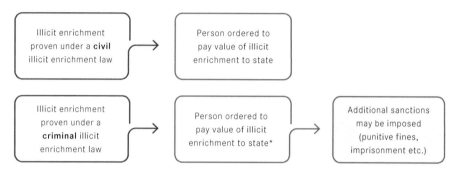

*this may sometimes be in the form of a fine

2.2.6.1 Sanctions under civil illicit enrichment laws

If illicit enrichment is proven under a civil illicit enrichment law, the respondent will be ordered to pay a civil debt to the state to the value of the proven illicit enrichment.

For example in Western Australia, if during proceedings the state proves that the 'total value of the respondent's wealth is greater than the value of the respondent's lawfully acquired wealth' then the court will issue an 'unexplained wealth declaration' under which 'the respondent is liable to pay to the State an amount equal to the amount specified in the declaration as the assessed value of the respondent's unexplained wealth'.[183]

Similarly, under the qualified illicit enrichment law in the Bahamas, if 'the Court is satisfied on a balance of probabilities that any part of the relevant person's wealth was not lawfully obtained or held' it may issue an 'unexplained wealth order, *absolute'* under which 'the relevant person is liable to pay to the Crown an amount equal to the amount that the Court is satisfied does not represent the relevant person's lawfully acquired property'.[184]

2.2.6.2 Sanctions imposed under criminal illicit enrichment laws

If a person is proven to have illicitly enriched themselves under a criminal illicit enrichment

---

183   Criminal Property Confiscation Act 2000 (Australia - Western Australia) Sections 10-14.

184   The Proceeds of Crime Act 2018 (Bahamas), Section 78.

law then they may be subjected to more severe sanctions, including potential imprisonment and / or fines.

Imprisonment

All criminal illicit enrichment laws identified in this publication (with the exception of Chile) outline the possibility of imprisonment as a potential sanction on the person found to have enriched themselves.

Many of these laws however do not specify that imprisonment is a compulsory sentence but that a punishment may include a prison sentence as an addition to, or in place of, a fine. For example in Uganda, if a person is proven to have illicitly enriched themselves then they are '... liable on conviction to a term of imprisonment not exceeding ten years or a fine not exceeding two hundred and forty currency points or both'.[185]

Potential prison sentences vary enormously from jurisdiction to jurisdiction. For instance, a person guilty of an illicit enrichment offence in Mexico[186] may face only three months' imprisonment, while a convicted person may face up to fifteen years in jail in Djibouti[187] or Moldova,[188] or even up to twenty years in Malaysia.[189]

Fines

Most jurisdictions with a criminal illicit enrichment law also outline a potential fine that may be imposed on a convicted person in place of, or in addition to, a sentence for imprisonment. For example, a convicted person in Sierra Leone[190] will be required to pay a fine of no less than 30,000,000 Leones while a convicted person in Tanzania[191] may be required to pay a fine of up to 10,000,000 Tanzanian Shillings. Furthermore, a person found to have benefited from an 'illegal gain' in Egypt will be required to 'pay a fine equal to the value of the illegal gain' in addition to the recovery of the gain itself.[192]

Administrative sanctions

A number of jurisdictions also impose additional sanctions on public officials who are convicted under criminal illicit enrichment laws, and will often disqualify a convicted public official from holding a public position either indefinitely, or for a specified period of time. For example, a convicted public official in Mongolia[193] may be deprived of the right to be

---

185 Anti Corruption Act 2009 (Uganda), Section 31.

186 Código Penal Federal (Mexico), Artículo 224.

187 Loi N° 111/AN/11/6ème L relative à la lutte contre le terrorisme et autres infractions graves (25.05.2011) (Djibouti), Article 11.

188 Criminal Code 2002 (as amended by the Criminal Law 326 as of 23.12.13) (Moldova), Article 330/2.

189 Malaysia Anti-Corruption Commission Act 2009, Section 36.

190 Anti-Corruption Act 2008 (Sierra Leone), Article 27.

191 Prevention and Combating of Corruption Act 2007 (Tanzania), Section 27.

192 Law no. 62 of 1975, Regarding Illegal Gains (Egypt), Article 18.

193 Criminal Code (Mongolia), Article 22.10.

appointed to public office for two years. A convicted public official in Antigua and Barbuda[194] will be disqualified from holding office for up to seven years, and may even forfeit any rights under existing pension schemes. Similarly in El Salvador,[195] an official may be prohibited from holding a public position for up to ten years – which was the sanction recently imposed on former president Elias Antonio Saca.[196]

Sanctions for companies involved in illicit enrichment

As noted previously, illicit enrichment laws in a few countries can also specifically be applied to 'legal persons', and consequently punishments directly relating to these legal persons may also be imposed. For instance, a Malagasy company may be forced to cease commercial operations for up to twenty years if it is found to have knowingly received wealth originating from someone who had illicitly enriched themselves.[197]

Scaling of imprisonment and fines: applying harsher sentences in certain circumstances

For some countries, the illicit enrichment law specifically provides a scale of punishment that should be imposed depending on the amount by which a person has enriched themselves. For example, in Mali, if someone is found to have enriched themselves by an amount less than or equal to 50,000,000 Francs, a sentence of one to three years and a fine equal to the value of enrichment can be imposed on them, while if they are found to have enriched themselves by a larger amount, then the punishment will include a prison sentence of three to five years and a fine twice the value of the enriched amount.[198] Similarly in Honduras, a public official who has illicitly enriched themselves by more than 500,000 Lempiras may face a punishment of four to six years' imprisonment, a fine of up to three times the value of enrichment and suspension from exercise of public office for a time period twice as large as the period of imprisonment. In contrast, a public official who has enriched themselves by more than 1,000,000 Lempiras will face a punishment of up to eight years' imprisonment, a fine of up to four times the value of enrichment and complete disqualification from holding a public position.[199]

Additionally, certain laws may impose different penalties on a person convicted of illicit enrichment depending on whether or not they are a public official – such as in Cuba,[200] where sentences of three to eight years may be imposed on public officials while sentences of only two to five years can be imposed on regular citizens. Alternatively, the level of punishment

---

194 The Prevention of Corruption Act (Law No.21 of 2004) (Antigua and Barbuda), Article 8.

195 Código Penal de la República de El Salvador, 26.04.1997 (29.01.2020), Artículo 333.

196 N. Renteria, 'Salvadoran court orders ex-president to return $4.4 million in stolen funds', Reuters, 6 January 2021, https://www.reuters.com/article/us-el-salvador-corruption-idUSKBN29B05W, accessed 10 March 2021.

197 Code pénal Malagasy (modifié par Loi No 2016-020 du 22 août 2016 sur la lutte contre la corruption), Article 183.1.

198 Loi N°2014-015/ Du 27 mai 2014 portant prévention et répression de l'enrichissement illicite (Mali), Article 37.

199 Código Penal (Decreto No. 130-2017) (Honduras), Artículo 484.

200 Ley no. 62, Código Penal de la República de Cuba, de 29.12.1987, Artículo 150.

imposed may depend on the level of seniority of a public official subjected to the charge. For example in Peru,[201] a convicted public official will potentially face a prison sentence of five to ten years, while a convicted public official holding certain senior management positions may face sentences of ten to fifteen years.

Finally, an accused person in Mali[202] may be able to reduce their punishment to a suspended sentence if they pay back the illicit wealth in full to the state while an accused person in Niger[203] may be able to nullify any potential punishment completely if they voluntarily return the full amount of illicit enrichment to the state before a judgement is made.

Recovery of the illicit wealth under criminal illicit enrichment proceedings

Besides imprisonment, fines or administrative sanctions, a person convicted under a criminal illicit enrichment law will also be required to return the amount of wealth deemed to have been illicitly acquired. The mechanisms through which such compensatory orders are made varies from jurisdiction to jurisdiction. Some laws overlap an obligation to repay the value of illicit wealth with an obligation to pay a fine by including the value of the illicit wealth as part of the fine. Laws in other jurisdictions however, impose an obligation to repay the value of the illicit wealth separately from any additional fines that may also be imposed. For instance, fines for convictions under the Tanzanian[204] and Sierra Leonean[205] laws may be imposed in addition to separate measures that require a convicted person to also repay the value of the proven amount of illicit enrichment.

---

201 Código Penal del Estado Peruano, Decreto Legislativo N°635, Artículo 401.

202 Loi N°2014-015/ Du 27 mai 2014 portant prévention et répression de l'enrichissement illicite (Mali), Article 37.

203 Ordonnance no. 92-024 du 18 Juin 1992 portant répression de l'enrichissement illicite (Niger), Article 10.

204 Prevention and Combating of Corruption Act 2007 (Tanzania), Section 27.

205 Anti-Corruption Act 2008 (Sierra Leone), Article 27.

2.3 Safeguards contained in some illicit enrichment laws

As illicit enrichment laws do not require the state to prove the existence of criminal activity, and instead often allow for presumptions that criminal activity has taken place, it is often argued that they can potentially violate established legal rights or can be abused by the state.

To address these concerns, a number of illicit enrichment laws have been drafted to include certain safeguards to minimise the chance of these laws being applied unjustly:

- The civil illicit enrichment law in Australia (at the federal level) and the two qualified civil enrichment laws in the state jurisdictions of New South Wales and Queensland all include an additional provision that allow a court to refuse to make an unexplained wealth order if it deems that making an order would not be in the 'public interest'. While this term is not defined by these laws, has not been tested, and is generally a flexible concept throughout common law, the inclusion of this safeguard within these laws should theoretically allow a court to invoke this power should the application of these illicit enrichment laws in certain circumstances amount to a gross violation of justice.[206]

- For the purpose of conducting legislative reviews, the federal-level Australian law also includes an entire section on 'oversight'. This section empowers a parliamentary body, the Parliamentary Joint Committee on Law Enforcement, to collect information from law enforcement agencies regarding their application of the unexplained wealth focused mechanisms in the law.[207] The committee can launch formal inquiries into the overall use of the law under which it can receive submissions from law enforcement agencies, other government agencies and

---

206 It is important to note that the question of whether or not something is in the public interest is not straightforward, as the definition of the 'public interest' is a fluid one. As outlined in C Wheeler, 'The Public Interest: We Know It's Important, but Do We Know What it Means', AIAL Forum, No. 48, 2006, the Australian Federal Court has recognised that the concept is difficult to define (referencing Right to Life Association (NSW) Inc v Secretary, Department of Human Services and Health (1995) 128 ALR 238): "The public interest is a concept of wide meaning and not readily limited by precise boundaries. Opinions have differed, do differ and doubtless always will differ as to what is or is not in the public interest...'. Ultimately, the determination of what exactly is in the public interest will differ depending on the various interests that need to be balanced under the specific circumstances of each case (referencing McKinnon v Secretary, Department of Treasury [2005] FCA FC142): 'The public interest is not one homogenous undivided concept. It will often be multi-faceted and the decision-maker will have to consider and evaluate the relative weight of these facets before reaching a final conclusion as to where the public interest resides. This ultimate evaluation of the public interest will involve a determination of what are the relevant facets of the public interest that are competing and the comparative importance that ought to be given to them so that 'the public interest' can be ascertained and served. In some circumstances, one or more considerations will be of such overriding significance that they will prevail over all others. In other circumstances, the competing considerations will be more finely balanced so that the outcome is not so clearly predictable. For example, in some contexts, interests such as public health, national security, anti-terrorism, defence or international obligations may be of overriding significance when compared with other considerations'. Consequently, until this concept is tested within the context of the relevant unexplained wealth laws in Australia, it is unclear how the court will assess when it is appropriate to invoke the 'public interest' safeguard available to them under these laws.

207 Proceeds of Crime Act 2002 (Australia - Federal), Section 179U.

special interest groups, and can make recommendations for necessary legislative amendments.[208]

- The qualified civil illicit enrichment law in the jurisdiction of South Australia includes a provision to cover situations where 'it is not reasonably possible for the person to establish that a component of his or her wealth was lawfully acquired (due to the effluxion of time, the circumstances in which that component was acquired or any other reason)'.[209] Providing the person in question also acts 'in good faith', the court is able to exclude this component of the person's wealth when assessing whether the person has illicitly enriched themselves.

- To counter concerns of possible self-incrimination, the qualified civil illicit enrichment law in the Bahamas includes an explicit provision specifying that any information disclosed in statements during the illicit enrichment process cannot be used in a separate criminal proceeding against the person (except in a proceeding that directly relates to the falsity of the statement).[210]

- Before making an application for an unexplained wealth order under the civil illicit enrichment law of Mauritius, the director of the Integrity Reporting Services Agency (the enforcement agency in charge of applying for such orders) must first justify the action to an independent board for review and approval. This board is made up of a chairperson, who must be a retired judge, and two other members, who all must be appointed by the President of Mauritius on the advice of the Prime Minister.[211]

- The illicit enrichment law of the Philippines specifically safeguards against the abuse of the law for political purposes by including a provision that prohibits an initiating complaint being made against public officials within one year of a general election and three months of a special election. It also further prohibits any judgments being made within six months of a general election and three months of a special election.[212]

---

208 See for example the Parliamentary Joint Committee on Law Enforcement, *Inquiry into Commonwealth Unexplained Wealth Legislation and Arrangements*, 19 March 2012.

209 Serious and Organised Crime (Unexplained Wealth) Act 2009 (Australia - South Australia), Section 9(11).

210 The Proceeds of Crime Act 2018 (Bahamas), Section 75(3).

211 The Good Governance and Integrity Reporting Act (Mauritius), Sections 5, 7 and 8.

212 Republic Act No. 1379, An Act Declaring Forfeiture in Favor of the State Any Property Found to have been Unlawfully Acquired by any Public Officer or Employee and Providing for the Proceedings Therefor (18 June 1955) (Philippines), Sections 2 and 6.

2.4 Overarching legislative instruments for illicit enrichment laws

Illicit enrichment laws are rarely stand-alone legislative instruments. Instead, an illicit enrichment law in a particular jurisdiction is often constituted by one or more provisions contained in a broader legislative instrument. The overarching legislation will often depend on whether the illicit enrichment law is civil or criminal in nature, as well as whether or not the illicit enrichment provisions were brought in to target the proceeds of a specific category of crime, such as corruption.

If the illicit enrichment law of a particular country is civil in nature, then the relevant provisions will most likely be included in the jurisdiction's overarching statute outlining recovery mechanisms regarding the proceeds of crime. For example, Western Australia's illicit enrichment provisions are contained in its Criminal Property Confiscation Act while the illicit enrichment provisions of the Bahamas are contained in its Proceeds of Crime Act.[213] There are exceptions of course, with the illicit enrichment provisions of Kenya and Zanzibar (Tanzania) instead contained in each jurisdiction's key anti-corruption statutes, namely the Anti-Corruption and Economic Crimes Act and the Zanzibar Anti-Corruption and Economic Crimes Act respectively.

If the illicit enrichment law of a particular country is criminal in nature, then the relevant provisions will most likely be included in either the jurisdiction's overarching criminal code or in the predominant anti-corruption statute. For instance in South America, the illicit enrichment offences of Argentina, Chile, Colombia, Ecuador, Peru and Suriname are contained in the respective jurisdictions' criminal code while the offences of Bolivia, Guyana and Venezuela are contained in anti-corruption focused statutes.

There are some jurisdictions throughout the world, however, that have enacted legislative instruments that are primarily focused on illicit enrichment. For example, Mali's illicit enrichment law is the Loi N°2014-015/ Du 27 mai 2014 portant prevention et repression de l'enrichissement illicite, which is a statute that criminalises illicit enrichment and also covers asset declaration obligations.

---

213 Criminal Property Confiscation Act 2000 (Australia - Western Australia); The Proceeds of Crime Act 2018 (Bahamas).

2.5 Common legislative formats for illicit enrichment laws

It is quite easy to gauge from the explanations of the key characteristics above that there is certainly no archetypal 'one size fits all' mould for an illicit enrichment law, and each jurisdiction has used a slightly different format when drafting its own legislative instrument. Nonetheless, there are a number of general approaches that have been used throughout the world, albeit of course with minor tweaks. These more common models are explained below.

2.5.1 Formats of criminal illicit enrichment laws

2.5.1.1 A broad illicit enrichment provision

The wording of the criminal illicit enrichment offence in many countries combines all the applicable actions that could be considered as illicit enrichment under one primary provision. This approach is more frequently used in countries with civil law systems rather than common law systems.

An example of this format is Niger's Ordonnance no. 92-024 du 18 Juin 1992 portant répression de l'enrichissement illicite:[214]

> [Unofficial translation] The offence of illicit enrichment is constituted when it is established that a person possesses assets and/or leads a lifestyle that his lawful income does not allow him to justify.

Another example is São Tomé and Príncipe, with its Código Penal[215] reading as follows:

> [Unofficial translation] An official who, during the period of performing public duties or during the three years following termination of such duties, acquires assets or a way of life which are manifestly disproportionate to his income and which do not result from any other lawful means of acquisition, with the result that such assets or way of life may be derived from advantages obtained by committing crimes committed in the exercise of public functions, shall be punishable by imprisonment for a maximum of five years.

---

214 Ordonnance no. 92-024 du 18 Juin 1992 portant répression de l'enrichissement illicite (Niger), Article 1 (Original text: 'Le délit d'enrichissement illicite est constitué lorsqu'il est établi qu'une personne possède un patrimoine et / ou mène un train de vie que ses revenus licites ne lui permettent pas de justifier.').

215 Código Penal, Aprovado pela Lei 6/2012 (São Tomé and Príncipe), Artigo 455(1) (Original text: 'O funcionário que, durante o período do exercício de funções públicas ou nos três anos seguintes à cessação dessas funções, adquirir um património ou um modo de vida que seja manifestamente desproporcionais ao seu rendimento e que não resultem de outro meio de aquisição lícito, com perigo de aquele património ou modo de vida provir de vantagens obtidas pela prática de crimes cometidos no exercício de funções públicas, é punível com pena de prisão até 5 anos.').

As can be seen from the two texts above, all the actions, or all the types of wealth that can be taken into consideration when determining the existence of illicit enrichment, are included under a single provision. Specifically, Niger's provision covers both the possession of unjustifiable assets and the leading of an unjustifiable lifestyle, while São Tomé and Príncipe's provision covers both the acquisition of disproportionate assets and the enjoyment of a disproportionate 'way of life'.

This approach is often used by jurisdictions in South and Central America as well as West Africa, and somewhat reflects the phrasing of the illicit enrichment articles contained in international treaties.

2.5.1.2 Split provisions for different forms of enrichment

Other criminal illicit enrichment laws divide the offence into two or more provisions that cover different types of enrichment, based on the types of wealth that a person has acquired or enjoyed. This format exists mostly in common law countries.

An example is Hong Kong's Prevention of Bribery Ordinance:[216]

---

10. Possession of unexplained property

(1) Any person who, being or having been the Chief Executive or a prescribed officer –

(a) maintains a standard of living above that which is commensurate with his present or past official emoluments; or

(b) is in control of pecuniary resources or property disproportionate to his present or past official emoluments,

shall, unless he gives a satisfactory explanation to the court as to how he was able to maintain such a standard of living or how such pecuniary resources or property came under his control, be guilty of an offence.

The phrasing used in the above law has been emulated almost exactly by a number of other countries, such as Brunei Darussalam's Prevention of Corruption Act:[217]

---

216   Cap.201 Prevention of Bribery Ordinance 1971 (China - Hong Kong), Section 10.

217   Prevention of Corruption Act 1982 (Brunei Darussalam), Section 12.

12. Possession of Unexplained Property

(1) Any person who, being or having been a public officer –

(a) maintains a standard of living above that which is commensurate with his present or past emoluments; or

(b) is in control of pecuniary resources or property disproportionate to his present or past emoluments,

shall, unless he gives a satisfactory explanation to the court as to how he was able to maintain such a standard of living or how such pecuniary resources or property came under his control, be guilty of an offence: Penalty, a fine of B$30,000 and imprisonment for 7 years.

And in Antigua and Barbuda's Prevention of Corruption Act:[218]

7. Possession of unexplained property

(1) A person who, being or having been a public official:

(a) maintains a standard of living above that which is commensurate with his present or past official emoluments; or

(b) is in control of pecuniary resources or property disproportionate to his present or past official emoluments,

unless he gives a satisfactory explanation to the court as to how he was able to maintain such standard of living or how such pecuniary resources or property came under his control, commits an offence.

The exact same or similar phrasing is also used in the laws of Bhutan,[219] Botswana,[220] Eswatini,[221] Ethiopia,[222] Fiji,[223] Lesotho,[224] Malawi,[225] the Marshall Islands,[226] the

---

218 The Prevention of Corruption Act (Law No.21 of 2004) (Antigua and Barbuda), Article 7.

219 Anti-Corruption Act of Bhutan 2011, Section 60.

220 Corruption and Economic Crime Act 1994 (Botswana), Section 34.

221 The Prevention of Corruption Act 2006 (Eswatini), Section 34.

222 The Criminal Code of the Federal Democratic Republic of Ethiopia Proclamation no.414/2004, Article 419.

223 Prevention of Bribery Act (Promulgation No.12 of 2007) (Fiji).

224 Prevention of Corruption and Economic Offences Act 1999 (as amended by the Prevention of Corruption and Economic Offences (Amendment) Act of 2006) (Lesotho), Section 31.

225 Corrupt Practices Act 1995 (as amended in 2004) (Malawi), Section 32.

226 Criminal Code 2011 (Marshall Islands), Section 240.8.

Seychelles,[227] Sierra Leone,[228] Tanzania,[229] and Uganda.[230]

As can be seen in the examples, these illicit enrichment laws contain several different provisions that relate to the type of wealth that has been acquired or enjoyed.

> **Author's note: One advantage of the broad provision format over the split provision format**
>
> While on the face of it the split provision format appears to be more specific in its approach by providing separate provisions for particular situations, its operation in practice has given rise to some uncertainties. This is because judicial interpretations will often overlap with regards to the items of wealth that should fall under each specific provision. For example, expenses incurred for traditional assets that help improve a person's standard of living, such as the purchase of a large house, can often be considered under both sub-sections of the split offence format.
>
> Additionally, there has been some confusion as to whether a person who both owns disproportionate traditional assets and has also maintained an incommensurate standard of living should be charged under one or all of the provisions that are specified in the illicit enrichment law.
>
> For instance, these ambiguities were raised within the jurisdiction of Hong Kong, where the courts have acknowledged that the dividing line between an illicit enrichment action based on the acquisition of property and an illicit enrichment action based on the enjoyment of a standard of living is very 'narrow' – as the property acquired by an accused person may also form part of their standard of living.[231]
>
> Consequently, it could be argued that the broad provision format, under which all types of wealth are considered under one offence, is a simpler and clearer legislative construction, as it does not create any confusion as to which types of wealth should be considered under which specific provision. Instead, all the wealth that has been acquired or enjoyed by an accused person is assessed under one single provision to determine whether or not the person has acquired or enjoyed a disproportionate amount of wealth as compared to their lawful income, either through the acquisition of property or the enjoyment of a certain lifestyle, or both.

---

227 Anti-Corruption Act 2016 (Seychelles), Section 25.

228 Anti-Corruption Act 2008 (Sierra Leone), Section 27.

229 Prevention and Combating of Corruption Act 2007 (Tanzania), Section 27.

230 Anti Corruption Act 2009 (Uganda), Section 31.

231 Ian McWalters SC et al., *Bribery and Corruption Law in Hong Kong*, 3rd Edition, Hong Kong, LexisNexis, 2015, pp. 386-387.

2.5.2   Formats of civil illicit enrichment laws

Most civil illicit enrichment laws are structured similarly, in that they outline an application and hearing procedure for a proceeds of crime based order (often called an unexplained wealth order or something similar) which, if granted, will require a respondent to pay the amount of proven illicit enrichment to the state.

The main differentiating factor between civil illicit enrichment laws is the number of procedural steps that need to be taken before a final compensatory order can be issued for the amount of illicit enrichment.

For example, the Western Australian law outlines a very straightforward approach, under which the state is permitted to apply directly for an 'unexplained wealth declaration' by filing an originating summons (and an accompanying affidavit).[232] This application will lead directly to a hearing on whether or not an unexplained wealth declaration should be made against a person, and if so, a declaration will be issued compelling the person in question to pay to the state the amount of unexplained wealth. This is similarly the case in a number of other Australian jurisdictions, including the Northern Territory[233] and Tasmania.[234]

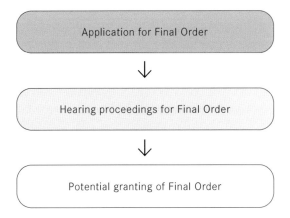

Several other jurisdictions, however, add an extra level of procedure. Rather than applying directly for a final order, the state is first required to make an application for a preliminary order which will summon a person to court for the purpose of determining whether a final order should be made. Interestingly, when applying for a preliminary order, the applicants in these jurisdictions can also request the court to compel the respondent to provide information regarding their properties and sources of income. For example, during the application for an 'unexplained wealth order *nisi*' in the Bahamas, the applicant (the state) may 'apply to a Court

---

232   Criminal Property Confiscation Act 2000 (Australia - Western Australia), Sections 11 and 12; Rules of the Supreme Court 1971 (Australia - Western Australia), Order 81FA, Sections 3 and 4.

233   Criminal Property Forfeiture Act 2002 (Australia - Northern Territory), Section 67.

234   Crime (Confiscation of Profits) Act 1993 (Australia - Northern Territory), Section 141.

in writing for an order requiring the relevant person to file declarations and answer questions as required in relation to their assets'.[235] Similarly, before applying for an unexplained wealth order under the qualified illicit enrichment law in Trinidad and Tobago, the state may apply for a preliminary order 'requiring the respondent to file a declaration and answer questions as required in relation to his assets.'[236]

> **Application for Preliminary Order**
> (requiring respondent to provide information/attend hearing for final order)

> **Potential granting of Preliminary Order**
> (includes time limit in which respondent can seek a revocation of the order)

> **Hearing proceedings for Final Order**

> **Potential granting of Final Order**

Notably, the civil illicit enrichment law in Mauritius, the Good Governance and Integrity Reporting Act[237] takes a different approach again and adds even further levels of procedure that need to be followed by the agency empowered with bringing applications for unexplained wealth orders, the Intergrity Reporting Services Agency. Specifically, before a court proceeding can be commenced, this agency must first seek the approval of the independent and impartial Integrity Reporting Board. A more detailed analysis and overview of this law is contained in Part 5.

---

235 The Proceeds of Crime Act 2018 (Bahamas), Section 75.

236 Civil Asset Recovery and Management and Unexplained Wealth Act, 2019 (Trinidad and Tobago), Section 58.

237 The Good Governance and Integrity Reporting Act 2015 (Mauritius).

2.6 Other laws that share substantial similarities with illicit enrichment laws

There are a number of laws that exist in jurisdictions which do not quite fit this publication's classifications for illicit enrichment laws, but which should be highlighted nonetheless due to the fact that they share a number of key similarities.

2.6.1 The UK's Unexplained Wealth Order

The UK introduced an Unexplained Wealth Order (UWO) regime into its Proceeds of Crime Act in 2017.[238] There is some confusion over the classification of the UK's UWO regime, and many publications and media articles often categorise the UK's UWO as the same type of recovery mechanism as unexplained wealth orders in other jurisdictions.

Unlike the other 'unexplained wealth' focused laws covered in this publication, however, the UK's UWO is not a stand-alone mechanism for the recovery of assets. Instead, it is only an investigative mechanism that can be used to acquire evidence that can then be presented under a separate civil recovery proceeding that seeks to establish that certain property was unlawfully acquired and can be recovered by the state. This separate proceeding is a non-conviction based confiscation regime under which the state must prove to a civil standard that the property in question was, more likely than not, 'obtained through unlawful conduct'.[239] A presumption may be made by the court in this subsequent proceeding that certain property was not obtained lawfully. However, this presumption is based on a lack of compliance regarding the production of information in response to the initial UWO, not on a disproportion between the assets and lawful income.

At the time of its enactment, the UK's UWO was a new and unique legislative mechanism. In recent years, however, it has been largely reproduced in the jurisdictions of Barbados[240] and Zimbabwe.[241] Excerpts of these laws are contained in Annex 1 under the heading 'Investigational Unexplained Wealth Order Laws'.

The UK's UWO mechanism operates as follows:

---

238   Proceeds of Crime Act 2002 (United Kingdom), Sections 362A-362T.

239   Proceeds of Crime Act 2002 (United Kingdom), Sections 266, 304.

240   Proceeds and Instrumentalities of Crime Act, 2019-17 (Barbados).

241   Money Laundering and Proceeds of Crime Act No.4 of 2013 (as amended by the Money Laundering and Proceeds of Crime (Amendment) Act 2019) (Zimbabwe).

STEP 1

The enforcement authority makes an application for a UWO

An enforcement authority applies to the court to issue a UWO against a person.

The application for the UWO must:

- Specify the property in respect of which the order is sought; and
- Specify the person whom the enforcement authority thinks holds the property (the respondent);

STEP 2

The court decides whether to issue a UWO

In order for the application for the UWO to succeed, the court must be satisfied that:

- The respondent holds the property outlined in the application; and
- The value of the property is greater than GBP 50,000; and
- There are reasonable grounds for suspecting that the known sources of the respondent's lawfully obtained income would have been insufficient for the purposes of enabling the respondent to obtain the property; and
- The respondent is a politically exposed person; or
- There are reasonable grounds to suspect the respondent was involved in serious crime or connected to a person involved in serious crime.

STEP 3

The court issues a UWO

If the application is successful, the court issues a UWO, and the respondent must provide a statement as a response to the order which, at the very least:

- Outlines the nature and extent of the respondent's interest in the property in respect of which the order is made; and
- Explains how the respondent obtained the property (including, in particular, how any costs incurred in obtaining it were met).

STEP

4

The respondent does or does not provide a statement and a potential separate civil proceeding for a recovery order is commenced by the enforcement authority

If the respondent **does not comply** with the UWO, or **does not purport to comply**[242] with the UWO, then...

If the respondent **does comply** with the UWO, or **purports to comply** with the order, and provides a statement of the requested information, then...

...the enforcement authority may commence a separate civil proceeding for a 'recovery order' and the fact that the respondent did not comply, or purport to comply, to the original unexplained wealth order will give rise to a presumption in this subsequent proceeding that the property in question was not obtained lawfully (this presumption can be rebutted by the respondent).

...the enforcement authority must decide within 60 days whether or not to commence a separate civil proceeding for a 'recovery order' in which they can potentially use the evidence in the statement provided by the respondent in an attempt to establish that the property in question was, more likely than not, obtained unlawfully.

As evidence acquired under a UK UWO has yet to be used in a separate civil proceeding for a recovery order at the time of writing, it is unclear how much weight it will be accorded when determining whether or not the property in question was obtained unlawfully. As the court in a recovery order proceeding must be satisfied, on the balance of probabilities, that the property in question is connected to unlawful conduct, it is unclear how much additional evidence a state will need to produce beyond that which is acquired through a response to an unexplained wealth order.

---

242 It is unclear at this stage what would constitute a 'purported' compliance. There is no definition in the legislation for this term. One commentary suggests that '[t]aken in context, and considering the object of the UWO regime, purported compliance would appear to mean a response which, on its face, appears to be in compliance with the UWO, but in fact is not, or may not be. It would not seem to matter whether the respondent is aware of the falsity of the response and so a deliberately fabricated response would seem to be in purported compliance with a UWO provided that, on its face, it appeared to be compliant.' (A Mitchell et. al, 'Mitchell, Taylor and Talbot on Confiscation and Proceeds of Crime', Vol. 2, Thomson Reuters, 2019 at [XIII 162]).

2.6.2   Ireland's Proceeds of Crime Act 1996

The Irish Proceeds of Crime Act[243] contains a widely lauded asset recovery mechanism that is extremely similar to illicit enrichment laws. The law, which is based in civil procedure, outlines that certain property may be forfeited if 'it appears to the court' that a person is 'in possession or control' of property that 'constitutes, directly or indirectly, proceeds of crime' or 'was acquired, in whole or in part, with or in connection with property that, directly or indirectly, constitutes proceeds of crime'.[244] In determining this, the court may rely on 'belief' evidence tendered by a law enforcement officer.[245] Furthermore, the law also includes a reverse onus mechanism similar to other illicit enrichment laws, in that a court will make an order if the respondent is unable to satisfy it 'that particular property does not constitute, directly or indirectly, proceeds of crime'.[246] Finally, the law also contains a provision whereby a court can issue an order to a respondent to submit an affidavit outlining the property they control and their sources of income.[247]

The law is a unique mechanism and is difficult to classify. Previous publications have in fact classified Ireland's law as an 'unexplained wealth order'.[248] However, as the property in question must be categorically proven to constitute, on the balance of probabilities, 'proceeds of crime', this publication has not classified this law as a civil illicit enrichment law. This categorisation is further reinforced by the fact that in practice, Irish courts do not rely purely on 'belief' evidence to make a determination that property is the proceeds of crime, unless it is corroborated by other evidence.[249] In any case, the law contains many similar characteristics to other laws classified in this publication as 'illicit enrichment laws' and the precise classification of this law will no doubt be subjected to future debates. A more detailed explanation and analysis of this law is contained in Part 5.

In addition to this, Ireland has another provision that is similar to an illicit enrichment law in Section 16 of the Criminal Justice (Corruption Offences) Act.[250] Under this provision, a 'presumption of corrupt enrichment' can be made regarding the origins of property held by a public official if, during proceedings for a separate corruption offence (e.g. active or passive bribery) the public official is found to hold property that they failed to declare in their

---

243 Proceeds of Crime Act 1996 (Ireland).

244 ibid., Section 3.

245 ibid., Sections 3, 8.

246 ibid., Section 3. Note that in practice, the reverse onus is only triggered once a prima facie case is made against the respondent (F. McK v GWD [2004] 2 I.R. 470).

247 Proceeds of Crime Act 1996 (Ireland), Section 9.

248 See for example: Booz Allen Hamilton, *Comparative Evaluation of Unexplained Wealth Orders*, 2012.

249 Gilligan v Criminal Assets Bureau [1997] IEHC 106.

250 Criminal Justice (Corruption Offences) Act 2018 (Ireland).

'statement of registrable interests'.[251] In such a case, a presumption will be made that the property in question 'derives or derived, either directly or indirectly, from a gift, consideration or advantage received as an inducement to, or reward for, or otherwise on account of, the Irish official doing an act in relation to his or her office, employment, position or business, unless the contrary is proved'.[252] However, as the operation of this law requires the existence of proceedings for a separate corruption offence, this law has also not been classified as an illicit enrichment law within this publication.

2.6.3 Switzerland's Law on the Freezing and the Restitution of Illicit Assets Held by Foreign Politically Exposed Persons

Switzerland's Loi fédérale du 18 décembre 2015 sur le blocage et la restitution des valeurs patrimoniales d'origine illicite de personnes politiquement exposées à l'étranger is another example of a law that does not quite fit the classification of an illicit enrichment law, but nonetheless contains some key similarities.

The law allows the Swiss Federal Council to freeze assets held in Switzerland by foreign politically exposed persons (and their close associates) in anticipation of confiscation proceedings under certain conditions, namely when:

a. The assets have been made subject to a provisional seizure order within the framework of international mutual legal assistance in criminal matters instigated at the request of the country of origin;

b. The country of origin is unable to satisfy the requirements for mutual legal assistance owing to the total or substantial collapse, or the impairment, of its judicial system (failure of state structures); and

c. The safeguarding of Switzerland's interests requires the freezing of the assets.[253]

Following an asset freeze, the Federal Administrative Court may then be permitted to confiscate the frozen assets if they are found to be of 'illicit origin'.[254] Interestingly, the illicit origin of the assets can be presumed, providing the following conditions are met:

a. The wealth of the individual who has the power of disposal over the assets or who is the beneficial owner thereof increased inordinately, facilitated by the exercise of a public function by a foreign politically exposed person; and

b. The level of corruption in the country of origin or surrounding the foreign politically exposed person in question was notoriously high during his or her term of office.[255]

---

251 ibid., Section 16(1)(a); the offences for which proceedings may trigger the presumption include 'active and passive bribery', 'active and passive trading in influence', 'corruption in relation to office, employment, position or business' and 'giving gift, consideration or advantage that may be used to facilitate an offence under this Act', contained in Sections 5-8 of the same legislative instrument.

252 Criminal Justice (Corruption Offences) Act 2018 (Ireland), Section 16(1)(b).

253 Loi fédérale du 18 décembre 2015 sur le blocage et la restitution des valeurs patrimoniales d'origine illicite de personnes politiquement exposées à l'étranger (Switzerland), Article 4.

254 ibid., Article 14.

255 ibid., Article 15(1).

The law further specifies that an 'increase' of the person's wealth 'shall be considered inordinate where there is a significant disproportion, inconsistent with ordinary experience and the prevailing circumstances in the country, between the income legitimately earned by the person with the power of disposal over the assets and the growth in that person's wealth'. [256]

Finally, if a presumption is made, then the affected person is able to reverse the presumption through demonstrating 'with overwhelming probability that the assets in question were acquired legitimately'.[257]

As demonstrated by these above provisions, the Swiss mechanism shares some notable similarities with illicit enrichment laws. Specifically, it does not require the state to establish a link between the assets and a precise crime – instead it allows the court to presume that certain assets held in Switzerland by a person have been acquired through illicit origins if it can be demonstrated that the person's overall wealth increased disproportionately in relation to their legitimate income.

Nonetheless, the Swiss legislation also differs somewhat from illicit enrichment laws in that it requires a number of significant conditions to be met before assets can be considered 'illicit'. Specifically the state must also demonstrate that the level of corruption in the country of origin of the person in question was notoriously high during the person's time in office. Moreover, before assets can be confiscated, a freezing order for the assets must be issued by a political body, the Swiss Federal Council, and this order can only be issued if the country of origin is unable to satisfy the requirements for mutual legal assistance owing to the total or substantial collapse, or the impairment, of its judicial system.

2.6.4   France's Criminal Code (Article 321-6)

Under Article 321-6 of France's Criminal Code, a person commits a crime if they:

- Are in a habitual relationship with one or more persons who engage in the commission of offences (punishable by at least five years' imprisonment); and

- Cannot justify the resources corresponding to their standard of living or the property they hold.[258]

---

256 ibid., Article 15(2).

257 ibid., Article 15(3).

258 Code pénal (France), Article 321-6 (Original text: 'Le fait de ne pas pouvoir justifier de ressources correspondant à son train de vie ou de ne pas pouvoir justifier de l'origine d'un bien détenu, tout en étant en relations habituelles avec une ou plusieurs personnes qui soit se livrent à la commission de crimes ou de délits punis d'au moins cinq ans d'emprisonnement et procurant à celles-ci un profit direct ou indirect, soit sont les victimes d'une de ces infractions, est puni d'une peine de trois ans d'emprisonnement et de 75 000 euros d'amende. Est puni des mêmes peines le fait de faciliter la justification de ressources fictives pour des personnes se livrant à la commission de crimes ou de délits punis d'au moins cinq ans d'emprisonnement et procurant à celles-ci un profit direct ou indirect.').

In light of this, this Article is extremely similar to illicit enrichment laws, in that a prosecutor does not have to prove that the wealth in question was derived from a separate criminal offence, nor do they have to prove that the charged person committed a criminal act. Moreover, sanctions may be imposed if the person is unable to justify the origins of their wealth, or is unable to justify their amount of wealth in reference to their lawful sources of income.

Despite these similarities, however, the law can be differentiated from illicit enrichment laws on the basis that a prosecutor must be able to demonstrate that another person committed an offence and that the person charged under Article 321-6 has a habitual relationship with this convicted person. Consequently, the presumption of illicit origin under this Article is not solely made on the basis that the charged person is unable to justify the sources of their wealth, but also on the basis that the charged person has a relationship with a person who has been convicted of an offence. Nonetheless, techniques used to establish illicit enrichment offences will also be relevant to investigations and prosecutions regarding this Article as well.

2.6.5   Similar laws connected to asset declaration obligations

In some jurisdictions, illicit enrichment-type mechanisms sometimes exist within the context of asset declaration obligations. For example, under the North Macedonian criminal code, if a public official provides false or incomplete data during obligatory reporting procedures, and it can be proven that the public official possesses property that is significantly disproportionate to their legal revenues, then the public official will have committed an offence, and the excess property will be confiscated.[259] Similarly, in Gabon, while there is no stand-alone illicit enrichment offence, if a public official fails to comply with asset reporting procedures then this may also result in asset confiscation.[260] Although these laws have not been specifically classified as illicit enrichment laws within this publication, similar investigational techniques could also be applied to these laws to determine the credibility of information contained in asset declarations made by public officials.

2.6.6   Similarities between illicit enrichment laws and tax legislation

A number of commentators have also noted the similarities between illicit enrichment legislation and tax legislation, or more specifically the investigation and prosecution of tax

---

259 Criminal Code (as amended up until 2018) (North Macedonia), Article 359-a.

260 Loi N°002/2003 du 7 mai 2003, instituant un régime de prévention et de répression de l'enrichissement illicite en République Gabonaise.

evasion offences in certain countries.[261] An interesting example is the United States (US), which has repeatedly issued reservations on the illicit enrichment provisions in international treaties, but which has for decades permitted the prosecution of disproportionate wealth under tax evasion laws.[262] For instance, in the case of *Holland v United States,*[263] prosecutors managed to convict the accused persons of tax evasion under the US internal revenue code by demonstrating that the value of their wealth had increased disproportionately to their reported income over a three-year period. However, unlike illicit enrichment laws, an element of 'wilfulness' must also be established in such cases, which must 'be proven by independent evidence' and 'cannot be inferred from a mere understatement of income'.[264]

261 For example, this document notes that similar legislative models to illicit enrichment laws exist in Czechia, Greece and Ireland: European Commission, *Commission Staff Working Document - Analysis of non-conviction based confiscation measures in the European Union*, European Commission, Brussels, 2019; The similarities in operation between US tax law and illicit enrichment legislation is also noted in R. Messick, 'Will the United States Please Admit It has an Illicit Enrichment Law', The Global Anti Corruption Blog, 24 April 2019 https://globalanticorruptionblog.com/2019/04/24/will-the-u-s-please-admit-it-has-an-illicit-enrichment-law/, accessed 21 March 2021 while the relationship between tax regimes and unexplained wealth-related mechanisms is also discussed in R. Julien, *Unexplained wealth orders (UWOs) under the UK's Criminal Finances Act 2017: The role of tax laws and tax authorities in its successful implementation*, WU International Taxation Research Paper Series No.2019-02, 2019.

262 R. Messick, 'Will the United States Please Admit It has an Illicit Enrichment Law', The Global Anti Corruption Blog, 24 April 2019, https://globalanticorruptionblog.com/2019/04/24/will-the-u-s-please-admit-it-has-an-illicit-enrichment-law/, accessed 21 March 2021.

263 Holland v United States, 348 U.S. 121 (1954), referenced by R. Messick, 'Will the United States Please Admit It has an Illicit Enrichment Law', The Global Anti Corruption Blog, 24 April 2019, https://globalanticorruptionblog.com/2019/04/24/will-the-u-s-please-admit-it-has-an-illicit-enrichment-law/, accessed 21 March 2021.

264 Holland v United States, 348 U.S. 121 (1954) at [15].

A quick comparison of illicit enrichment laws and other similar laws

Criminal / civil illicit enrichment laws	• Empower a court to impose a criminal or civil sanction if they are satisfied that illicit enrichment has taken place (i.e. that a person has enjoyed an amount of wealth that has not been justified through reference to lawful income). • No separate or underlying criminal activity needs to be established before the sanction can be imposed.
Qualified criminal / civil illicit enrichment laws	• Empower a court to impose a criminal or civil sanction if they are satisfied that illicit enrichment has taken place. • No separate or underlying criminal activity needs to be established before the sanction can be imposed, but the state must establish a 'reasonable suspicion' or a 'reasonable belief' that some sort of underlying or separate criminality has taken place.
Investigational unexplained wealth order laws (e.g. unexplained wealth orders from the UK, Barbados and Zimbabwe)	• Only empower a court to impose an obligation on a person to provide information to the court regarding the sources of income used to acquire certain wealth. • Separate or underlying criminal activity does not need to be established before the order can be imposed if the targeted person is a politically exposed person (UK / Barbados). • After an unexplained wealth order is issued, a separate 'civil recovery' proceeding must take place before any assets can be confiscated, and the information obtained through the unexplained wealth order may be used in this proceeding.
Ireland's Proceeds of Crime Act 1996 recovery mechanism	• Property may be forfeited if 'it appears to the court' that a person is 'in possession or control' of property that 'constitutes, directly or indirectly, proceeds of crime' or 'was acquired, in whole or in part, with or in connection with property that, directly or indirectly, constitutes proceeds of crime.' • Permits a court to order a person to furnish an affidavit specifying the property that they own and the incomes that they have received. • Court may rely on the 'belief' of a law enforcement officer as evidence, but in practice this needs to be corroborated.

Switzerland's Federal Act of 18 December 2015 on the Freezing and the Restitution of Illicit Assets held by Foreign Politically Exposed Persons	• Assets initially frozen by the Federal Council (the executive branch of the Swiss government system) providing certain conditions are met (including that the country of origin of the relevant assets is unable to satisfy traditional MLA requirements). • Assets will subsequently be confiscated by the courts if they are considered of 'illicit origin', with the 'illicit' nature of assets presumed if the wealth of the relevant individual has increased 'inordinately' and if the level of corruption in the country of origin or surrounding the relevant person was 'notoriously high'.
France's Criminal Code (Art. 321-6)	• Sanctions may be imposed if a person is unable to justify the origins of their wealth, or is unable to justify their amount of wealth in reference to their lawful sources of income and if the state can also demonstrate that the person has a habitual relationship with another person who has been convicted of an offence.
Confiscation laws triggered by contraventions of asset declaration laws	• May permit the confiscation assets that cannot be justified in reference to lawful income. • Can only be triggered if it is first established that a person has contravened asset declaration laws.

Part 3

Establishing that illicit enrichment has taken place

Part 3 Summary

The specific elements that need to be established under illicit enrichment laws are not universal. As covered in the previous Part, illicit enrichment laws vary drastically in form and wording, and consequently, the elements outlined in one jurisdiction's law are not always outlined in another's. For example whereas one illicit enrichment law may require a state to establish the 'standard of living' of a 'public official' that cannot be 'explained', another illicit enrichment law may require the state to prove that 'a person' has 'acquired property' that is 'incommensurate' with their lawful income.

Moreover, due to the varied approaches towards reverse onus mechanisms, the party burdened with the obligation to address a certain element may also differ between jurisdictions. For example, the onus to establish a person's total lawful income may fall on the state in one jurisdiction but on the accused person/respondent in another jurisdiction (for simplicity the accused person/respondent will be referred to as the 'targeted person' in this publication).

In light of these differences, this Part does not seek to devise a comprehensive and universally applicable list of elements that need to be proven to obligate a court to impose a judicial sanction for illicit enrichment. This is impossible. Instead, this Part will focus on outlining:

- The two common elements that exist, in some form, in all illicit enrichment laws requiring the introduction of evidence to determine a person's total wealth and total lawful income over a relevant period of time;

- Burdens of proof regarding the two common elements, and the different applications of reverse onus mechanisms present in illicit enrichment proceedings;

- The simple formula courts will use to assess the existence of a disproportionality between a person's wealth and their income;

- What a 'satisfactory explanation' may include;

- The types of evidence that can be brought to establish the total wealth that someone has benefited from and the total lawful income received by them; and

- Other specific elements that are often included in particular illicit enrichment laws, such as value thresholds, intent, and the need to prove someone is a public official.

3.1 Who needs to prove what? The two common elements that need to be addressed in illicit enrichment proceedings

As covered in previous sections, this publication defines an illicit enrichment law as one which imposes a judicial sanction if a person has illicitly enriched themselves, or more specifically, has **enjoyed an amount of wealth** that **is not justified through reference to lawful income**.

In line with this definition, it is possible to infer that all criminal and civil laws categorised as 'illicit enrichment laws' by this publication have, at the very least, two common elements that must be addressed in proceedings to determine if someone has illicitly enriched themselves and can be sanctioned under the law, namely:

The Wealth Element	A person has enjoyed an amount of **wealth**
The Inadequate Income Element	The lawful origin of the amount of wealth demonstrated under the Wealth Element is not justified or explained through reference to the same person's **lawful income**

3.1.1 How is the Wealth Element expressed in illicit enrichment laws?

The Wealth Element is the most straightforward of the two elements above. It refers to a general requirement that exists in all illicit enrichment laws for the state to establish that the targeted person enjoyed (or 'acquired', 'controlled' or 'benefited' from) a certain amount of 'wealth' over the claimed period of illicit enrichment.

As alluded to previously, this element is expressed in a multitude of different ways throughout illicit enrichment laws, depending on how the particular country classifies or refers to the issue of 'wealth' and how it can be enjoyed. For example, the criminal illicit enrichment laws in Nicaragua[265] and Afghanistan[266] express this element as a requirement on the state to establish an 'increase' in 'assets'. Both the criminal illicit enrichment law in Hong Kong[267]

---

265 [Unofficial translation] Código Penal, Ley N°. 641, Aprobado el 13 de Noviembre de 2007 (Nicaragua), Artículo 448 (Original text: 'La autoridad, funcionario o empleado público, que sin incurrir en un delito más severamente penado, obtenga un incremento de su patrimonio con significativo exceso, respecto de sus ingresos legítimos, durante el ejercicio de sus funciones y que no pueda justificar razonablemente su procedencia, al ser requerido por el órgano competente señalado en la ley, será sancionado de tres a seis años de prisión e inhabilitación por el mismo período para ejercer cargo o empleo público.').

266 Penal Code (Afghanistan), Article 419(1).

267 Cap.201 Prevention of Bribery Ordinance 1971 (China - Hong Kong), Section 10.

and the criminal and civil illicit enrichment laws in Fiji[268] express this element as a need to demonstrate that a person has 'maintained' a 'standard of living' or 'is in control of pecuniary resources or property'. The civil illicit enrichment law in Western Australia[269] outlines this element as a requirement to prove a 'total value of the respondent's wealth' – which includes 'the sum of the values of all the items of property, and all the services, advantages and benefits, that together constitute the person's wealth'.

3.1.2   How is the Inadequate Income Element expressed in illicit enrichment laws?

The way in which the Inadequate Income Element is expressed in an illicit enrichment law will depend largely on which party or parties bear the burden of addressing the element. In principle, this element will require a court to be satisfied that the value of wealth established in the Wealth Element has not been explained by reference to the person's lawful income, either because:

A. the **state** has shown that the targeted person's total wealth established under the Wealth Element is disproportionate to the targeted person's 'official' or 'known' income, and the **targeted person** has not or cannot explain this disproportion (despite there being an express obligation under the law to do so);

B. the **state** alone has shown that the targeted person's total wealth established under the Wealth Element cannot possibly be explained by the targeted person's total income; or

C. the **targeted person** alone has not offered an explanation, or has not given an adequate explanation of the wealth established under the Wealth Element by reference to their lawful income (despite there being an express obligation under the law to do so).

As can be gauged from the above options, illicit enrichment laws may place the burden of addressing the Inadequate Income Element partially on the state and the targeted person (example A above), wholly on the state (example B above), or wholly on the targeted person (example C above).

In line with this, the actual wording of the Inadequate Income Element in illicit enrichment legislation will take one of three common models, depending on which party the law tasks with addressing the element:

---

268 Prevention of Bribery Act (Promulgation No.12 of 2007) (Fiji), Section 10; Proceeds of Crime Act 1997 (as amended by the Proceeds of Crime Amendment Act No.7 of 2005 and by the Proceeds of Crime (Amendment) Decree 2012 (Decree No.61 of 2012)) (Fiji), Section 71F.

269 Criminal Property Confiscation Act 2000 (Australia - Western Australia), Sections 12, 144.

Model A: A requirement that the state establishes that the wealth in the Wealth Element is disproportionate to (or 'greater than' or 'incommensurate to' or 'exceeds' or 'could not have been acquired with') aspects of the targeted person's lawful income (e.g. only their 'official' or 'known' income) before an express reverse onus mechanism is triggered which requires the targeted person to provide an 'explanation' or 'justification' for this established disproportionality.

Model B: A requirement that the state establishes that the wealth in the Wealth Element is 'disproportionate to' (or 'greater than' or 'incommensurate to' or 'exceeds' or 'could not have been acquired with') all of the targeted person's lawful income, with no express burden placed on the targeted person to provide any evidence whatsoever of any income to justify their wealth (though the targeted person has the option to provide a defence if they choose to).

Model C: A requirement that the targeted person provides evidence of sufficient lawful income to explain the total amount of wealth established by the state under the Wealth Element (under this option the express reverse onus is activated once the state establishes the Wealth Element and there is no obligation on the state to provide any evidence of lawful income). The wording of the law will often include an express provision stating that the burden of proving sufficient lawful income is solely that of the targeted person.

Regardless of whether the Inadequate Income Element is expressed in a particular illicit enrichment law as Model A, B, or C, if a court is satisfied that **there has not been an adequate explanation** for the total wealth established in the Wealth Element through reference to the targeted person's lawful income, then it will impose a sanction.

Express burdens under the three "Inadequate Income Element" options

	Burden to address the Wealth Element (and provide evidence of the targeted person's wealth)	Burden to address Inadequate Income Element (and provide evidence of the targeted person's lawful income)
Model A	State	State & Targeted Person
Model B	State	State
Model C	State	Targeted Person

3.2 Comparing the elements and burdens of proof in the three models of illicit enrichment laws

3.2.1 Examples of legislation following 'Model A' (laws imposing shared burdens)

This model of elements is by far the most common contained in illicit enrichment laws, and there are examples of both criminal and civil illicit enrichment laws which have taken this approach.

Laws containing this model of elements will first include a requirement that the state establishes that the targeted person has enjoyed a certain amount of wealth (the Wealth Element). Following this, the law will also require the state to partially address the Inadequate Income Element and demonstrate a discrepancy (or a 'disproportion' or 'incommensurateness') between the 'official' or 'known' lawful income of the targeted person and the value of total wealth that has been established. The standard to which this needs to be proven will depend on whether the illicit enrichment law is criminal or civil in nature. Furthermore, the degree to which a state will need to evidence a targeted person's income over the relevant period of time will depend on the wording of the particular law. For example, while the law in Hong Kong requires a state to only demonstrate the total amount of 'official emoluments' that a targeted person received during the relevant time, the law in India requires the state to establish the targeted person's 'known sources of income'. [270] The former category of income generally refers to the salary and allowances a person receives from their employment as a public official. In contrast, the latter category of income is wider and refers to the 'sources [of income] known to the prosecution on a thorough investigation of the case'.[271]

Once the state has established the requisite amount of income, and has demonstrated a discrepancy between this income and the value of wealth established under the Wealth Element, a reverse onus mechanism is triggered which will then require the targeted person to effectively disprove the Inadequate Income Element by satisfactorily 'explaining' or 'justifying' the discrepancy through evidence of additional lawful income.

This extra burden distinguishes this style of illicit enrichment elements from those in Model B, which do not, under any circumstances, place a burden on the targeted person to provide any such explanation, and Model C, which place the entirety of the burden for addressing the Inadequate Income Element on the person being targeted by the law.

---

270 Cap.201 Prevention of Bribery Ordinance 1971 (China - Hong Kong), Section 10; Prevention of Corruption Act 1988 (as amended by the Prevention of Corruption (Amendment) Act 2018) (India), Section 13.

271 N. Pasupathy v State 2018 (1) MLJ (Crl) 745 at [44] quoting C.S.D. Swami v The State, 1960 Crl.L.J. 131 at [6]; Note that while the prosecution is required to establish incomes beyond the person's official salary, the prosecution is also not expected to know all 'the affairs of an accused person'.

**Model A: The Wealth Element (State) and the Inadequate Income Element
(State / Targeted Person)**

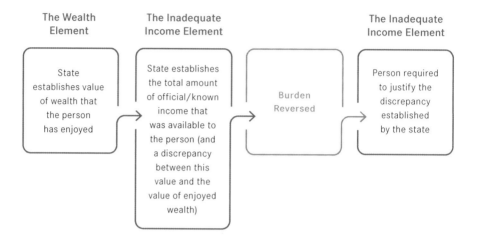

One example of a law containing this style of elements is that of Hong Kong:[272]

10 (1) Any person who, being or having been the Chief Executive or a prescribed officer –

(a) maintains a standard of living above that which is commensurate with his present or past official emoluments; or

(b) is in control of pecuniary resources or property disproportionate to his present or past official emoluments,

shall, unless he gives a satisfactory explanation to the court as to how he was able to maintain such a standard of living or how such pecuniary resources or property came under his control, be guilty of an offence.

As can be seen from the text, the Wealth Element is clearly expressed as a requirement that the state establishes that the targeted person either 'maintains a standard of living' of a certain value or 'is in control or possession of pecuniary resources or property' of a certain value.

The Inadequate Income Element however is less straightforward, and is expressed as:

- Firstly, a requirement on the state to establish that the 'standard of living' or 'pecuniary resources or property' is 'incommensurate' or 'disproportionate' to the targeted person's 'present or past official emoluments'; and

---
272 Cap.201 Prevention of Bribery Ordinance 1971 (China - Hong Kong), Section 10.

- Secondly, if this is achieved by the state, as a reversed onus on the targeted person to provide 'a satisfactory explanation to the court as to how he was able to maintain such a standard of living or how such pecuniary resources or property came under his control'.

The practical application of this law was examined in the case of *Ernest Percival Max Hunt v the Queen*, in which the Supreme Court of Hong Kong assessed an allegation under Section 10(1)(b) relating to a public official's standard of living. The court held that firstly, the state is required to 'prove beyond reasonable doubt that an accused person has maintained a standard of living above that commensurate with his present or past official emoluments'.[273] Then, if the prosecution manages to do this, an 'explanation by the person accused becomes necessary', which must be established 'on the balance of probabilities'.[274]

With regards to what needs to be proven by the parties to discharge these burdens, the case of *Attorney General v Hui Kin-hong*[275] outlined that in order for the state to establish that a person's standard of living is 'above that commensurate' with their income, they must show 'that the standard of living maintained by the accused could not reasonably, in all the circumstances, have been afforded out of his total official emoluments during that period'.[276] With regards to what is required for a targeted person's explanation to be deemed satisfactory, *Ernest Percival Max Hunt v the Queen* outlined that the explanation must show that the established difference between a person's standard of living and their official emoluments was paid for by the targeted person using funds that were not the proceeds of crime:

> Thus "satisfactory explanation", for the purposes of this case, means an explanation which shows, upon a balance of probabilities, that the difference between an accused person's standard of living over the period charged and that which would have been commensurate with his present or past official emoluments has, if the standard of living actually maintained has been the higher of the two standards, been paid for with money the ultimate source of which was untainted by any corruption on the part of the accused.[277]

The Hong Kong approach to applying its illicit enrichment law has been mirrored in other jurisdictions with similarly styled laws. For instance in applying the law in India,[278] courts

---

273 Ernest Percival Max Hunt v the Queen [1974] HKCA 111.

274 ibid.

275 Attorney General v Hui Kin-hong [1995] 1 HKCLR 227.

276 ibid.

277 Ernest Percival Max Hunt v the Queen [1974] HKCA 111.

278 Prevention of Corruption Act 1988 (as amended by the Prevention of Corruption (Amendment) Act 2018) (India), Section 13; Note before the amendment of 2018, the phrasing of the illicit enrichment provision was almost identical, and read: '13(1) A public servant is said to commit the offence of criminal misconduct... (e) if he or any person on his behalf, is in possession or has, at any time during the period of his office, been in possession for which the public servant cannot satisfactorily account, of pecuniary resources or property disproportionate to his known sources of income. Explanation. For the purposes of this section, "known sources of income" means income received from any lawful source and such receipt has been intimated in accordance with the provisions of any law, rules or orders for the time being applicable to a public servant'. Before the introduction of the Prevention of Corruption Act 1988, the illicit enrichment law was contained in the Section 5(1)(e) of the Prevention of Corruption Act 1947 with the same wording as the pre-amended Prevention of Corruption Act 1988.

have consistently ruled that the primary burden in proceedings is first on the prosecution to prove, beyond reasonable doubt, that the public servant had 'been in possession of pecuniary resources or property disproportionate to his known sources of income' and that once this burden had been discharged, a burden was then placed on the targeted person to satisfactorily account for this disproportion on the balance of probabilities.[279]

In Malawi, the Chief Resident's Magistrate's Court has also mirrored this interpretation. In *Republic v Wesley Mzumara*,[280] the court held that in proceedings to determine illicit enrichment, 'the state is under a duty to establish prima facie control or possession by the accused of pecuniary resources and property held in his name or alias for his apparent benefit' and that this must be done to the standard 'beyond reasonable doubt'.[281] Furthermore, if the state achieves this, then 'the accused at this moment has the burden of satisfying this honourable court upon the balance of probabilities that there is a satisfactory explanation to each of these pecuniary resources and property and to bring the same within reach of his past or present official emoluments and other known sources of income'.[282]

Applications along these lines have also been mirrored in the criminal illicit enrichment proceedings of Pakistan[283] and Sierra Leone.[284]

The application of this style of elements in civil proceedings is similar, but with different standards of proof that must be reached. For example, the Kenyan qualified civil illicit enrichment law defines unexplained wealth as assets 'whose value is disproportionate to his known sources of income...and for which there is no satisfactory explanation' and empowers courts to issue a civil sanction, namely a value-based forfeiture order, against a person under the following circumstances:[285]

---

279 Vasant Rao Guhe v State of Madhya Pradesh (AIR 2017 SC 3713); Also see: N. Pasupathy v State 2018 (1) MLJ (Crl) 745; State Of Maharashtra vs Wasudeo Ramchandra Kaidalwar 1981 AIR 1186.

280 Republic v Wesley Mzumara (Criminal Case No.47 of 2010).

281 ibid.

282 ibid.

283 Khalid Aziz v the State 2011 SCMR 136; Ghani-Ur-Rehman v National Accountability Bureau and others, PLD 2011 Supreme Court 1144.

284 The State v Solomon Katta, Idrissa Fornah, Elizabeth King, Momoh Turay, Emmanuel Sesay, Catherine Katta, Santigie Kargbo before Hon. Mr. Justice M.A. Paul (3 April 2014).

285 Anti-Corruption and Economic Crimes Act 2003 (Kenya), Sections 2 and 55(5); Note also that Kenya's law is a qualified illicit enrichment law and in accordance with Section 2(b) unexplained wealth must also be shown to be assets that were 'acquired at or around the time the person was reasonably suspected of corruption or economic crime...'.

> 55(5) If after the Commission has adduced evidence that the person has unexplained assets the court is satisfied, on the balance of probabilities, and in light of the evidence so far adduced, that the person concerned does have unexplained assets, it may require the person, by such testimony and other evidence as the court deems sufficient, to satisfy the court that the assets were acquired otherwise than as the result of corrupt conduct.

In applying the above law, the court has confirmed that if the state satisfies the court that a person has unexplained wealth then 'the burden shifts so that the court may require the defendant to satisfy it that the assets were acquired otherwise than as a result of corrupt conduct'.[286]

3.2.2 Examples of legislation following 'Model B' (laws imposing the sole burden for both common elements on the state)

These types of illicit enrichment laws place the entirety of the burden of proof on the state to establish both the total wealth enjoyed by the person (the Wealth Element) and the fact that the targeted person did not have sufficient lawful income to justify the enjoyment of this amount of wealth (the Inadequate Income Element). Under this option, there is no express obligation on the targeted person to provide any evidence whatsoever, and there is no express reverse onus mechanism like those present in 'Model A' and 'Model C' laws.

This model has only been adopted by criminal illicit enrichment laws; at the time of writing there are no civil illicit enrichment laws that exist in this format. Consequently the threshold of proof that needs to be reached under these types of laws is the criminal standard of proof (i.e. beyond reasonable doubt).

---

286 Kenya Anti-Corruption Commission v Stanley Mombo Amuti [2017] eKLR at [95]. Peculiarly though, while jurisprudence outlines that the state is only required to prove their case on the balance of probabilities, if a person is required to satisfy the court that their assets were acquired lawfully, then Kenyan jurisprudence indicates that the person will need to do so to a 'higher threshold than one of [the] balance of probabilities' (see: Ethics and Anti-Corruption Commission (The legal successor of Kenya Anti - Corruption Commission) v Stanley Mombo Amuti [2015] eKLR at [34]). Specifically, courts have repeatedly held that the 'amount of proof that produces the court's satisfaction must be that which leaves the court without reasonable doubt.' (see: Kenya Anti-Corruption Commission v Stanley Mombo Amuti [2017] eKLR at [95] referencing Ethics and Anti-Corruption Commission (The legal successor of Kenya Anti - Corruption Commission) v Stanley Mombo Amuti [2015] eKLR at [34] which in turn references Col. Dr. Besigye Kiiza v Museveni Yoweri Kaguta, Election Petition No. 1 of 2001).

Model B: The Wealth Element (State) and the Inadequate Income Element (State)

The Wealth   The Inadequate
Element   Income Element

| The State establishes the value of wealth the person has enjoyed | The State establishes the total amount of income available to the person to spend on items of wealth (and a discrepancy between this value and the value of wealth enjoyed) |

An example of this option is the criminal illicit enrichment law in Lithuania:[287]

189-1(1) A person who holds by the right of ownership the property whose value exceeds 500 MSLs, while being aware or being obliged and likely to be aware that such property could not have been acquired with legitimate income, shall be punished by a fine or by arrest or by a custodial sentence for a term of up to four years.

As can be seen from the text above, this law expresses the Wealth Element as a requirement on the state to establish that a person 'holds by the right of ownership property whose value exceeds 500 MSLs' and expresses the Inadequate Income Element as a requirement on the state to demonstrate that this established wealth 'could not have been acquired with legitimate income'. (There are also other elements contained above, including a value threshold and a requirement to show awareness, and these issues will be discussed further under Section 3.4.) In other words, under this law, if the court is satisfied that the targeted person's total wealth (as established by the state) has not been adequately explained or justified by the targeted person's total proven lawful income (which also must be established by the state) then it will impose a sanction (assuming the other elements are also established of course).

The method for applying this law was outlined thoroughly by Lithuania's Constitutional Court in *Case No KT4-N3/2017*,[288] which confirmed that the targeted person does not bear any burden whatsoever in a proceeding under this provision. In this case, the court ruled that 'the

---

287 Law on the Approval and Entry into Force of the Criminal Code 26 September 2000 No VIII-1968 (as amended 21 November 2017 No XIII-791) (Lithuania), Article 189(1).

288 Case no. 14/2015-1/2016-2/2016-14/2016-15/2016- The Constitutional Court of the Republic of Lithuania in the name of the Republic of Lithuania ruling on the compliance of Paragraph 1 of Article 1891 of the Criminal Code of the Republic of Lithuania with the Constitution of the Republic of Lithuania 15 March 2017, no KT4-N3/2017.

prosecutor has the obligation to prove that the crime... has been committed, inter alia, that the property above 500 MSLs in value held by the person by right of ownership could not have been acquired with legitimate income.'[289] They also further clarified that the law 'does not shift the burden of proof to a person suspected of (charged with) illicit enrichment' and that '[t]he suspect/accused is not obliged to provide evidence and prove that the criminal act ... has not been committed and that he/she is not guilty of its commission, but has the right to do so in the exercise of his/her right to defence...'.[290] Furthermore, the court specified that 'the situations where the suspect/accused opts to be silent may not be treated as aggravating his/her situation in criminal proceedings'.[291]

Another example of a law containing the Inadequate Income Element in the style of Model B, and which also does not expressly place any burden on a targeted person, is the criminal illicit enrichment law in Uganda:[292]

31(1) The Inspector General of Government or the Director of Public Prosecutions or an authorised officer, may investigate or cause an investigation of any person where there is reasonable ground to suspect that the person—

(a) maintains a standard of living above that which is commensurate with his or her current or past known sources of income or assets; or

(b) is in control or possession of pecuniary resources or property disproportionate to his or her current or past known sources of income or assets.

31(2) A person found in possession of illicitly acquired pecuniary resources or property commits an offence and is liable on conviction to a term of imprisonment not exceeding ten years or a fine not exceeding two hundred and forty currency points or both.

The method to apply this law was covered in the case of *Uganda v B.D Wandera*,[293] where the High Court of Uganda outlined that the state has the responsibility of demonstrating the following elements of the above Subsection 1(b) provision:

The ingredients of this offence...are that:

(i)   The accused must be in control or possession of pecuniary resources or property;

(ii) The pecuniary resources or property must be disproportionate to his or her current or past known sources of income or assets.[294]

289 ibid., at [22] and [39.3].
290 ibid., at [20] and [39.3].
291 ibid., at [39.3].
292 Anti Corruption Act 2009 (Uganda), Section 31.
293 Uganda v B.D Wandera HCT-00-AC-SC-0012/2014.
294 ibid.

In doing so, the court further stated that 'the prosecution...has the burden of proof to prove their case beyond reasonable doubt', and that if they are successful then an 'inference' would be drawn 'that the accused has illicitly enriched himself if there was no plausible defence'.[295]

Of course, as alluded to in both the above Ugandan and Lithuanian cases, even if the laws in both these jurisdictions do not expressly place a burden on the targeted person to provide evidence, if the state manages to establish the elements required by the law, then it will be prudent for a targeted person to provide evidence in their defence as a failure to do so will likely lead to conviction.

3.2.3   Examples of legislation following 'Model C' (laws imposing a sole burden on the targeted person to address the Inadequate Income Element)

Illicit enrichment laws containing this model of elements only require the state to establish that the targeted person has benefited from an amount of wealth before a burden of proof is then automatically placed on the targeted person to demonstrate an adequate amount of lawful income to justify this established wealth.

This is the model of choice for the majority of civil illicit enrichment laws.[296] Consequently the thresholds of proof that need to be reached under these types of laws are the civil standards of proof (e.g. the balance of probabilities).

Model C: The Wealth Element (State) and the Inadequate Income Element (Targeted Person)

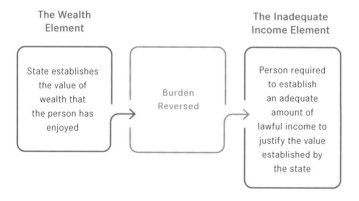

The Wealth Element

The Inadequate Income Element

State establishes the value of wealth that the person has enjoyed

Burden Reversed

Person required to establish an adequate amount of lawful income to justify the value established by the state

---

295   ibid.

296   The wording of Côte d'Ivoire's criminal law appears to takes this approach as well, stating: [Unofficial translation] 'The burden of proving the lawful origin of his wealth rests with the person prosecuted.' (Original text: 'Il appartient à la personne poursuivie d'enrichissement illicite de prouver l'origine licite de son patrimoine.') – see Ordonnance n° 2013-660 du 20 septembre 2013 relative à la prévention et à la lutte contre la corruption et les infractions assimilées, Article 56. Note however that published judicial decisions confirming how the burdens under this particular law apply in practice were not located during research for this publication.

An example of this style of illicit enrichment law is that of Western Australia:[297]

> 12(1) On hearing an application under section 11(1), the court must declare that the respondent has unexplained wealth if it is more likely than not that the total value of the respondent's wealth is greater than the value of the respondent's lawfully acquired wealth.
>
> 12(2) Any property, service, advantage or benefit that is a constituent of the respondent's wealth is presumed not to have been lawfully acquired unless the respondent establishes the contrary.

As can be seen from the text above, this law expresses the Wealth Element as a requirement for the state to establish 'the total value of the respondent's wealth' and the Inadequate Income Element as a requirement for the targeted person to establish sufficient 'lawfully acquired wealth' to explain the amount of wealth that has been established, with '...any property, service, advantage or benefit that is a constituent of the respondent's wealth... presumed not to have been lawfully acquired unless the respondent establishes the contrary'.[298] By nature of the reverse onus provision contained in Section 12(2), this law does not place any responsibility on the state to establish a person's 'lawfully acquired wealth', and instead places the entirety of the burden on the targeted person.

The method for applying this law was covered in the District Court of Western Australia case of *Director of Public Prosecutions v Morris*,[299] which confirmed that the respondent bears the onus of establishing the lawful sources of the relevant property in a proceeding under this provision.

In justifying his application of the law, Wager DCJ quoted the explanatory notes of the law itself, which explained that:

> ...it is easier for a person to establish that his wealth is lawfully acquired rather than for the state to establish the contrary... Failure to include such a provision would place heavy resource obligations on the state in seeking to establish that a person's wealth was not lawfully acquired.[300]

3.2.4 Laws that take one model of elements but which are judicially applied in accordance with another model of elements

It is important to also highlight that even if the wording of a law appears to allocate burdens for the two common elements in one way, the courts may distribute the relevant burdens in a different way when applying the law.

---

297 Criminal Property Confiscation Act 2000 (Australia - Western Australia), Section 12.

298 ibid.

299 Director of Public Prosecutions v Morris [No2] [2010] WADC 148.

300 Explanatory Notes, Criminal Confiscation Bill 2000 (Australia - Western Australia) as referenced in Director of Public Prosecutions v Morris [No2] [2010] WADC 148.

For example, a literal reading of the criminal illicit enrichment law of Argentina would suggest that a person has at least a partial burden to justify the source of their wealth:[301]

> 268(2) Any person who, upon being duly requested, does not justify the origin of appreciable enrichment of his or her own wealth or that of a third party seeking to conceal it... shall be punished...

The Argentinian courts however have interpreted this provision differently, and have instead ruled that it does not in fact place any burden on the accused to explain their wealth. For instance, in the case of *Alsogaray*,[302] the National Chamber of Criminal Cassation stated that:

> ...it should be noted that Article 268(2) of the Criminal Code does not imply or define a reversal of the burden of proof by placing on the suspect the burden of proving his innocence by justifying the origin of the enrichment, because the truth is that the proof of enrichment in this unjustified sense is the responsibility of the court and the Public Prosecutor's Office, which are not replaced by the defendant.[303]

Furthermore, the court also stated that the requirement of 'justification' contained in the law can only be logically understood as an '...opportunity for the defendant to prove the lawfulness of his enrichment' and '[i]f the accused makes use of his right to remain silent, in this case too the judicial bodies will have the burden of proof'.[304]

This interpretation was confirmed by a subsequent appeal in this case to the Supreme Court in 2008,[305] and more recently, by the Federal Criminal and Correctional Court in the 2017

---

301 [Unofficial translation] Código Penal de la Nación Argentina Ley 11.179, Artículo 268(2) (Original text: 'Será reprimido con prisión de dos (2) a seis (6) años, multa de dos (2) a cinco (5) veces del valor del enriquecimiento, e inhabilitación absoluta perpetua, el que al ser debidamente requerido, no justificare la procedencia de un enriquecimiento patrimonial apreciable suyo o de persona interpuesta para disimularlo, ocurrido con posterioridad a la asunción de un cargo o empleo público y hasta dos (2) años después de haber cesado en su desempeño.').

302 Cámara Nacional de Casación Penal, sala IV, 'Alsogaray', causa n°4787 (2005).

303 [Unofficial translation] Cámara Nacional de Casación Penal, sala IV, 'Alsogaray', causa n°4787 (2005) (Original text: 'Teniendo en cuenta todo lo antes referido, no se advierte que el artículo 268 (2) del Código Penal implique o defina una inversión de la carga de la prueba poniendo en cabeza del sospechado el deber de demostrar su inocencia mediante la justificación de la procedencia del enriquecimiento, porque lo cierto es que la prueba del enriquecimiento en tal sentido injustificado corresponde al órgano jurisdiccional y al Ministerio Público Fiscal, quienes no son sustituidos en esa carga por el imputado.').

304 [Unofficial translation] Cámara Nacional de Casación Penal, sala IV, 'Alsogaray', causa n°4787 (2005) (Original text: 'En similar sentido se ha sostenido que el requerimiento de 'justificación', usado por el legislador, sólo puede ser entendido lógicamente como una notificación para que el acusado pueda hacer uso de una oportunidad formal de probar la licitud de su enriquecimiento; que se ha mal interpretado ese concepto, confundiéndoselo con la noción procesal de 'prueba positiva'; y que el tipo es avalorado, neutro y respeta plenamente el derecho de abstención que se deriva, en materia procesal, de la presunción de inocencia. Si el imputado hiciere uso de su derecho a callar, también en este caso serán las instancias judiciales las que tendrán la carga de probar –idéntica a la de otros tipos penales en los casos en que los imputados se abstienen de declarar- (cfr.: C.N.C. y C.C.F., Sala I, voto del doctor Elbert en el precedente 'Cullota', ya citado')).

305 Corte Suprema de Justicia de la Nación Argentina, 'Alsogaray', Fallos 331:2799 (2008).

case of *César Santos Gerardo del Corazón de Jesús Milani*,[306] which also held that the burden of proof is not reversed and that '[i]n essence, it is the State that has the burden of proving an appreciable and unjustified increase in the assets of the official or employee'.[307] Rather than reversing the burden of proof, the law gives the targeted person 'the possibility of justifying the origin of his enrichment as well as the power to refuse to testify'.[308]

In a contrasting example, the criminal illicit enrichment law of Peru reads as follows:[309]

> 401 ... Illicit enrichment is considered to exist when the increase in the wealth or personal economic expenditure of the civil servant or public official, in consideration of his or her sworn declaration of assets and income, is notoriously greater than that which he or she would normally have had by virtue of his or her salaries or emoluments received or increases in his or her capital or income for any other lawful cause.

As can be seen from the text above, the law does not appear to expressly place any burden on the targeted person to provide evidence regarding the legitimate source of their funds at any point in a potential proceeding. Nonetheless, Peruvian courts have interpreted this law to include a reverse burden mechanism. In the Supreme Court case regarding *Manuel Enrique Cárdenas Valseca*,[310] the judges reference international legal instruments including the illicit enrichment provisions in IACAC and UNCAC in ruling that an application of the Peruvian illicit enrichment law did in fact include a reverse burden mechanism. Specifically, the judges ruled that a prosecutor's burden is limited to establishing the increase in assets of the targeted person in regards to their lawful income, and once this has been established, the burden of proof is reversed onto the targeted person 'with the official having the duty to prove that this

---

306 Poder Judicial de la Nación, Juzgado Criminal y Correccional Federal 3, 'César Santos Gerardo del Corazón de Jesús Milani', CFP 6734/2013 (2017/09).

307 [Unofficial translation] Poder Judicial de la Nación, Juzgado Criminal y Correccional Federal 3, 'César Santos Gerardo del Corazón de Jesús Milani', CFP 6734/2013 (2017/09) (Original text: 'En definitiva, es el Estado quien tiene a su cargo acreditar el aumento apreciable y no justificado del patrimonio del funcionario o del empleado.').

308 [Unofficial translation] Poder Judicial de la Nación, Juzgado Criminal y Correccional Federal 3, 'César Santos Gerardo del Corazón de Jesús Milani', CFP 6734/2013 (2017/09) (Original text: 'De esta forma, con el llamamiento efectuado, no se invirtió la carga de la prueba ni fue violatorio de la prohibición de declarar en contra de uno mismo, sino que, con dicha convocatoria, se le brindó a Milani la posibilidad de justificar el origen de su enriquecimiento como así también la facultad de negarse a declarar (cfr. C.N.C.P., in re: 'Alsogaray', ya citado).'). As mentioned in footnote 171 however, this position has proven to be contentious amongst legal commentators.

309 [Unofficial translation] Código Penal del Estado Peruano, Decreto Legislativo N°635, Artículo 401° Enriquecimiento ilícito (Original text: 'Se considera que existe indicio de enriquecimiento ilícito cuando el aumento del patrimonio o del gasto económico personal del funcionario o servidor público, en consideración a su declaración jurada de bienes y rentas, es notoriamente superior al que normalmente haya podido tener en virtud de sus sueldos o emolumentos percibidos o de los incrementos de su capital o de sus ingresos por cualquier otra causa lícita.').

310 Corte Suprema de Justicia de la República, Sala Penal Transitoria Casación, Manuel Enrique Cárdenas Valseca, n° 953-2017 (2018).

disproportionate increase has had just cause'.[311]

3.2.5   Providing a satisfactory explanation

As alluded to above, many illicit enrichment laws often require a targeted person to provide an explanation for either their total amount of wealth or an established discrepancy between their total amount of wealth and their known or official sources of income – either through an obligation to do so or voluntarily as part of a defence.

In a general sense, this will require a person to prove, usually to the civil standard (e.g. on the balance of probabilities) that the relevant amount of wealth was not sourced through criminality, but was derived from legitimate sources.

Throughout the world, people subjected to illicit enrichment proceedings have often sought to explain the alleged disproportion in their wealth by claiming that they had received income from sources such as side businesses, gifts from family, or substantial gambling wins. However, such explanations have only been deemed satisfactory if they are substantiated through credible evidence.

For instance, in the Argentinian criminal case of *L., C. y otro*,[312] the defendant's claims that the difference in income and wealth was actually through the receipt of donations from family members was rejected on the basis that no documentation was provided to evidence this. Similarly, in the Argentinian case *Omar Daniel Carreiras*,[313] the defendant's claims that he had received additional income from livestock farming was rejected on the basis that the income was not documented. In the Kenyan civil case of *Stanley Mombo Amuti v Kenya Anti-Corruption Commission*,[314] the respondent's claim that a cash deposit into his bank account was for professional fees from a deceased Sudanese national was deemed unsatisfactory on the basis that the respondent could not prove the nature of the professional services rendered, nor the duration of the work done, and did not tender any evidence of a fee note related to the work.[315]

On the other hand, adequately evidenced explanations are often accepted by courts. For instance, in the criminal case of *Kedari Lal v State of M.P. and Ors*,[316] the Supreme Court of

---

311 [Unofficial translation] Corte Suprema de Justicia de la República, Sala Penal Transitoria Casación, Manuel Enrique Cárdenas Valseca, n° 953-2017 (2018) (Original text: '5.5. Las fuentes internacionales antes citadas, hacen mención a la naturaleza del delito de enriquecimiento ilícito, y nos muestra de un modo relativo la inversión de la carga de la prueba. En donde la carga de probar, está circunscrita a demostrar la existencia del incremento patrimonial de un funcionario público, cuando son muy superiores a los que regularmente hubiera podido alcanzar como resultado de sus ingresos legítimos; y es a partir de ese instante, en que se invierte la carga de la prueba, correspondiendo al funcionario el deber de acreditar que ese incremento desmesurado, ha tenido una causa justificada lícita.').

312 Cámara Nacional de Apelaciones en lo Criminal y Correccional, sala VII, 'L., C. Y otros', Fallos 45793 (2017).

313 Tribunal en lo Criminal n° 4 De La Plata, Omar Daniel Carreiras, causa n° 4618 (2017).

314 Kenya Anti-Corruption Commission v Stanley Mombo Amuti (Civil Appeal No.184 of 2018).

315 ibid.

316 Kedari Lal v State of M.P. and Ors MANU/SC/0343/2015.

India ruled that an alleged disproportion between the defendant's total value of wealth and his sources of income had in fact been justified by reference to gifts, inheritances and loans that he claimed to have received from friends and family. The ruling was based on the fact that the defendant had provided substantial verbal and documentary evidence to support 'every single amount received'.[317]

Moreover, in the Western Australian civil case of *Director of Public Prosecutions v Morris*, the respondent was able to satisfactorily explain the legitimate origin of AUD 108,390 in cash found during a police search of his car. In doing so, the respondent pointed to sufficient records of income from his gym and other sources, provided a plausible excuse for having the cash in his car when he was searched, and further justified his habit of keeping his savings in the form of cash by referring to a previous incident where he lost funds from his savings account due to the collapse of a bank.[318]

---

317 ibid., at [12].
318 Director of Public Prosecutions v Morris [No 2][2010] WADC 148 at [41].

3.3 How courts assess the elements to determine if illicit enrichment has taken place

3.3.1 A matter of 'mathematical calculation'

In assessing whether the Wealth Element and the Inadequate Income Element have been established, and illicit enrichment has occurred, the courts will often conduct a mathematical exercise. In doing so, they will assess the evidence presented and will seek to determine two precise figures that can be put into a simple formula to determine whether or not the targeted person has illicitly enriched themselves. These two figures are derived directly from the evidence presented to establish the two common elements, and are as follows:

Figure 1: The **total amount of wealth** that the person has enjoyed over a certain period of time (as derived from the state's evidence regarding the Wealth Element); and

Figure 2: The **total amount of lawful income** received by the person over the same period of time (as derived from the state's and/or person's evidence of income regarding the Inadequate Income Element).

Once these two figures have been determined, the court can then conduct a simple mathematical exercise to determine if the elements have been successfully established and that:

- A person enjoyed an amount of wealth; and

- The lawful origin of this amount of wealth has not been justified or explained by reference to the same person's lawful income.

This mathematical exercise can be summarised as a simple formula:

FIGURE 1

Total amount of wealth
(enjoyed by the person over a certain period of time)

—

(minus)

FIGURE 2

Total amount of lawful income
(received by/available to the person over the same period of time)

=

(equals)

TOTAL ILLICIT ENRICHMENT

If the total amount of wealth (Figure 1) is larger than the total amount of lawful income (Figure 2), then the resulting number will be positive and this will mean that the elements have been established and that illicit enrichment has occurred. Providing of course that any other elements required by the particular law (e.g. that the person is a public official) have also been established, then the court will impose a sanction.

In addition to demonstrating the fact that illicit enrichment has taken place, a final positive figure will also represent the precise value of this illicit enrichment.

If zero, or a negative figure, is produced by the formula, illicit enrichment has obviously not been established. This idea of processing evidence mathematically has been highlighted in jurisprudence throughout the world. In the case of *Queen v Mok Wei-Tak and Another*,[319] the Hong Kong Court of Appeal described the analysis of evidence in an illicit enrichment proceeding as 'accounting exercises' and the 'computation of figures'.[320] Moreover, in the *Uganda v B.D Wandera* case mentioned previously in this section, Justice Keitirima described Uganda's criminal illicit enrichment law as 'an offence of mathematical calculation' under which the value of the property or pecuniary resources of the accused needs to be established (i.e. Figure 1), followed by the accused's income (i.e. Figure 2), and finally that the value of the former is disproportionate to the value of the latter.[321]

Even in jurisdictions where jurisprudence doesn't exist, the need to conduct a computation of sorts is intrinsically required by the wording of the illicit enrichment legislation itself, which will expressly necessitate the establishment of some sort of disparity, disproportion, or incommensurateness. Take for instance the civil illicit enrichment law of Fiji, which empowers a court to impose a civil sanction if the 'value of the person's total wealth is greater than the value of the person's lawfully acquired wealth'.[322] It is impossible for a court to precisely determine whether or not this is the case without performing some sort of calculation and comparison of the two mentioned values.

3.3.2 Defining a 'period of interest' in which to calculate potential illicit enrichment

In order to be able to calculate if illicit enrichment has occurred under the above formula, a court will usually be required to set time parameters for its analysis. The period of time between the two set dates is often referred to as a 'period of interest', a 'period of check' or a 'period of reckoning', and is necessary for an accurate calculation and comparison of a person's total wealth and income. If such parameters did not exist, then it would be possible for:

---

319 Queen v Mok Wei-Tak and Another [1985] HKLR 1054.

320 ibid., at [1059].

321 Uganda v B.D Wandera HCT-00-AC-SC-0012/2014.

322 Proceeds of Crime Act 1997 (as amended by the Proceeds of Crime Amendment Act No.7 of 2005 and by the Proceeds of Crime (Amendment) Decree 2012 (Decree No.61 of 2012)) (Fiji), Section 71H.

1) The targeted person to argue that they paid for certain wealth that they enjoyed during the period of interest using income that they received before or after the period of interest that wasn't actually available to them at the time; or

2) The state to argue that a person acquired additional wealth before or after the period of interest that is disproportionate to a certain amount of income received during the period of interest.

The period of interest does not necessarily refer to the total period of time that someone could be targeted by an illicit enrichment law (for example, the total period of time someone was a public official or the time period that falls within a legislation's limitation period). Instead, it refers to the time period in which the claimed illicit enrichment occurred (for example, one year in which a public official inexplicably acquired a significant amount of wealth).

For instance, although the Indian illicit enrichment law requires those who illicitly enrich themselves to be public officials, this does not mean that the period of interest used by the court to calculate an alleged disproportion in wealth versus income needs to span the entire period the person was a public official. As explained in *State of Marashtra v Pollonji Darabshaw Daruwalla*:

> ...it is not imperative that the period of reckoning be spread-out for the entire stretch of anterior service of the public-servant... However, the period must be such as to enable a true and comprehensive picture of the known sources of income and the pecuniary resources and property in possession of the public-servant either by himself or through any other person on his behalf, which are alleged to be so disproportionate.[323]

Of course, if a certain jurisdiction's criminal illicit enrichment law specifically targets public officials, the period of interest that a court will often use will coincide directly with the first date that the person entered the public service up until the date the investigation was commenced or the person left office.

In practice, the period will usually be set by the prosecution in the details of the allegation or claim against the targeted person.

3.3.3   How a court determines a person's total amount of wealth (Figure 1)

As covered under Section 2.2.2.2, different illicit enrichment laws target different types of wealth. While some laws only target actual assets and pecuniary resources, others take a much wider approach and target any benefit a person may have received that contributed to their overall standard of living.

In practice, the specific types of items that can potentially be assessed by courts as contributing

---

323 State of Marashtra v Pollonji Darabshaw Daruwalla, 1988 AIR 88 (case originally referenced by L. Muzila et al., *On the Take: Criminalizing Illicit Enrichment to Fight Corruption*, The World Bank, Washington, 2012, p.17).

to a person's wealth during a period of interest are almost limitless – providing of course that they fall under the general umbrella of the type of wealth targeted by a particular law.

To give an example, when totalling the value of pecuniary resources held by the appellant in the *Indian case of Krishnanand v The State of Madhya Pradesh*,[324] the Supreme Court of India tallied the total values of the appellant's bank balances, investment instruments, car, firearms and even his radio and furniture. In determining the value of day-to-day expenditures that the appellant had made over the relevant period, the Supreme Court also took into account money spent by the appellant on such items as insurance premiums, education fees, rent, car maintenance, electricity bills, phone bills, vacations, food, clothing, club memberships and even money spent on smoking and the consumption of alcohol.[325]

To give a second example: in the Senegalese case of *Karim Meïssa Wade*,[326] when calculating whether the son of the former president had illicitly enriched himself, the Court of Repression of Illicit Enrichment (La Cour de Répression de l'Enrichissement Illicite) counted the value of a number of significant assets towards the defendant's total wealth. This included the value of a number of luxury vehicles, large sums in foreign bank accounts, numerous items of jewellery, a number of Swiss-made watches and several real estate properties.

Of course, as mentioned above, the exact items that can be included towards the total value of enjoyed wealth in one jurisdiction may not be considered in another. For instance, whereas Indian courts will consider day-to-day purchases of food and clothing or other household expenditures,[327] courts in several Australian jurisdictions are legislatively prohibited from including 'necessary food, clothing and other items reasonably necessary for the ordinary daily requirements of living' when conducting the same calculations.

A more thorough examination of the types of items that investigators and prosecutors may want to consider is found in Annex 2.

> **Author's note: Asset declaration systems and illicit enrichment laws**
>
> In the context of illicit enrichment laws targeting public officials, asset declaration laws can play a key role in the establishment of disproportionate wealth in illicit enrichment investigations and proceedings. In fact, many illicit enrichment provisions exist in legislative instruments alongside asset declaration provisions. While the credibility of information contained in such asset declarations must always be verified, such declarations can often

---

324 Krishnanand v The State of Madhya Pradesh MANU/SC/0134/1976.

325 ibid., at [9] and [20].

326 The original decision could not be obtained, an unofficial reproduction of this decision by La Cour de Répression de l'Enrichissement Illicite was accessed at 'Condamnation de Karim Wade: L'arrêt de la Cour de Répression de l'Enrichissement Illicite', aDakar, 27 March 2015, http://news.adakar.com/d/14066. asp, accessed 10 March 2021. Also note, excerpts from this decision are also contained in a subsequent ruling of France's Cour D'Appel de Paris: CA Paris, 14 mars 2018, n°17/03650.

327 Vasant Rao Guhe v the State Of Madhya Pradesh AIR 2017 SC 3713.

provide a useful starting point in the assessment of a person's wealth. The evidential value of such declarations is covered in Annex 2 (Section 2.5.1).

3.3.3.1 Legal issues that may arise surrounding the establishment of the total wealth enjoyed by a person

There are some common legal issues that have been considered by courts when determining if certain items can be counted towards the total amount of wealth enjoyed by a person.

Assets held or enjoyed by other people

Those seeking to conceal their ownership of illegally acquired assets often place the ownership of these assets under the names of other parties. When this occurs, contentions often arise in asset recovery proceedings when the state seeks to establish that items of wealth held or enjoyed by a separate person are actually items of wealth that should be considered as part of the targeted person's total wealth. As mentioned in Section 2.2.2.2, many illicit enrichment laws attempt to address this issue before it arises in the courts by expressly stating that assets proven to be held 'on trust or otherwise' by people closely connected to a targeted person can be considered in wealth calculations. For instance, the criminal illicit enrichment law in Hong Kong states:

> Where a court is satisfied in proceedings for an offence under subsection (1)(b) that, having regard to the closeness of his relationship to the accused and to other circumstances, there is reason to believe that any person was holding pecuniary resources or property in trust for or otherwise on behalf of the accused or acquired such resources or property as a gift from the accused, such resources or property shall, in the absence of evidence to the contrary, be presumed to have been in the control of the accused.[328]

The above provision allows a court to make a presumption that certain resources or property held by a separate party are in the control of the targeted person in certain situations. While the court in *Ho Shing Tuen v R*[329] subsequently clarified that the 'closeness of the relationship' between the targeted person and the separate party is not enough in itself to invite a presumption of control, other cases have demonstrated that this presumption can be made if additional circumstances also exist. For example, in the case of *Queen v Chung Cheong*,[330] the court found that there was overwhelming evidence that shares registered in the name of the accused's brother were in fact under the control of the accused, due in part to the fact that payments for the shares could be traced to a bank account held by the accused.[331]

---

328 Cap.201 Prevention of Bribery Ordinance 1971 (China - Hong Kong), Section 10(2).

329 Ho Shing Tuen v R [1980] HKC 289 (as referenced in I. McWalters SC et al., *Bribery and Corruption Law in Hong Kong*, LexisNexis, Hong Kong, 2015, p.413).

330 Queen v Chung Cheong DCCC000137/1977.

331 Interestingly, while the court specified that the preconditions to make a presumption of control had been met in this case, they even further clarified that the evidence of 'control' was so overwhelming that the prosecutors had proven the accused's 'control' over the asset beyond reasonable doubt, and that therefore there wasn't even a need to make a presumption in this case.

This concept has also been addressed in other jurisdictions. For example, in the Pakistani case of *Muhammad Yaqub v The State*,[332] the court held that agricultural land in the name of the accused's brother could actually be attributed to the accused on the basis that the purchase price for this land had been paid for in person by the accused. Furthermore, this case also held that land in the accused's wife's name could also be attributed to the accused on the basis that his wife did not have any independent sources of income to justify the parcel of land in her name.[333]

Similarly, in the Indian Supreme Court case of *K. Poonuswamy v State of Tamilnadu*,[334] significant assets held by the accused's wife and daughter, including large bank deposits, were deemed to be part of the accused's total wealth on the basis that neither his wife nor his daughter had sufficient income or any other feasible excuse to justify the acquisition of these assets.

> **Author's note: Considerations regarding the rights of third parties over unexplained assets**
>
> Issues may arise if a bona fide third party has received the benefits of another person's illicit enrichment, and the state seeks to recover these assets. For example, if a person acquires a house from unexplained sources and then uses this house to obtain a mortgage with a bank, questions may arise surrounding the rights of this bank with regards to any efforts by the state to confiscate this house. Similar questions may also arise if the person had acquired a car from unknown sources and then sold it to an innocent party. Some criminal and civil illicit enrichment laws do include safeguards to ensure that a bona fide third party can make their interest in property known during enforcement proceedings (e.g. Section 179S of the Australian (Federal) Proceeds of Crime Act 2002, Sections 12AA(3)-(4) of Hong Kong's Prevention of Bribery Ordinance 1971 and Section 12AA of Fiji's Prevention of Bribery Act (Promulgation No.12 of 2007)). However, there are many laws that are silent on this issue.

When and how to value assets

Questions have also sometimes arisen surrounding the appropriate date on which a certain item of wealth should be valued.

In general, when calculating a targeted person's total wealth during proceedings, courts refer to the value of the item at the moment it was acquired or enjoyed by the targeted person. For instance, in *Uganda v B.D Wandera*, the court specifically states that a proper valuation of assets should refer to 'the cost at the time they were acquired'. [335]

---

332 Muhammad Yaqub v The State 1988 SCMR 282.

333 ibid.

334 \ AIR 2001 SC 2464.

335 Uganda v B.D Wandera HCT-00-AC-SC-0012/2014.

In determining the value of a subsequent pecuniary based recovery order, however, the value of the assets at the charge date (for criminal illicit enrichment laws) or the date of application for a civil order (for civil illicit enrichment laws) have also been used to determine the appropriate amount of any such order.[336] The justification for this is to ensure that the person is stripped of the total value of the proceeds of their illicit enrichment (e.g. where a house has been purchased from unexplained sources and has risen in value in the period up until the court proceedings).

3.3.4   How a court determines the total amount of a person's lawful income (Figure 2)

In illicit enrichment proceedings, either the state or the targeted person will be required to bring evidence to establish the targeted person's total lawful income during the period of interest. As explained previously in this Part, the purpose for this will be:

- To provide a satisfactory explanation as to how certain items of wealth were lawfully acquired or enjoyed (e.g. when the targeted person has the burden under a Model C law); or

- To establish a discrepancy between the total value of this income and the total value of the wealth enjoyed by the person (e.g. when the state has the burden under a Model B law); or

- Both of the above (e.g. when there is a shared burden under a Model A law).

In the broadest sense, a person's income will include any provably legitimate receipt of wealth. Most commonly this will include the salary received from employment, but like with items of wealth, the legitimate sources of income for a person may be almost limitless.

For example, when calculating the total income of the defendant in the case of *Krishnanand v The State of Madhya Pradesh*, the Supreme Court of India also took into account job-related allowances, interest earned from bank accounts, insurance claims, income tax refunds, monetary payments from family members and money received through the sale of a bond.[337] In the case of *Director of Public Prosecutions v Morris* mentioned previously, the District Court of Western Australia took into account the total amount of income Morris had earned from his gym business and personal training services, funds he had received through the sale of a car, a motorbike and shares, plus an additional sum he had received through a bank loan.[338] In *Case No KT4-N3/2017*, the Constitutional Court of Lithuania noted that when determining the legitimacy of a person's enrichment, the court may also consider taking into account the income

---

336   For an example see the Hong Kong case of Chung Cheong v The Queen CACC001364/1977. Also note, that the laws in the Australian jurisdictions of the Northern Territory, Western Australia, and Tasmania also specifically outline that the value to be used should be the greater of the value of the item at the time it was acquired or the value of the item on the date the civil application was made by the state.

337   Krishnanand v The State of Madhya Pradesh MANU/SC/0134/1976.

338   Director of Public Prosecutions v Morris [No2][2010] WADC 148.

of family members – including any loans or inheritances from which they may have benefited.[339]

Legitimate income earned before a defined period of interest in the form of savings may also be included in the calculation of a person's total income, if the targeted person used these savings during the period of interest towards the acquisition of items of wealth. In *Uganda v B.D Wandera*, the accused claimed that he had managed to acquire certain assets by using savings from income earned before the period of interest, and the court held that at the very least, the prosecution should have sought to verify this. The court stated that it was 'imperative for the prosecution to establish whether the accused indeed had those savings as he had declared...' and that 'the evidence could have easily been established either from his bank statements during that period or from interviewing the accused'.[340]

3.3.5 Final step – Assessing the discrepancy between Figure 1 and Figure 2

The final determination of whether there is a discrepancy (or disproportion or incommensurateness) between the total wealth enjoyed by the person and the total income available to the person during the period of interest is a simple process that is completed using the mathematical formula explained previously in this Part.

In practice, the state will usually perform its own mathematical calculations as part of the case it presents to court. However at the conclusion of proceedings, the court will also conduct its own independent calculation based on the evidence that has been presented by both parties.[341] This sometimes leads to the court determining a different figure to that of the state, due to the fact that the court may adjust its calculations to take into account any items of wealth that have not been adequately proven by the state or any additional income that may have been proven by the targeted person.

---

339 Case no. 14/2015-1/2016-2/2016-14/2016-15/2016- The Constitutional Court of the Republic of Lithuania in the name of the Republic of Lithuania ruling on the compliance of Paragraph 1 of Article 189¹ of the Criminal Code of the Republic of Lithuania with the Constitution of the Republic of Lithuania 15 March 2017, no KT4-N3/2017 at [20].

340 Uganda v B.D Wandera HCT-00-AC-SC-0012/2014; The failure on behalf of the prosecution to verify this evidence was a key factor in the acquittal of the defendant in this case.

341 In practice, providing a jurisdiction's procedure allows for the pre-trial agreement of certain facts, both the state and the targeted person may seek to agree on certain values of incomes and items of wealth pre-trial to reduce the amount of time required to conduct actual court proceedings.

3.4 Other elements contained in illicit enrichment laws in addition to the Wealth Element and the Inadequate Income Element

While the Wealth Element and the Inadequate Income Element are fundamental elements that need to be addressed in some form under all criminal and civil illicit enrichment laws, they may not be the only elements that need to be established during proceedings to compel a court to issue a judicial sanction.

3.4.1 Requirement to prove the enrichment was above a defined value or was 'significant'

As outlined in Section 2.2.2.3, some illicit enrichment laws include thresholds that require the state to establish either a minimum value of:

- The overall wealth of the targeted person;

- The increase in the overall wealth of a person over a certain period of time; or

- The increase in the wealth of a person over and above their lawful income.

These thresholds can be either clearly defined, with stated monetary amounts, or less specific.

Defined value thresholds

Value thresholds with a defined amount are often clearly stated in an illicit enrichment law, and as such are not particularly open to interpretation by the courts. Examples of these types of laws include the qualified civil illicit enrichment law of Trinidad and Tobago[342] as well as the criminal illicit enrichment laws of Afghanistan[343] and Honduras[344], which all include specific monetary-based value amounts in the wording of their law that need to be established by the state before sanctions can be imposed.

Unspecific value thresholds

Value thresholds also exist in other laws, however, that are not so specific. Rather than mentioning an exact minimum monetary value that needs to be proven, these laws instead require the state to demonstrate that a person's enrichment over a certain period of time was 'significant' or 'appreciable'.

For example, the illicit enrichment law in Argentina requires that an 'appreciable enrichment' be proven – and a precise, value-based definition for this threshold has not been established. Instead, in the case of *Alsogaray*, the court held that whether or not the enrichment in question is 'appreciable' should be determined on a case-by-case basis through reference to

---

342 Civil Asset Recovery and Management and Unexplained Wealth Act 2019 (Trinidad and Tobago), Section 58.

343 Penal Code (Afghanistan), Article 419(2).

344 Código Penal (Decreto No. 130-2017) (Honduras), Artículo 484.

the unique economic situation of the targeted person to determine if any proven enrichment could be 'considered normal or not' in reference to the person's lawful income.[345]

Value thresholds created through jurisprudence

Even when a defined or unspecific value threshold is not included in the law, some jurisdictions have introduced a requirement to establish a certain minimum amount of illicit enrichment through jurisprudence. In the Indian case of *Krishnanand v The State of Madhya Pradesh*, the Supreme Court of India found that the excess assets held by the appellant were 'comparatively small' and 'less than 10 percent of the total income', and consequently set aside the conviction, despite the fact that the law itself does not include any express thresholds that need to be considered.[346] This notion was further reinforced in the later case of *Kedari Lal v State of M.P. and Ors*, in which the same ten percent threshold was referred to in order to justify an acquittal.[347] Similarly, the criminal illicit enrichment law of Hong Kong does not include any reference to value thresholds, yet the courts have still sought to emphasise that a requirement for an accused person to explain a discrepancy in wealth versus income is not 'triggered by trifling incommensurateness or disproportion' in accordance with the legal maxim 'de minimis non curat lex: the law does not concern itself with trifles'.[348]

3.4.2 Requirement to prove the targeted person is a public official

The majority of illicit enrichment laws specifically seek to target proceeds of corruption. Consequently, as outlined in Section 2.2.2.1, many illicit enrichment laws can only be applied to public officials or people directly connected to a public official (e.g. immediate family).

In practice, the question of whether or not someone is a public official is rarely in dispute, and most overarching legislative instruments that contain illicit enrichment laws include a specific definition on the types of roles that will be included under the umbrella of 'public official'.

---

345 [Unofficial translation] Cámara Nacional de Casación Penal, sala IV, 'Alsogaray', causa n°4787 (2005) (Original text: 'Este adjetivo está tomado del Proyecto de 1941 -el de 1960 dice incremento 'considerable' y el Decreto-Ley 4778/63 incremento 'importante'-, y por tal debe entenderse el que 'resulta considerable con relación a la situación económica del agente en el momento de asumir el cargo y que no está de acuerdo con las posibilidades de evolución normal de aquélla durante el tiempo del desempeño de la función' o después de haber cesado en la función 'pero vinculado antes a ese ejercicio' (cfr.: Creus: 'Delitos contra la Administración Pública', ya citado, pág. 420, y Núñez: 'Tratado de Derecho Penal', Ed. Marcos Lerner Editora Córdoba, Bs. As., junio de 1992, pág. 145). Coincide con esa idea Fontán Balestra, quien ha sostenido con meridiana claridad que dicha palabra es de significado relativo, como lo son sus sinónimos, por lo que una guía aceptable para determinar ese carácter apreciable del enriquecimiento 'la constituiría el análisis de la proporción que resulte al relacionar el volumen del enriquecimiento con las entradas y bienes de fortuna que se le conocen al funcionario; de modo que el aumento pueda ser considerado como normal o no en la evaluación económica de ese patrimonio', por lo que sólo la apreciación de cada caso particular podrá dar la pauta'. Ese aumento patrimonial, entonces, debe ser el desproporcionado respecto de sus ingresos legítimos (cfr.: 'Tratado de Derecho Penal',T. VII, Ed. Abeledo-Perrot, Bs. As., 1990, pág. 357).').

346 Krishnanand v The State of Madhya Pradesh MANU/SC/0134/1976.

347 Kedari Lal v State of M.P. and Ors MANU/SC/0343/2015.

348 Attorney General v Hui Kin-hong [1995] HKCLR 227 at [235] (as referenced in I. McWalters SC et al., *Bribery and Corruption Law in Hong Kong*, LexisNexis, Hong Kong, 2015, p.397).

Laws will also generally apply to people that have left the public service to ensure that an illicitly enriched person can't simply achieve immunity from legal action by retiring. This extended application of the law is often expressly included in the wording of the law itself, such as in Guatemala,[349] where a public official can be proven to have illicitly enriched themselves during the first five years after leaving office, or Burkina Faso,[350] where the act of illicit enrichment is considered a 'continuous' offence.

Interestingly, illicit enrichment laws may even be applied to people who were public officials, but who retired before the law itself was enacted. For instance, in the Hong Kong case of *Lai Man-Yau v Attorney General (No.2)*,[351] the Privy Council examined whether Hong Kong's illicit enrichment law could be applied to a former police officer who retired almost two years before the law came into force, but who still controlled the illicitly acquired assets after the date of enactment. In his judgement, Lord Salmon noted that the wording of the relevant provision extended the application of the law to any person who, 'being or having been a Crown servant', controlled disproportionate assets, and interpreted this phrase in accordance with its plain language meaning. He rejected the appellant's arguments that the phrase 'since the coming into operation of this Ordinance' should be read into the provision as it would be 'a strong thing to read into an Act of Parliament or an Ordinance words which are not there; and in the absence of clear necessity it is a wrong thing to do.'[352] Consequently, the court deemed that the illicit enrichment law in Hong Kong could be applied to a person who held a public position even before the law itself came into force, providing of course that they still controlled the acquired assets after the date of enactment. The issue of the potential retroactive application of illicit enrichment laws is discussed in more detail in Part 4.

3.4.3   Requirement to prove that the enrichment occurred within a limited time period

As alluded to above, a number of illicit enrichment laws require the state to establish that the enrichment took place within a certain limited period of time. This time period will often be directly related to when the targeted person was a public official, and will often run a certain number of years after the person's retirement date.

3.4.4   Requirement to prove reasonable suspicion of criminality

As discussed in detail in Sections 1.4.2 and 2.2.5, some illicit enrichment laws (referred to in this publication as qualified illicit enrichment laws) include an additional element which

---

349   Código Penal, Decreto Número 17-73 (modificado por Ley Contra La Corrupción, Decreto Número 31-2012) (Guatemala), Artículo 448 bis.

350   [Unofficial translation] Loi N° 004-2015/CNT Portant prévention et répression de la corruption au Burkina Faso, Article 63 (Original text: 'Le délit d'apparence, ainsi visé, est une infraction continue caractérisée par la détention des biens illicites ou leur emploi d'une manière directe ou indirecte.').

351   Lai Man-Yau v Attorney General (No.2) [1978] HKCU 79.

352   ibid.

requires the state to establish a reasonable suspicion or belief that the wealth in question has been derived from crime or that some sort of criminality has taken place.

3.4.5   No need to demonstrate knowledge or intent

As a final note on elements, while the UNCAC Article 20 on illicit enrichment includes a requirement to show the offence was committed 'intentionally', such specifically worded elements regarding 'intent' or 'knowledge' are not common in domestic illicit enrichment laws.

Even when 'intent' is referenced in a law, it is not outlined as a separate element, but one which can be presumed on the basis of facts required to be proven in other elements.

For instance, while India's law outlines that a public servant commits an offence if 'he intentionally enriches himself illicitly during the period of his office', the law further stipulates that:

> A person shall be presumed to have intentionally enriched himself illicitly if he or any person on his behalf, is in possession of or has, at any time during the period of his office, been in possession of pecuniary resources or property disproportionate to his known sources of income which the public servant cannot satisfactorily account for.[353]

Therefore, if the Wealth Element and the Inadequate Income Element in this particular law are established, the court will presume that the targeted person intended to illicitly enrich themselves.

Similarly, requirements to demonstrate 'knowledge' have also been limited in practice. For example, although the law in Lithuania requires that a targeted person is 'aware' or 'likely to be aware that such property could not have been acquired with legitimate income', the Constitutional Court has further clarified that the offence can still be committed through 'negligence' or 'criminal carelessness'.[354]

While almost all illicit enrichment laws are silent on the issue of mens rea, defendants have still on occasion sought to test the issue in courts. For instance, in the Hong Kong case of *Roy Sturgeon v the Queen*,[355] the defendant sought to argue that in order to establish that he had acquired disproportionate property, the state needed to demonstrate that he had knowledge of the property allegedly under his control. The court disagreed, stating that 'prima facie evidence of mens rea is entirely unnecessary' and if a prosecution establishes control of certain property, the absence of knowledge of this property would be a matter to be addressed in any explanation or defence put forward by the defendant.[356]

---

353 Prevention of Corruption Act 1988 (as amended by the Prevention of Corruption (Amendment) Act 2018) (India), Section 13(1)(b).

354 Case no. 14/2015-1/2016-2/2016-14/2016-15/2016- The Constitutional Court of the Republic of Lithuania in the name of the Republic of Lithuania ruling on the compliance of Paragraph 1 of Article 189¹ of the Criminal Code of the Republic of Lithuania with the Constitution of the Republic of Lithuania 15 March 2017, no KT4-N3/2017, at [22].

355 Roy Sturgeon v the Queen [1975] HKLR 677 (as referenced in I. McWalters SC et al., *Bribery and Corruption Law in Hong Kong*, LexisNexis, Hong Kong, 2015, p.409).

356 Roy Sturgeon v the Queen [1975] HKLR 677 at [683].

Part 4

Common legal challenges to illicit enrichment laws

Part 4 Summary

Illicit enrichment laws often raise concerns regarding their compatibility with established legal principles surrounding fair legal process.

The majority of these concerns relate to the fact that these laws often place (or appear to place) burdens on a person to provide evidence during proceedings. Those challenging illicit enrichment laws have argued that such burdens infringe on the presumption of innocence, remove a person's ability to remain silent in proceedings, and expose them to the risk of self-incrimination.

Further concerns relate to the fact that some illicit enrichment laws can potentially apply retroactively, and can be used to target wealth that was acquired by a person even before the law itself came into force.

This Part will examine the existing jurisprudence regarding three of the major legal questions that have been raised in this context, namely:

- Whether illicit enrichment laws unfairly reverse the burden of proof and infringe on the presumption of innocence principle;

- Whether illicit enrichment laws are compatible with the right to silence and the privilege against self-incrimination; and

- Whether illicit enrichment laws can be applied retroactively.

4.1 Illicit enrichment laws, reversed burdens of proof and the presumption of innocence

Unlike other legal mechanisms focused on proceeds of crime, such as money laundering offences or non-conviction based forfeiture provisions, illicit enrichment laws do not require an accusing party to establish even a probable link between the assets in question and a 'proceeds-generating' crime. On the contrary, illicit enrichment legislation generally permits a court to make a presumption that certain items of wealth have not come from lawful sources if the court has not seen evidence of an adequate amount of lawfully sourced income to justify the total value of the evidenced wealth.

In addition to this, many illicit enrichment laws expressly require a person to satisfactorily 'explain' how certain items of wealth have been derived from legal sources once they have been established by the state to be disproportionate to the person's known sources of income. For example under Hong Kong's criminal illicit enrichment law, a person who maintains a standard of living or controls resources that are disproportionate to past or present official emoluments will be guilty of an offence 'unless he gives a satisfactory explanation to the court as to how he was able to maintain such a standard of living or how such pecuniary resources or property came under his control.'[357] Similarly under Kenya's civil illicit enrichment law, if a court is satisfied that the state has demonstrated that a person controls unexplained assets, then the person may be required 'to satisfy the court that the assets were acquired otherwise than as the result of corrupt conduct.'[358]

Such presumptions of fact regarding the origin of a person's wealth, and such statutory obligations to 'explain', have often been used as a basis to challenge the legitimacy of many illicit enrichment laws. These challenges claim that the statutory obligations unfairly reverse the burden of proof onto the person subjected to proceedings and, in the case of criminal illicit enrichment laws, that they contravene the principle of the presumption of innocence.

In general, courts around the world have overwhelmingly disagreed with such challenges and have consistently held that both criminal and civil illicit enrichment laws do not place unfair burdens on persons subjected to proceedings. The following text will examine:

- Jurisprudence addressing whether or not criminal illicit enrichment laws unfairly reverse the burden of proof and violate the principle of the presumption of innocence; and

- Jurisprudence addressing whether or not civil illicit enrichment laws unfairly reverse the burden of proof onto respondents to justify the lawful sources of their wealth.

---

357 Cap.201 Prevention of Bribery Ordinance 1971 (China - Hong Kong), Section 10.

358 Anti-Corruption and Economic Crimes Act 2003 (Kenya), Section 55.

4.1.1 Do criminal illicit enrichment laws violate the presumption of innocence principle by unfairly reversing the burden of proof?

The presumption of innocence principle ensures that 'everyone charged with a criminal offence shall have the right to be presumed innocent until proved guilty according to law'.[359] As explained by the United Nations Human Rights Committee:

> The presumption of innocence, which is fundamental to the protection of human rights, imposes on the prosecution the burden of proving the charge, guarantees that no guilt can be presumed until the charge has been proved beyond reasonable doubt, ensures that the accused has the benefit of doubt, and requires that persons accused of a criminal act must be treated in accordance with this principle.[360]

The principle has been enshrined in multiple international instruments including the Universal Declaration of Human Rights (UDHR),[361] the International Covenant on Civil and Political Rights (ICCPR),[362] the African Charter on Human and Peoples' Rights (ACHPR),[363] the American Convention on Human Rights (ACHR),[364] the European Convention on Human Rights (ECHR),[365] the Charter of Fundamental Rights of the European Union[366] and the Rome Statute of the International Criminal Court.[367] It is an almost universal legal principle that has been established in both common law and civil law jurisdictions, and which has been expressly included in many domestic constitutions.

4.1.1.1 Substance of challenges on this issue

It is a common claim that criminal illicit enrichment legislation violates the principle of the presumption of innocence. Challenges on this basis generally include a similar line of argument: that the wording of the illicit enrichment provision may give rise to a presumption that certain items of wealth were obtained through unlawful sources, and that this unfairly reverses the burden of proof onto an accused person, requiring them to produce evidence, to a certain standard, that establishes the non-criminal sources of their wealth.

As a basis for these claims, those challenging illicit enrichment legislation often point to

---

359 The International Covenant on Civil and Political Rights, Article 14(2).

360 The United Nations Human Rights Committee General Comment No. 32 (on the International Covenant on Civil and Political Rights, Article 14: Right to equality before courts and tribunals and to a fair trial) CCPR/C/GC/32, 23 August 2007.

361 The Universal Declaration of Human Rights, Article 11(1).

362 The International Covenant on Civil and Political Rights, Article 14(2).

363 The African Charter on Human and Peoples' Rights, Article 7(1)(b).

364 The American Convention on Human Rights, Article 8(2).

365 The European Convention on Human Rights, Article 6(2).

366 The Charter of Fundamental Rights of the European Union, Article 48.

367 The Rome Statute of the International Criminal Court, Article 66.

statutory obligations contained in these laws that require an accused person to provide some sort of satisfactory 'explanation' as to the source of their wealth before a verdict is delivered (such as the Hong Kong example referred to previously). They argue that these express obligations contravene one of the fundamental requirements of the presumption of innocence principle, namely that the responsibility for proving the key elements of an offence must be that of the accusing party.

Challenges have also been made against criminal illicit enrichment laws even if they do not contain an express obligation to 'explain'. In such cases, those opposed have argued that while the law doesn't contain a literal reverse onus mechanism, the wording itself implies that assumptions can be made surrounding the illicit nature of certain property which similarly places an unfair burden on the owner of these properties to establish the contrary.[368]

4.1.1.2 Prevailing judicial view in response to these challenges: the presumption of innocence principle is not absolute

Most courts acknowledge that the illicit enrichment law in their jurisdiction can give rise to a presumption that certain items of wealth were not lawfully sourced, and that a burden can be placed on an accused person to rebut this presumption. Most courts also acknowledge that this presumption and the resulting reversal of burdens run contrary to the presumption of innocence principle. The overwhelming majority of these courts however also take the view that the presumption of innocence principle is not absolute in nature, and that the deviation from this principle prevalent in illicit enrichment laws is an acceptable one for a number of reasons.

This view is in line with the broader jurisprudence on this issue (outside of an illicit enrichment context), which has established that limitations can be imposed on the presumption of innocence principle in certain circumstances.

The European Court of Human Rights (ECtHR) decision of *Salabiaku v France*[369] is a key precedent on this point of law. In this case, the court considered a provision in France's Customs Code that presumes that a person in possession of an imported suitcase is legally liable for its undeclared contents, and assessed whether the presumption contained in this

---

368 For example in Case no. 14/2015-1/2016-2/2016-14/2016-15/2016- The Constitutional Court of the Republic of Lithuania in the name of the Republic of Lithuania ruling on the compliance of Paragraph 1 of Article 189¹ of the Criminal Code of the Republic of Lithuania with the Constitution of the Republic of Lithuania 15 March 2017, no KT4-N3/2017 at [7.3.1] the petitioners argued that: 'the formulation of the object of the crime by using a negative statement ("property that could not have been acquired with legitimate income") inevitably creates a situation where the illegality of income is determined on the basis of the lack of officially received income and the inability of the accused to provide a credible explanation for the sufficiency of his/her officially received income enabling him/her to acquire the property that he/she possesses. The conclusion regarding the illegality of income is based on the assumption that everything that could not have been acquired by lawful means has been acquired illegally. In criminal justice, such a manner of establishing facts can be assessed as placing the burden of proof on the accused and drawing on assumptions in determining the guilt of the person. This may violate the principle of the presumption of innocence, enshrined in Paragraph 1 of Article 31 of the Constitution, as well as the prohibition, consolidated in Paragraph 3 of this article, on giving evidence against himself/herself.'.

369 Salabiaku v France (Application no. 10519/83) ECHR 7 October 1988.

law was incompatible with the presumption of innocence principle contained in Article 6(2) of the ECHR. In determining that the statutory presumption was compatible, the court held that the presumption of innocence principle is not an absolute right, and should not be seen to prevent individual legal systems from implementing legislation that contains rebuttable presumptions of fact or law, providing such presumptions are within 'reasonable limits' and 'maintain the rights of the defence'.[370]

This position has been further reinforced by the more recent ECtHR decisions of *Phillips v United Kingdom*,[371] *Falk v the Netherlands*[372] and *Krumpholz v Austria*.[373] It has also been echoed repeatedly in domestic courts throughout the world.[374]

The case of *Salabiaku v France* has been cited frequently in judicial proceedings considering whether the reverse onus mechanisms contained specifically in criminal illicit enrichment laws are compatible with the presumption of innocence principle.[375] For instance, in the case of *Attorney General v Hui Kin-hong*, the Hong Kong Court of Appeal sought to determine whether the jurisdiction's illicit enrichment offence could be considered a legitimate exception to the right to the presumption of innocence outlined in Hong Kong's Bill of Rights Ordinance.[376] In deeming that the law was consistent, the court specifically noted the ruling in *Salabiaku v France* and agreed that:

> There are exceptional situations in which it is possible compatibly with human rights to justify a degree of deviation from the normal principle that the prosecution must prove the accused's guilt beyond reasonable doubt.[377]

4.1.1.3 Tests for justifying a deviation from the presumption of innocence principle

While *Salabiaku v France* and other cases have clearly established that certain laws can in fact run contrary to the presumption of innocence principle, jurisprudence to date has not conclusively established a universal test to determine how and when such 'deviations' or

---

370 ibid., at [28].

371 Phillips v the United Kingdom (Application no. 41087/98) ECHR 5 July 2001.

372 Falk v the Netherlands (Application no. 66273/01) ECHR 19 October 2004.

373 Krumpholz v Austria (Application no. 13201/05) ECHR 18 March 2010 at [34].

374 For instance in R v Lambert [2001] UKHL 37; Attorney General v Lee Kwong-kut [1993] AC 951; R v Johnstone [2003] 1 WLR 1736.

375 Cámara Nacional de Casación Penal, sala IV, 'Alsogaray', causa n°4787 (2005); Republic v Wesley Mzumara (Criminal Case No.47 of 2010); Attorney General v Hui Kin-hong [1995] HKCLR 227; Case no. 14/2015-1/2016-2/2016-14/2016-15/2016 - The Constitutional Court of the Republic of Lithuania in the name of the Republic of Lithuania ruling on the compliance of Paragraph 1 of Article 189¹ of the Criminal Code of the Republic of Lithuania with the Constitution of the Republic of Lithuania 15 March 2017, no KT4-N3/2017.

376 Hong Kong Bill of Rights Ordinance, Cap. 383, Section 8, Article 11(1), which states that: 'Everyone charged with a criminal offence shall have the right to be presumed innocent until proved guilty according to law'.

377 Attorney General v Hui Kin-hong [1995] HKCLR 227.

'exceptions' can be considered 'reasonable'. Instead, a variety of different approaches and tests have been used around the world to assess the acceptability of potential statutory exceptions, taking into account one or more of a common assortment of considerations.[378]

In the specific context of illicit enrichment, however, courts have generally limited their considerations to four key issues. Namely, in determining whether reverse burdens contained specifically in these laws are a justifiable exception to the presumption of innocence principle, courts have commonly considered one or more of the following:

- Whether the accusing party is still required to prove the fundamental facts of their accusation in proceedings under the law (referred herein as the 'primary burden assessment');

- Whether the facts proven by the accusing party in proceedings under the law rationally prove the presumed fact (referred herein as the 'rational connection assessment');

- Whether the infringement imposed by the law on the principle of the presumption of innocence is in the public interest (referred herein as the 'public interest assessment'); and

- Whether the facts that must be proven to rebut the arising presumption are particularly within the knowledge of the accused (referred herein as the 'particular knowledge assessment');

The approach taken by courts in assessing these considerations is explained in the following sections.[379]

---

378 For instance, as explained in N. Kofele-Kale, *Combating Economic Crimes - Balancing Competing Rights and Interests in Prosecuting the Crime of Illicit Enrichment*, Routledge, Milton Park, 2013, courts in different jurisdictions have applied different 'tests' in this context. The European Court of Human Rights adopted a two-step test in Falk v the Netherlands (Application no. 66273/01) ECHR 19 October 2004 under which a limitation on the presumption of innocence can be deemed compatible if it firstly pursues a legitimate aim, and secondly if there is a reasonable relationship of proportionality between the means employed (that infringe on the right) and the aim sought to be achieved. In a similar vein, other versions of a 'proportionality' test have been established in Canada (see R v Oakes [1986] 1 SCR 103) and South Africa (S v Manamela [2000] 5 LRC 65). As explained later in this section, another test to assess potential rights infringements by statutory presumptions was also established by the Privy Council decision in Attorney General v Hui Kin-hong [1995] HKCLR 227.

379 It should be noted that these are the considerations that are mostly taken into account in the context of illicit enrichment laws, and that they are not the only considerations that have been taken into account by courts when assessing the acceptability of other reverse burden provisions with regards to the presumption of innocence principle. For example, a number of courts have considered other, somewhat overlapping, considerations such as whether or not the reversed burden relates to an element of the offence that is essential to 'culpability' – which is considered a significant encroachment on the presumption of innocence. For a further discussion on this issue, see the Australian Law Reform Commission, *Traditional Rights and Freedoms—Encroachments by Commonwealth Laws*, ALRC Report 129, Tabled 2 March 2016 at [9.42] as well as R v Whyte (1988) 51 DLR 4th 481 and R v Lambert [2002] 2 AC 545. Additionally academics have discussed whether potential infringements on the presumption of innocence in illicit enrichment laws would be considered more acceptable if any burdens placed on a defendant in illicit enrichment proceedings were evidential burdens rather than legal burdens. As evidential burdens are considered less onerous on a defendant, some have suggested that courts should 'read down' any apparent legal burdens contained in illicit enrichment laws to evidential burdens to limit any potential incursions on the presumption of innocence. For a further discussion on this issue, see N. Kofele-Kale, *Combating Economic Crimes - Balancing Competing Rights and Interests in Prosecuting the Crime of Illicit Enrichment*, Routledge, Milton Park, 2013, p.13 and the Australian Law Reform Commission, *Traditional Rights and Freedoms—Encroachments by Commonwealth Laws*, ALRC Report 129, Tabled 2 March 2016 at [9.12].

4.1.1.3.1 Primary burden assessment

When considering the legitimacy of illicit enrichment laws, courts often assess whether the state retains the primary responsibility of proving the guilt of the accused in any proceedings under the law, despite the existence of a reversed burden mechanism. If the court is satisfied that the state is still required to establish the 'essential ingredients' or the 'foundational facts' of the actual accusation before any such mechanisms are triggered, then this will often be considered a major justification in holding that the particular law is an acceptable deviation from the presumption of innocence principle.

For example, this consideration was given serious weight by the Hong Kong Court of Appeal in the case of *Attorney General v Hui Kin-hong* whilst assessing the acceptability of the reverse burden mechanism contained in the illicit enrichment provisions of the Prevention of Bribery Ordinance.[380] In determining the issue, the court followed a test previously outlined by the case of *Attorney General v Lee Kwong-kut*,[381] in which the Privy Council had assessed whether presumptions made under Hong Kong's Summary Offences Ordinance[382] were justifiable exceptions to the presumption of innocence principle, and held:

> Whether [such exceptions] are justifiable will in the end depend upon whether it remains primarily the responsibility of the prosecution to prove the guilt of an accused to the required standard and whether the exception is reasonably imposed... The less significant the departure from the normal principle, the simpler it will be to justify an exception. If the prosecution retains responsibility for proving the essential ingredients of the offence, the less likely it is that an exception will be regarded as unacceptable. In deciding what are the essential ingredients, the language of the relevant statutory provision will be important. However what will be decisive will be the substance and reality of the language creating the offence rather than its form.[383]

In assessing these considerations within the context of Hong Kong's illicit enrichment law, the Court of Appeal sought to determine the 'essential ingredients' a prosecutor was obligated to prove under this law to trigger a presumption against the accused, and whether or not these obligations satisfied the above reasoning.

In doing so, the court followed the decision of another Privy Council case, *Attorney General v Ho Pui-yiu*,[384] and determined that the illicit enrichment law obligates a prosecutor to prove the following:

> Having proved the amount of pecuniary resources and other assets in the accused's control at [the charge] date, the prosecution must go on to prove his total official emoluments up to the same date, and finally it must establish a disproportion between the two. The words

---

380 Cap.201 Prevention of Bribery Ordinance 1971 (China - Hong Kong), Section 10.

381 Attorney General v Lee Kwong-kut [1993] AC 951.

382 Cap. 228 Summary Offences Ordinance (1933) (China - Hong Kong).

383 Attorney General v Hui Kin-hong [1995] HKCLR 227 at [232] citing Attorney General v Lee Kwong-kut [1993] AC 951 at [969G]-[970B].

384 Attorney General v Ho Pui-yiu [1981] HKLR 110.

"disproportionate to" convey the idea that the acquisition of the total assets under the accused's control could not reasonably, in all the circumstances, have been afforded out of the total official emoluments up to that date.[385]

In taking this into account, the court reasoned that the ingredients the prosecutor was required to prove to trigger the reverse burden mechanism went beyond what was likely to be a 'formality in the majority of cases' and that they were also 'complex' enough in nature to justify an exception.[386]

India has also given significant weight to this issue. In a broader context, the Supreme Court of India has held on multiple occasions that there can be exceptions to the principle of the presumption of innocence, and that reverse burdens can permissibly be applied onto an accused in certain circumstances.[387] A key condition for the application of such reverse burdens, however, is that the prosecution must still be required to prove the 'foundational facts' regarding the accusation.[388]

This reasoning has also been applied specifically to the reverse burdens contained in the illicit enrichment provisions of India's Prevention of Corruption Act. For example in the case of *Vasant Rao Guhe vs The State Of Madhya Pradesh*,[389] Amitava Roy J held that '…even in a case when the burden is on the accused, the prosecution must first prove the foundational facts' and that these facts must be established 'beyond reasonable doubt'.[390]

The Supreme Court of Pakistan has also taken this line of interpretation with regards to the application of the illicit enrichment provisions contained in the jurisdiction's National Accountability Ordinance.[391]

In *Syed Qasim Shah v the State*,[392] the court acknowledged that the presumption and reversed burden arising under the wording of these provisions were an 'exception' to the presumption of innocence. The court held however that this exception was justifiable, as the reverse burden is only triggered once the prosecution discharges a 'prima facie burden of proof' to make a 'reasonable' case against the accused.[393] The court cited the reasoning in a previous case, *Rehmat v the State*,[394] which stated:

It is only after the prosecution has on the evidence adduced by it, succeeded in raising

---

385 Attorney General v Hui Kin-hong [1995] HKCLR 227 at 233-234 referencing Attorney General v Ho Pui-yiu [1981] HKLR 110 at p.112 F-H.

386 Attorney General v Hui Kin-hong [1995] HKCLR 227 at 234; Of course it should be noted that other considerations were also taken into account, which are also discussed in this section.

387 For example, see Noor Aga vs State Of Punjab & Anr on 9 July, 2008; Krishna Janardhan Bhat vs Dattatraya G. Hegde on 11 January, 2008.

388 State Of Maharashtra vs Dnyaneshwar Laxman Rao Wankhede on 29 July, 2009; Noor Aga vs State Of Punjab & Anr on 9 July, 2008.

389 Vasant Rao Guhe vs The State Of Madhya Pradesh (Criminal Appeal No.1279 of 2017).

390 ibid., at [21].

391 National Accountability Ordinance (XVIII of 1999) (Pakistan), Sections 9(a)(v), 14.

392 Syed Qasim Shah v the State 2009 SCMR 790.

393 Syed Qasim Shah v the State 2009 SCMR 790 citing Khan Asfandyar Wali v Federation of Pakistan PLD 2001 SC 607.

394 Rehmat v the State PLD 1977 SC 515.

reasonable inference of the guilt of the accused, unless the same is rebutted, that this section wherever applicable, comes into play and the accused may negative the inference by proof of some facts within his special knowledge. If, however, the prosecution fails to prove the essential ingredients of the offence, no duty is cast on the accused to prove his innocence.[395]

The Malawian case of *Republic v Wesley Mzumara* also established the acceptability of reverse burden mechanisms contained in the illicit enrichment provisions of Malawi's Corrupt Practices Act.[396] In his decision, CRM Usiwa Usiwa noted that the concept of shifting the burden of proof in exceptional circumstances had already been recognised in Malawi in the Supreme Court decision of *Malombe v Rep*.[397] In line with this, he held that the illicit enrichment provision could also be considered a legitimate exception provided that the prosecution proves, beyond reasonable doubt, that the accused person 'was in prima facie control' of disproportionate property.[398]

4.1.1.3.2 Rational connection assessment

A number of courts have also used a 'rational connection' assessment to evaluate whether certain statutory presumptions amount to acceptable deviations from the presumption of innocence principle.

This assessment requires a court to determine whether the presumed fact that triggers the reverse burden (e.g. that a person's wealth was not lawfully sourced) is a rational conclusion that can be made from the facts that have already been proven (e.g. that the value of this wealth is disproportionate to the person's lawfully sourced income).

Such assessments are not unique to the context of illicit enrichment, and have been used by courts to assess the justifiability of other types of presumptions for over a century. For instance, the US Supreme Court case of *Mobile, Jackson & Kansas City R. Co. v Turnipseed*,[399] was one of the first decisions to refer to this type of assessment. In this civil case, the court was asked to determine whether proof of an injury inflicted from the operation of a locomotive could acceptably be considered prima facie evidence of negligence on behalf of servants of the railway company without affecting due process of the law. The court held:

> That a legislative presumption of one fact from evidence of another may not constitute a denial of due process of law or a denial of the equal protection of the law, it is only essential that there shall be some rational connection between the fact proved and the ultimate fact presumed, and that the inference of one fact from proof of another shall not be so unreasonable as to be a purely arbitrary mandate.[400]

395 Syed Qasim Shah v the State 2009 SCMR 790 citing Rehmat v the State PLD 1977 SC 515.
396 Corrupt Practices Act 1995 (as amended in 2004) (Malawi), Section 32.
397 Malombe v Rep [1993] 16 (2) MLR 561.
398 Republic v Wesley Mzumara (Criminal Case No.47 of 2010).
399 Mobile, Jackson & Kansas City R. Co. v Turnipseed, 219 U.S. 35 (1910).
400 ibid., at [43].

The concept of the above civil case was subsequently upheld in a criminal law context in *Tot v United States*,[401] where the court considered a contention that a person's unregistered possession of a firearm in one state (where firearm ownership was usually registered) could lead to a presumption that the firearm was acquired from another state. The court in this case held that the presumption was not permissible, on the basis that it did not satisfy a rational connection test, noting that there were numerous other non-interstate sources from which a person may have acquired the firearm. In applying the test, the court highlighted that a conclusion regarding a rational connection can be drawn from common experience:

> Under our decisions, a statutory presumption cannot be sustained if there be no rational connection between the fact proved and the ultimate fact presumed, if the inference of the one from proof of the other is arbitrary because of lack of connection between the two in common experience.[402]

This decision was reinforced again in *Leary v the United States*,[403] which further held that:

> ...a criminal statutory presumption must be regarded as "irrational" or "arbitrary," and hence unconstitutional, unless it can at least be said with substantial assurance that the presumed fact is more likely than not to flow from the proved fact on which it is made to depend.[404]

Moving beyond the United States, the principles in these cases were confirmed with approval by the Judicial Committee of the Privy Council in the Hong Kong case of *Attorney General v Lee Kwong-kut*, which cited the above passage from *Leary v the United States* whilst assessing the acceptability of presumptions under Hong Kong's Summary Offences Ordinance.[405] In the context of illicit enrichment, the Privy Council's citation of *Leary v the United States* was a key consideration in the subsequent decision of *Attorney General v Hui Kin-hong* mentioned above. In this case, the Hong Kong Court of Appeal followed the guidance in *Attorney General v Lee Kwong-kut* and confirmed that the rational connection principle should also be a key consideration in assessing whether the presumption of innocence 'exception' contained in Hong Kong's illicit enrichment law was justifiable:

> ...If the exception requires certain matters to be presumed until the contrary is shown, then it will be difficult to justify that presumption unless, as was pointed out by the United States Supreme Court in Leary v United States (1969) 23 L Ed (2d) 57, 82, "it can at least be said with substantial assurance that the presumed fact is more likely than not to flow from the proved fact on which it is made to depend'.[406]

In line with this principle, the court held that if the state is able to prove a level of disproportion

---

401   Tot v United States, 319 U.S. 463 (1943).

402   ibid., at [468].

403   Leary v the United States 395 US 6 (1969).

404   ibid., at [36].

405   Cap. 228 Summary Offences Ordinance (1933) (China - Hong Kong).

406   Attorney General v Hui Kin-hong [1995] HKCLR 227 at [232] citing Attorney General v Lee Kwong-kut [1993] AC 951 at 969G-970B.

between the accused person's wealth and their official emoluments that is 'unreasonable in the circumstances', then this will be enough to trigger an acceptable presumption against the person.[407]

The rational connection test has also been used in other jurisdictions in assessing their own illicit enrichment laws. For instance, in *Republic v Wesley Mzumara*, the court highlighted the submission that 'it has to be shown that there is a rational connection between the proved fact of the accused person's accumulation of property and the presumed fact that the same were obtained corruptly or at least in general violation of the Corrupt Practices Act'.[408] Furthermore, whilst not referencing the assessment by name, the High Court of Uganda engaged a similar logic to a rational connection assessment in *Uganda v B.D Wandera* in assessing that it was acceptable to make an inference that a person had illicitly enriched themselves if it were established that assets held by the person were disproportionate to their income.[409]

4.1.1.3.3 Public interest assessment

Arguably one of the most significant considerations taken into account by courts when determining the legitimacy of infringements on the presumption of innocence principle is whether or not the deviation serves to protect a wider societal interest. Courts have often discussed at length the difficulty of attempting to strike the 'balance' noted in *Salabiaku v France* between taking into account 'the importance of what is at stake' and 'maintaining the rights of the defence'.[410]

For instance in *R v Johnstone*,[411] the UK's House of Lords expressed the following:

> Identifying the requirements of a reasonable balance is not as easy as might seem. One is seeking to balance incommensurables. At the heart of the difficulty is the paradox noted by Sachs J in State v Coetzee [1997] 2 LRC 593, 677, para 220: the more serious the crime and the greater the public interest in securing convictions of the guilty, the more important the constitutional protection of the accused becomes. In the face of this paradox all that can be said is that for a reverse burden of proof to be acceptable there must be a compelling reason why it is fair and reasonable to deny the accused person the protection normally guaranteed to everyone by the presumption of innocence.[412]

In line with this thinking, courts around the world have sought to consider whether the underlying objective behind a reverse burden is 'compelling' enough, and is sufficiently in the public interest to justify an infringement on the presumption of innocence principle.

---

407 Attorney General v Hui Kin-hong [1995] HKCLR 227 at [234].

408 Republic v Wesley Mzumara (Criminal Case No.47 of 2010).

409 Uganda v B.D Wandera HCT-00-AC-SC-0012/2014.

410 Salabiaku v France (Application no. 10519/83) ECHR 7 October 1988, at [28].

411 R v Johnstone [2003] 1 WLR 1736.

412 ibid., at [49].

For instance in the renowned Canadian Supreme Court case of *R v Oakes*,[413] the court discussed the limitation on the presumption of innocence principle posed by a reverse onus in the Canadian Narcotic Control Act[414] under which a court can presume that a person found in control of a narcotic was possessing this substance for the purpose of trafficking it. The court determined that a key criteria to evaluating if such a presumption is 'reasonable and demonstrably justified in a free and democratic society' is that its overarching objective:

> ...must be sufficiently important to warrant overriding a constitutionally protected right or freedom. The standard must be high to ensure that trivial objectives or those discordant with the principles of a free and democratic society do not gain protection. At a minimum, an objective must relate to societal concerns which are pressing and substantial in a free and democratic society before it can be characterized as sufficiently important.[415]

In this case the court held that 'protecting society from the grave ills of drug trafficking' could potentially justify such a limitation on the presumption of innocence principle (though the limitation in this particular case was not considered justifiable on the basis that it failed another key consideration – the rational connection test).[416]

There are other cases in which presumptions have been deemed acceptable. For example, in the *R v Johnstone* case mentioned above, the House of Lords assessed that the public interest with regards to protecting the system of trademark protection justified a limitation on the presumption of innocence principle. Additionally, in the subsequent case of *Sheldrake v the DPP*,[417] the House of Lords also held that reverse burdens regarding drink driving could be justified by the overarching public interest to prevent 'the death, injury and damage caused by unfit drivers'.[418]

In the context of illicit enrichment laws – and particularly those that target public officials – courts have considered whether the reverse burdens contained in these laws are justified by a public interest to combat corruption.

For example, in *Attorney General v Hui Kin-hong*, Bokhary JA considered the need to find a balance between protecting the rights of those accused of corruption and protecting the victims of corruption (namely the public):

> If the law only protected persons accused of corruption, but failed to protect members of the general public from the evils and perils of corruption, then it would deny them equal protection.

---

413 R v Oakes [1986] 1 SCR 103.

414 Narcotic Control Act RSC 1970 (Canada), Section 4(2).

415 R v Oakes [1986] 1 SCR 103.at [76].

416 The court held that there was 'no rational connection between the basic fact of possession and the presumed fact of possession for the purpose of trafficking' and that '[t]he possession of a small or negligible quantity of narcotics would not support the inference of trafficking'.

417 Sheldrake v the DPP [2004] UKHL 43.

418 ibid., at [41].

> Whenever two imperatives of a legal system rub against each other, simply sacrificing one for the other is not a real option. Nor is compromising both. An acceptable balance which works in practice has to be found. That may not be easy to do. But it must be done if society is to be truly secure: both clean and free.[419]

In his subsequent reasoning, Bokhary JA further highlighted the specific difficulties faced by those combating corruption in order to justify the reverse burden in Hong Kong's illicit enrichment law:

> Where corruption is concerned, one can readily see the need - within reason of course - for special powers of investigation and provisions such as ones requiring an accused to provide an explanation. Specific corrupt acts are inherently difficult to detect let alone prove in the normal way. The true victim, society as a whole, is generally unaware of the specific occasions on which it is victimized. And, unlike in dangerous drugs cases for example, there is no obviously unlawful commodity, like the drugs themselves, which the criminals can be caught in possession of... There is nothing unreasonable in what is required of an accused here.[420]

Consequently, the court held that the reverse onus provisions contained in Hong Kong's illicit enrichment law were acceptable in view of the wider public interest and the particular undetectable nature of corruption offences themselves.

The High Court of Madras (India) in *N. Pasupathy v State*[421] also briefly considered the issue with regards to the reverse burden contained in India's illicit enrichment law. The court cited the reasoning in a previous Indian Supreme Court decision, *M. Narayanan Nambiar v State of Kerala*,[422] and highlighted that the reverse onus in the Prevention of Corruption could be construed as 'a socially useful measure conceived in [the] public interest.'[423]

4.1.1.3.4 Particular knowledge assessment

When assessing the acceptability of reverse burdens, some courts around the world have also placed significant weight on whether or not a reverse burden requires an accused to prove a matter that is particularly within their own knowledge.

For instance, in *R v Johnstone*, the UK's House of Lords considered the 'extent to which the burden on the accused related to facts' that are 'readily provable by him as matters within his own knowledge or to which he has ready access' in their evaluation of a reverse burden made under the UK's Trade Marks Act.[424]

---

419 Attorney General v Hui Kin-hong [1995] HKCLR 227.

420 ibid.

421 N. Pasupathy v State 2018 (1) MLJ (Crl) 745.

422 M. Narayanan Nambiar v State of Kerala (1963) Suppl. 2 SCR 724.

423 N. Pasupathy v State 2018 (1) MLJ (Crl) 745 at [212]. Note that India's illicit enrichment statute is the Prevention Of Corruption Act 1988, which superseded a previous illicit enrichment provision in the Prevention of Corruption Act 1947.

424 Trade Marks Act 1994 (United Kingdom), Section 92.

Furthermore, in *R v Oakes*, the Canadian Supreme Court emphasised that it is hard to justify a presumption if it places a burden on the accused to prove a fact that they 'cannot be reasonably expected to prove, being beyond his knowledge or being beyond what he may reasonably be expected to know...'.[425]

In the context of illicit enrichment, this was also a noted consideration in *Attorney General v Hui Kin-hong:*

> What does the accused have to do in order to give a satisfactory explanation as to how he was able to maintain an incommensurate standard of living or as to how disproportionate pecuniary resources or property came under his control? In the normal way, the primary facts on which the accused's explanation would be based - such as the existence of any capital or income of his independent of his official emoluments - would be peculiarly within his own knowledge. And it is for him to prove such facts, on a mere balance of probabilities of course.
>
> Such a position is normal where presumptions are concerned. And, as we have noted, presumptions are by no means invariably incompatible with human rights.[426]

This was also a consideration in *K. Veeraswami vs Union Of India And Others*,[427] in which the Supreme Court of India assessed the legitimacy of reversed burdens contained in the illicit enrichment provisions of the Prevention of Corruption Act:

> This procedure may be contrary to the well known principle of criminal jurisprudence laid down in Woolmington v Director of Public Prosecution, [1935] A.C. 462 that the burden-of proof is always on the prosecution and never shifts to the accused person. But Parliament is competent to place the burden on certain aspects on the accused as well and particularly in matters "specially within his knowledge"...Adroitly... the prosecution cannot, in the very nature of things, be expected to know the affairs of a public servant found in possession of resources of property disproportionate to his known sources of income. It is for him to explain. Such a statute placing burden on the accused cannot be regarded as unreasonable, unjust or unfair.[428]

It should be noted however that in a wider context some courts have also highlighted their concerns in relying solely on a particular knowledge assessment to evaluate the acceptability of a statutory presumption in criminal cases. For instance, in the previously mentioned case of *Tot v United States,* the US Supreme Court suggested that while the 'comparative convenience of producing evidence' should be a consideration, the fact that 'the defendant has a better means of information' cannot justify the creation of a presumption by itself:

> In every criminal case, the defendant has at least an equal familiarity with the facts, and, in most, a greater familiarity with them, than the prosecution. It might, therefore, be argued that to place upon all defendants in criminal cases the burden of going forward with the

---

425   R v Oakes [1986] 1 SCR 103 at [39] citing R v Shelley [1981] 2 S.C.R. 196.

426   Attorney General v Hui Kin-hong [1995] HKCLR 227.

427   K. Veeraswami vs Union Of India And Others 1991 SCR (3) 189.

428   ibid.

evidence would be proper. But the argument proves too much. If it were sound, the legislature might validly command that the finding of an indictment, or mere proof of the identity of the accused, should create a presumption of the existence of all the facts essential to guilt. This is not permissible.[429]

Instead the court held that this consideration should be a 'corollary' test to the rational connection test mentioned above.[430]

4.1.1.4 An alternative view: The burden of proof is never reversed so there is no violation of rights

An alternative interpretation of this issue is that of the Lithuanian and Argentinian courts. Rather than justifying presumptions in their illicit enrichment laws as acceptable limitations on the right to be presumed innocent, these courts have both held instead that their laws do not infringe on such rights at all, as they do not actually reverse the burden of proof at any point.

In *Case No KT4-N3/2017*, the Constitutional Court of Lithuania was petitioned to consider whether the illicit enrichment offence outlined in Article 189(1) of the Criminal Code (BK) violated the right to be presumed innocent contained in the Lithuanian Constitution.[431] Despite considering jurisprudence from the ECtHR on the issue (including the decision of *Salabiaku v France*), the court took a different approach altogether and held that law was in fact compatible with the presumption of innocence principle on the basis that it never actually reverses the burden of proof onto an accused person. During proceedings, the petitioners had argued that the provisions were unconstitutional on the following grounds:

> ..the formulation of the object of the crime by using a negative statement ("property that could not have been acquired with legitimate income") inevitably creates a situation where the illegality of income is determined on the basis of the lack of officially received income and the inability of the accused to provide a credible explanation for the sufficiency of his/her officially received income enabling him/her to acquire the property that he/she possesses. The conclusion regarding the illegality of income is based on the assumption that everything that could not have been acquired by lawful means has been acquired illegally. In criminal justice, such a manner of establishing facts can be assessed as placing the burden of proof on the accused and drawing on assumptions in determining the guilt of the person. This may violate the principle of the presumption of innocence...[432]

In response, the representative of the Seimas of the Republic of Lithuania[433] argued that the

---

429   Tot v United States, 319 U.S. 463 (1943) at 467-469.

430   ibid., at 467

431   Article 31 of the Constitution of the Republic of Lithuania (Adopted by citizens of the Republic of Lithuania in the Referendum of 25 October 1992) reads: 'A person shall be presumed innocent until proved guilty according to the procedure established by law and declared guilty by an effective court judgement'.

432   Case no. 14/2015-1/2016-2/2016-14/2016-15/2016 - The Constitutional Court of the Republic of Lithuania in the name of the Republic of Lithuania ruling on the compliance of Paragraph 1 of Article 189¹ of the Criminal Code of the Republic of Lithuania with the Constitution of the Republic of Lithuania 15 March 2017, no KT4-N3/2017, at [7.3.1].

433   The legislative branch of government of the Republic of Lithuania.

right to be presumed innocent is not violated as it is not an accused person's responsibility to substantiate the lawfulness of the property in question. Instead, it is the prosecutor's responsibility to prove the impossibility of the legality of the property:

> The formulation "property that cannot be reasonably explained in relation to legitimate income"... does not mean that a person must attempt to substantiate the lawfulness of the acquisition of the property, but, rather, it means that the prosecutor must prove by means of evidence the impossibility of the legality of such acquisition. The mere fact that, in the course of applying Article 189 of the BK, the prosecutors must prove circumstances that are somewhat different than usual (in most cases, the prosecutor must prove that the facts or actions have taken place, whereas in order to prove illicit enrichment, he/she must prove the impossibility of the fact that the acquisition of the property has been lawful), there are no grounds for asserting that the principle of the presumption of innocence is violated.[434]

The court agreed that the illicit enrichment offence is not in violation of the presumption of innocence principle on the basis that it 'does not shift the burden of proof to a person suspected of (charged with) illicit enrichment'.[435] In arriving at this decision, the court noted that provisions in Lithuania's Code of Criminal Procedure stipulate specifically that the responsibility of proving an illicit enrichment offence is the duty of a prosecutor. Consequently, the court concluded that an accused 'has no obligation to prove the legitimacy of his/her enrichment' and 'is not obliged to provide evidence and prove that the criminal act provided for in Paragraph 1 of Article 189(1) of the BK has not been committed and that he/she is not guilty of its commission, but has the right to do so in the exercise of his/her right to defence'.[436]

In Argentina, the case of *Alsogaray* examined whether Argentina's illicit enrichment law violated a number of rights, including the presumption of innocence principle, and held that the relevant article of the Criminal Code 'does not imply or define a reversal of the burden of proof by placing on the suspect the burden of proving his innocence by justifying the origin of the enrichment' as 'the proof of enrichment in this unjustified sense is the responsibility of the court and the Public Prosecutor's Office, which are not replaced by the defendant'.[437]

In clarifying their position, the National Chamber of Criminal Cassation held that the illicit

---

434 Case no. 14/2015-1/2016-2/2016-14/2016-15/2016- The Constitutional Court of the Republic of Lithuania in the name of the Republic of Lithuania ruling on the compliance of Paragraph 1 of Article 1891 of the Criminal Code of the Republic of Lithuania with the Constitution of the Republic of Lithuania 15 March 2017, no KT4-N3/2017, at [8.3].

435 ibid., at [39.3].

436 ibid., at [20], [22], [39.1].

437 [Unofficial translation] Cámara Nacional de Casación Penal, sala IV, 'Alsogaray', causa n°4787 (2005) (9 June 2005) (Original text: 'Teniendo en cuenta todo lo antes referido, no se advierte que el artículo 268 (2) del Código Penal implique o defina una inversión de la carga de la prueba poniendo en cabeza del sospechado el deber de demostrar su inocencia mediante la justificación de la procedencia del enriquecimiento, porque lo cierto es que la prueba del enriquecimiento en tal sentido injustificado corresponde al órgano jurisdiccional y al Ministerio Público Fiscal, quienes no son sustituidos en esa carga por el imputado.'). Note this case was upheld on appeal in Corte Suprema de Justicia de la Nación Argentina, 'Alsogaray', Fallos 331:2799 (2008).

enrichment offence should be considered a crime of 'commission' and not 'omission' and the responsibility for proving the elements of the crime remain with the prosecutor:

> ... we must bear in mind that we are dealing with a crime of commission, which consists of enriching oneself in an appreciable and unjustified manner during the exercise of public service and not - as the defence claims - with a crime of omission, which consists of "not justifying considerable enrichment when duly required".[438]

The court concluded that:

> The principle of innocence... remains unimpaired, as long as the accused is innocent until proven guilty and that proof of guilt is always in the hands of the Public Prosecutor's Office, which at the time of the request must already have the elements of the charge that show the existence of an appreciable enrichment, which prima facie is not justified by the legitimate income of the public official.[439]

4.1.1.5 Dissenting opinion: Criminal illicit enrichment laws do violate the presumption of innocence

At an international level, a number of countries have officially raised presumption of innocence-related concerns regarding the compatibility of illicit enrichment obligations in treaties. For instance, with regards to the IACAC, both Canada and the US reserved the right not to implement Article IX on the criminalisation of illicit enrichment on the basis that such a law would violate the presumption of innocence guaranteed by their respective constitutions.[440]

---

438 [Unofficial translation] Cámara Nacional de Casación Penal, sala IV, 'Alsogaray', causa n°4787 (2005) (Original text: 'Para aclarar este punto, debemos tener en cuenta que estamos ante un delito de comisión, consistente en enriquecerse de manera apreciable e injustificada durante el ejercicio de la función pública y no -como pretende la defensa- ante un delito de omisión, consistente en 'no justificar un enriquecimiento considerable al ser debidamente requerido'.').

439 [Unofficial translation] Cámara Nacional de Casación Penal, sala IV, 'Alsogaray', causa n°4787 (2005) (Original text: 'El principio de inocencia, y su importante correlato procesal -el in dubio pro reo-, quedan incólumes, en tanto el imputado es inocente mientras no se pruebe lo contrario y esa prueba de culpabilidad queda siempre en cabeza del Ministerio Público Fiscal, que al momento del requerimiento ya debe contar con los elementos de cargo que dan cuenta de la existencia de un enriquecimiento apreciable, que prima facie, no se encuentra justificado en los ingresos legítimos del funcionario;').

440 The United States stated that they would sign subject to the following understandings: '...The United States of America intends to assist and cooperate with other States Parties pursuant to paragraph 3 of Article IX of the Convention to the extent permitted by its domestic law. The United States recognizes the importance of combating improper financial gains by public officials, and has criminal statutes to deter or punish such conduct. These statutes obligate senior-level officials in the federal government to file truthful financial disclosure statements, subject to criminal penalties. They also permit prosecution of federal public officials who evade taxes on wealth that is acquired illicitly. The offense of illicit enrichment as set forth in Article IX of the Convention, however, places the burden of proof on the defendant, which is inconsistent with the United States constitution and fundamental principles of the United States legal system. Therefore, the United States understands that it is not obligated to establish a new criminal offense of illicit enrichment under Article IX of the Convention.' Canada similarly stated: 'Article IX provides that the obligation of a Stated Party to establish the offence of illicit enrichment shall be "Subject to its Constitution and the fundamental principles of its legal system'. As the offence contemplated by Article IX would be contrary to the presumption of innocence guarenteed by Canada's Constitution, Canada will not implement Article IX, as provided for by this provision.' (see: OAS, Signatories and Ratifications B-58, Inter-American Convention Against Corruption (B-58), http://www.oas.org/en/sla/dil/inter_american_treaties_B-58_against_Corruption_signatories.asp, accessed 10 December 2020).

At a domestic level, however, there is not a significant amount of jurisprudence to support the idea that illicit enrichment laws violate the presumption of innocence. One example is *Case No. 1-135/2018(5846/17)*,[441] in which the Constitutional Court of Ukraine declared that the illicit enrichment provisions contained in Article 368.2 of the Criminal Code were unconstitutional for a number of reasons, including that they violated the presumption of innocence principle. It should be noted though, that this decision was not without significant controversy, and even resulted in allegations of judicial corruption.[442]

Nonetheless, in its decision, the court ruled that it was not possible to 'narrow' or 'cancel' the guarantee provided by the presumption of innocence principle outlined in the Ukrainian Constitution and that by allowing the 'transfer of duties' from the state to an accused person, the illicit enrichment laws were not compatible with the Constitution:[443]

> The legislative definition of illegal enrichment as a crime, provided that the prosecution fails to fulfil its obligation to collect evidence of legality of the grounds for acquisition assets in a significant amount by a person, makes it possible to transfer such duty from the prosecution (the state) to the defence (suspect or accused), which is unacceptable in view of the constitutional principle of the presumption of innocence...[444]

Interestingly, while the decision referenced jurisprudence[445] from the ECtHR that highlighted the importance of the presumption of innocence principle, the court failed to consider the key ECtHR decision of *Salabiaku v France* and the reasoning outlined in this case that there can be exceptions to this principle, within reasonable limits.

---

441 Case No. 1-135/2018(5846/17), Decision of the Constitutional Court of Ukraine in the case upon the constitutional petition of 59 People's Deputies of Ukraine on conformity of Article 368.2 of the Criminal Code of Ukraine to the Constitution of Ukraine (February 26, 2019); An unofficial translation of the decision provided by the Constitutional Court of Ukraine is available at: http://web.ccu.gov.ua/en/docs/2541.

442 The nature of this decision prompted Ukraine's own anti-corruption body, the National Anticorruption Bureau of Ukraine, to release a statement alleging that the decision was 'politically motivated' (see: 'Abolition of "Illegal enrichment" article is a step back in the Ukrainian anti-corruption reform', National Anti-Corruption Bureau, 27 February 2019, https://nabu.gov.ua/en/novyny/abolition-illegal-enrichment-article-step-back-ukrainian-anti-corruption-reform, accessed 20 March 2021). At the time of publication, four justices of the court are also facing criminal investigation, and following subsequent decisions of the court relating to asset declarations and an amended illicit enrichment law, the country is experiencing a constitutional crisis (see: E. Channel-Justice, 'The Nature of Ukraine's Constitutional Crisis Explained', Harvard University Ukrainian Research Institute, https://huri.harvard.edu/ukraine-constitutional-court-crisis-explained, accessed 10 December 2020).

443 Case No. 1-135/2018(5846/17), Decision of the Constitutional Court of Ukraine in the case upon the constitutional petition of 59 People's Deputies of Ukraine on conformity of Article 368.2 of the Criminal Code of Ukraine to the Constitution of Ukraine (February 26, 2019). The English translation of this case was obtained from the Official Website of the Constitutional Court of Ukraine, https://web.ccu.gov.ua/en/docs/2541, accessed 31 March 2021.

444 ibid.

445 The court referenced [77] of the Judgement in the case of "Barberà, Messegué and Jabardo v. Spain" dated December 6, 1988, and [97] of the Judgement in the case of "Janosevic v Sweden" dated July 23, 2002 stating that 'The case law of the European Court of Human Rights shows that the principle of presumption of innocence requires, in particular, that in performing their duties the judges do not start the proceedings with a prejudice as to the offence having been committed by the defendant of which he is accused; the burden of proof lies with the prosecution, and any doubt is interpreted in favour of the accused; the prosecution must inform the defendant of the charge brought against him'.

4.1.2 Do civil illicit enrichment laws unfairly reverse the burden of proof?

Challenges have also been raised regarding the express reversal of burdens contained in some civil illicit enrichment laws.

In Kenya, the fairness of the reverse burden mechanism contained in the civil illicit enrichment provisions of the Anti-Corruption and Economic Crimes Act (ACECA) was scrutinised by the Court of Appeal in *Ethics and Anti-Corruption Commission (The legal successor of Kenya Anti - Corruption Commission) v Stanley Mombo Amuti*.[446] In this decision, the court noted that while the burden of proof could shift in proceedings under this law, this would only occur if it were discharged by the state on the balance of probabilities.[447] The court reasoned that this type of shift was 'not an alien process in civil litigation' and that it also occurs under defamation laws when a defence of justification is raised.[448]

This decision was subsequently upheld by the Court of Appeal in *Stanley Mombo Amuti v Kenya Anti-Corruption Commission*, which also held that the mechanism was in line with existing evidential rules:

> The Sections require the Anti- Corruption Commission to prove on balance of probability that an individual has assets disproportionate to his/her legitimately known sources of income. Section 55 (2) of the Act make provision for evidentiary burden which is cast upon the person under investigation to provide satisfactory explanation to establish the legitimate origin of his/her assets. This evidentiary burden is a dynamic burden of proof requiring one who is better able to prove a fact to be the one to prove it. Section 55 (2) of ACECA is in sync with Section 112 of the Evidence Act, Cap 80 of the Laws of Kenya. Section 112 of the Evidence Act, (Cap 80 of the Laws of Kenya) provides: "In civil proceedings when any fact is especially within the knowledge of any party to those proceedings the burden of proving or disproving that fact is upon him."[449]

Similar to the logic applied in some courts regarding criminal illicit enrichment laws, the court here also took into account the fact that the reverse burden requires a respondent to prove matters that are specifically within their knowledge. On this issue, the court further opined: 'In our considered view, a person with lawful income has no trouble proving the legal origin of his or her assets'.[450]

Finally, in addressing concerns that the reverse burden may conflict with the presumption of innocence principle outlined in Kenya's Constitution, the court further stated:

---

446 Ethics and Anti-Corruption Commission (The legal successor of Kenya Anti - Corruption Commission) v Stanley Mombo Amuti [2015] eKLR.

447 ibid., at [33].

448 ibid.

449 Stanley Mombo Amuti v Kenya Anti-Corruption Commission (Civil Appeal No. 184 of 2018) at [78].

450 ibid., at [80].

> The requirement to explain assets is not a requirement for one to explain his innocence. The presumption of innocence is a fundamental right that cannot be displaced through a Notice to explain how assets have been acquired.[451]

Questions have also been raised regarding the fairness of reverse burdens contained in the civil illicit enrichment provisions of Western Australia's Criminal Property Confiscation Act.[452] Similar to Kenya's approach, the Western Australian District Court has also given significant weight to the fact that the reverse burdens contained in these provisions obligate a person to prove facts that could be considered within their specific knowledge.

In *Director of Public Prosecutions v Morris*, Wager DCJ held that the reverse burden mechanism contained in the law was reasonable, as the evidence required for the defendant to discharge this burden should be easily obtainable.[453] In his reasoning, Wager DCJ referred to a previous case regarding a freezing order, *Director of Public Prosecutions for Western Australia v Gypsy Jokers Motorcycle Club Inc*,[454] and considered the views put forward by Templeman J:

> In my view a person who becomes the owner of substantial property by legitimate means ought reasonably to be expected to be able to prove that fact, on the balance of probabilities, without any great difficulties. If the route by which property came into the ownership of an objector is lawful, it will usually be documented in some way.[455]

Wager DCJ also took into account the original explanatory note of the legislation itself, and considered that a 'heavy resource obligation' would be placed on the state if it was expected to lead evidence to establish that a respondent's assets were not lawfully acquired:

> I considered that the Criminal Confiscation Bill 2000 - explanatory notes in relation to s 12(2) was of assistance because it noted:

>> Sub-clause (2) places an onus of proof onto the respondent to establish that his wealth was lawfully acquired. This is because it is easier for a person to establish that his wealth is lawfully acquired rather than for the state to establish the contrary. This provision is central to the advancement of the objectives of the Act. Failure to include such a provision would place heavy resource obligations on the

---

451   ibid., at [79].

452   Criminal Property Confiscation Act 2000 (Australia - Western Australia).

453   In Australia in particular, the idea that rules regarding the burden of proof can be relaxed for issues particularly within an accused person's knowledge is not a new one. In fact an authoritative decision issued by the Australian High Court almost a century ago, Williamson v Ah On, already permitted the application of such flexibility in certain cases: 'The broad primary principles guiding a Court in the administration of justice are that he who substantially affirms an issue must prove it. But, unless exceptional cases were recognized, justice would be frustrated and the very rules intended for the maintenance of the law would defeat their own objective. The usual path leading to justice if rigidly adhered to in all cases, would sometimes prove but the primrose path for wrongdoers and obstruct vindication of the law... the primary rule should be relaxed when the subject matter of the allegation lies peculiarly within the knowledge of one of the parties.' (see: Williamson v Ah On (1926) 39 LR 95 at 113–114, as referenced in Booz Allen Hamilton, *Comparative Evaluation of Unexplained Wealth Orders*, 2012, p.116).

454   Director of Public Prosecutions for Western Australia v Gypsy Jokers Motorcycle Club Inc (2005) WASC 61.

455   Director of Public Prosecutions for Western Australia v Gypsy Jokers Motorcycle Club Inc (2005) WASC 61 at [68], as referenced by Director of Public Prosecutions v Morris [No2][2010] WADC 148 at [19].

state in seeking to establish that a person's wealth was not lawfully acquired.[456]

At a federal level, while the reasonableness of reverse burdens contained in the civil illicit provisions of Australia's Proceeds of Crime Act[457] have yet to be judicially considered, concerns on this issue have been raised during parliamentary reviews of the legislation itself. In reviewing the appropriateness of these mechanisms, the Senate Standing Committee for the Scrutiny of Bills took a similar view to that held in *Director of Public Prosecutions v Morris* above, and justified the reverse burdens on the basis that '[d]etails of the source of a person's wealth will be peculiarly within his or her knowledge'.[458] The legislation was also subjected to review by the Parliamentary Joint Committee on Law Enforcement in 2012. In considering the issue, the Committee stated that 'it is difficult to conceive of scenarios by which an individual had significant amounts of unexplained wealth with no way of accounting for their legitimate accumulation, if that was in fact what had occurred.'[459] They further justified this opinion as follows:

> The committee sought evidence on whether there was any way that an individual could legitimately accumulate wealth without being able to explain or document how they accumulated that wealth. Several witnesses indicated that they could not think of any ways. The ACC noted one possible, but rare, scenario where a legitimate reason could be offered:
>
> > A couple [of] examples that have been brought to our notice would be if someone were fleeing persecution, liquidated their assets and arrived in Australia claiming refugee status with those assets. That might be a possibility.[460]

In light of this, the Committee concluded that 'with appropriate safeguards, unexplained wealth laws represent a reasonable, and proportionate response to the threat of serious and organised crime in Australia'.[461]

---

456 Director of Public Prosecutions v Morris [No2] [2010] WADC 148 at [6].

457 Proceeds of Crime Act 2002 (Australia - Federal).

458 Australian Law Reform Commission, *Traditional Rights and Freedoms—Encroachments by Commonwealth Laws*, ALRC Report 129, Tabled 2 March 2016 at [9.118] referencing the Senate Standing Committee for the Scrutiny of Bills, Parliament of Australia, 10th Report of 2009 (September 2009).

459 Parliamentary Joint Committee on Law Enforcement, Parliament of Australia, *Inquiry into Commonwealth Unexplained Wealth Legislation and Arrangements* (March 2012) at [2.24].

460 ibid., at [2.23].

461 ibid., at [2.24].

4.2 Illicit enrichment laws, the right to silence and the privilege against self-incrimination

The right to silence and the privilege against self-incrimination are two well-established principles that aim to guarantee fair judicial proceedings. They are based on the same underlying notion of the presumption of innocence principle, namely that it is the responsibility of the accusing party to prove their accusations.

The right to silence generally provides that an accused person cannot be compelled to provide evidence either in pre-trial proceedings or the proceedings themselves. It may also protect the person from any adverse inferences that may be drawn from the person's choice to remain silent.

The privilege against self-incrimination more specifically allows a person to refuse to answer any questions or produce any evidence if it would implicate them in the alleged action or would expose them to additional legal proceedings for other actions.

Like with the presumption of innocence, it has been argued that illicit enrichment legislation potentially violates these two principles by permitting the reversal of the burden of proof onto the person targeted by the law – removing their ability to remain silent, and making them vulnerable to additional legal proceedings based on the evidence that they are compelled to provide.

The two closely related legal principles are well entrenched at an international level. The ICCPR guarantees that a person cannot 'be compelled to testify against himself or to confess guilt.'[462] Furthermore, the Rome Statute of the International Criminal Court states that in proceedings for a charge before the International Criminal Court, a person cannot 'be compelled to testify or to confess guilt' and that they can 'remain silent, without such silence being a consideration in the determination of guilt or innocence.'[463] It also outlines that during an investigation, a person '[s]hall not be compelled to incriminate himself or herself or to confess guilt'.[464]

At a regional level, these principles were also expressly included in the ACHR, which similarly guarantees that an accused person has 'the right not to be compelled to be a witness against himself or to plead guilty'.[465] While not expressly included in the ECHR or the ACHPR, the principles have arguably been reinforced in both these regions through differing levels of jurisprudence.[466] For instance in Europe, the Grand Chamber of the European Court of Justice has confirmed that 'even though Article 6 of the ECHR does not explicitly mention the right to silence, that right is a generally recognised international

---

462 The International Covenant on Civil and Political Rights, Article 14(3)(g).

463 The Rome Statute of the International Criminal Court, Article 67 (1)(g).

464 The Rome Statute of the International Criminal Court, Article 55 (1)(a).

465 The American Convention on Human Rights, Article 8 (2)(g).

466 See N. Kofele-Kale, *Combating Economic Crimes – Balancing Competing Rights and Interests in Prosecuting the Crime of Illicit Enrichment*, Routledge, Milton Park, 2013, pp. 67-78.

standard which lies at the heart of the notion of a fair trial.'[467]

Finally, at a domestic level, many state jurisdictions have formally entrenched these principles through constitutional provisions, other legislative instruments or jurisprudence.[468]

4.2.1 Do criminal illicit enrichment laws infringe on the right to silence and the privilege against self-incrimination?

To date, only a small number of courts have addressed whether or not criminal illicit enrichment laws infringe on the right to silence or the privilege against self-incrimination. Nonetheless some specific guidance can be gauged from the existing jurisprudence covering this issue in the context of illicit enrichment law, while broader guidance can be drawn from wider jurisprudence that has dealt with the relationship between these rights and other laws.

4.2.1.1 Jurisdictions in which the criminal illicit enrichment law does reverse the burden of proof

As discussed previously in the context of the presumption of innocence principle, there are a number of courts that have acknowledged that their jurisdictions' criminal illicit enrichment laws do in fact permit the reversal of the burden of proof in some circumstances. At this stage though there is little to no jurisprudence on whether or not these reverse burden mechanisms acceptably infringe on the right to silence and/or the privilege against self-incrimination. Nonetheless, there are some cases that have discussed whether or not these principles can be infringed upon in a general sense.

Like with the presumption of innocence principle, there are a number of cases that have established that these principles are not absolute in nature. For instance, in *John Murray v the United Kingdom*,[469] the ECtHR examined whether a failure on behalf of the accused person to answer police questions or testify at court could give rise to adverse inferences being made against them during proceedings. While acknowledging that 'there can be no doubt that the right to remain silent under police questioning and the privilege against self-incrimination are generally recognised international standards which lie at the heart of the notion of a fair procedure', the court also determined that these principles are not absolute:

> What is at stake in the present case is whether these immunities are absolute in the sense that the exercise by an accused of the right to silence cannot under any circumstances be used against him at trial or, alternatively, whether informing him in advance that, under certain conditions, his silence may be so used, is always to be regarded as "improper compulsion".

---

467 DB v Commissione Nazionale per le Società e la Borsa (Consob) (Case C-481/19) 2 February 2021, at [38].

468 For example, in Malawi these rights have been enshrined specifically in Article 42 (2)(f)(3) of the Constitution, while conversely in Australia, these protections have been outlined in state legislative instruments, such as Section 89 of the Evidence Act 1995 (no 25) (Australia - New South Wales), and through jurisprudence, such as the High Court case of Petty and Maiden v R (1991) 173 CLR 95.

469 John Murray v the United Kingdom (Application No. 18731/91) 8 February 1996.

> On the one hand, it is self-evident that it is incompatible with the immunities under
> consideration to base a conviction solely or mainly on the accused's silence or on a refusal
> to answer questions or to give evidence himself. On the other hand, the Court deems it
> equally obvious that these immunities cannot and should not prevent that the accused's
> silence, in situations which clearly call for an explanation from him, be taken into account
> in assessing the persuasiveness of the evidence adduced by the prosecution.
>
> Wherever the line between these two extremes is to be drawn, it follows from this
> understanding of "the right to silence" that the question whether the right is absolute must
> be answered in the negative.[470]

The court went on to clarify that while adverse inferences can be drawn based on silence, this
can only occur providing:

- 'Appropriate warnings' were given to the accused as to 'the legal effects of
  maintaining silence';[471]

- The prosecutor has established 'a prima facie case against the accused, i.e. a
  case consisting of direct evidence which, if believed and combined with legitimate
  inferences based upon it, could lead a properly directed jury to be satisfied
  beyond reasonable doubt that each of the essential elements of the offence is
  proved';[472] and

- The established 'evidence against the accused "calls" for an explanation which
  the accused ought to be in a position to give' and that a failure to provide this
  information would 'as a matter of common sense allow the drawing of an inference
  that there is no explanation and that the accused is guilty'.[473]

This case is by no means the only interpretation of this issue, and other jurisprudence
from around the world has taken a stricter approach towards enforcing these principles.[474]
Nonetheless courts throughout several common law jurisdictions have accepted that it is
justifiable to draw inferences from a person's silence in circumstances similar to those
outlined above.[475]

The question of whether or not criminal illicit enrichment laws with reversed burdens
infringe on the right to silence or the privilege against self-incrimination has not been widely
addressed in courts to date. Nonetheless, there are some obvious parallels between the

---

470   ibid., at [46]-[47].

471   ibid., at [51].

472   ibid.

473   ibid.

474   Other ECtHR cases that address this issue include Funke v France (Application No. 10828/84) 25 February
      1993; Saunders v the United Kingdom (Application No. 19187/91) 17 December 1996; Jalloh v Germany
      (Application No. 54810/00) 11 July 2006.

475   See N. Kofele-Kale, Combating Economic Crimes – Balancing Competing Rights and Interests in Prosecuting
      the Crime of Illicit Enrichment, Routledge, Milton Park, 2013, pp. 122-125 discussing the United Kingdom
      decisions of Murray v Director of Public Prosecutions (1992) 97 Cr App R 151 and R v Cowan [1995] 3
      WLR; the New Zealand decision of Trompet v Police [1985] NZLR 357; and the Canadian case of R v Noble
      [1997] 1 SCR 874.

considerations taken into account by courts when assessing the justifiability of exceptions to the presumption of innocence principle and the reasoning outlined in the *John Murray v the United Kingdom* decision regarding exceptions to traditional rights on silence and self-incrimination. Specifically, the level to which such exceptions are permitted in both contexts may depend on whether the prosecution still needs to establish the essential elements of an offence, and whether the exception requires an accused to provide information specifically within their own knowledge. Consequently, there is weight to the argument that courts may take a similar approach to both issues.

This argument is reinforced by cases such as *Vasant Rao Guhe vs The State Of Madhya Pradesh,* in which the Supreme Court of India briefly discussed the reversal of the burden of proof in illicit enrichment proceedings and mentioned the conditions that must be met to compel an accused person to provide an explanation regarding the sources of their wealth:

> ...in case the prosecution fails to prove that the public servant either by himself or through anyone else had at any time during the period of his office been in possession of pecuniary resources or property disproportionate to his known sources of income, he would not be required in law to offer any explanation to satisfactorily account therefor. A public servant facing such charge, cannot be comprehended to furnish any explanation in absence of the proof of the allegation of being in possession by himself or through someone else, pecuniary resources or property disproportionate to his known sources of income.[476]

Of course, as criminal illicit enrichment laws containing reverse burden mechanisms become more widely tested in courts throughout the world, there is no doubt that courts will be compelled to shed further light on whether such mechanisms acceptably infringe on the right to silence and the privilege against self-incrimination.

4.2.1.2   Jurisdictions in which the criminal illicit enrichment law does not reverse the burden of proof

In jurisdictions where courts have held that their illicit enrichment laws do not reverse the burden of proof onto an accused person, the courts have relied on similar reasoning to that regarding the presumption of innocence principle. Specifically, the courts in Lithuania and Argentina have both maintained that their illicit enrichment legislation has no effect on these principles, as an accused person always maintains their right to remain silent throughout proceedings.

In Case No KT4-N3/2017, the Constitutional Court of Lithuania specified that in accordance with Lithuania's Criminal Procedure Code, in a proceeding for illicit enrichment 'the prosecutor is under the obligation to prove that the crime... has been committed' and that in 'implementing his/her right to defence, the suspect/accused has the right to give evidence

---

476   Vasant Rao Guhe vs The State Of Madhya Pradesh (Criminal Appeal No.1279 of 2017) at [21].

and challenge the suspicions (charges) brought against him/her.'[477] While the court noted that an accused person can choose to give evidence, it emphasised that they are in no way 'obliged to prove the fact that the criminal act of illicit enrichment has not been committed' and that 'situations where the suspect/accused opts to be silent may not be treated as aggravating his/her situation in criminal proceedings.'[478]

In the Argentinian case of Alsogaray, the National Chamber of Criminal Cassation took an analogous stance to that which it had taken regarding the presumption of innocence principle:

> ... the defence starts from the premise that "the requirement that the accused must justify his increase in assets means that the authority issuing the request does not have to prove his suspicion, but that the official [the accused] must prove that he is innocent; this implies the imperative need for the suspected person to 'testify', since if he chooses to remain silent he would have to pay the very high cost of automatically becoming involved in the crime in question". We have already said above that this is not so, since the crime we are studying is one of commission and consists not in "not justifying" -as the defence claims- but in enriching himself in an appreciable and unjustified way in his legitimate income as a civil servant, and that, on the other hand, at the moment of formulating the request it is up to the competent State organ to prove such extremes in a specific way.[479]

The court further clarified in this case that the apparent requirement to 'justify' present in the law should be interpreted only as an '...opportunity for the defendant to prove the lawfulness of his enrichment' and that '[i]f the accused makes use of his right to remain silent, in this case too the judicial bodies will have the burden of proof'.[480]

As noted previously in Section 3.2.4, this reasoning was subsequently confirmed by an appeal in

---

477 Case no. 14/2015-1/2016-2/2016-14/2016-15/2016- The Constitutional Court of the Republic of Lithuania in the name of the Republic of Lithuania ruling on the compliance of Paragraph 1 of Article 189¹ of the Criminal Code of the Republic of Lithuania with the Constitution of the Republic of Lithuania 15 March 2017, no KT4-N3/2017 at [39.3].

478 ibid.

479 [Unofficial translation] Cámara Nacional de Casación Penal, sala IV, 'Alsogaray', causa n°4787 (2005) (Original text: 'Asimismo, en cuanto a la inversión de la carga de la prueba, la defensa parte, para formular su agravio de inconstitucionalidad, de la premisa por la cual "la exigencia de que el imputado justifique su incremento patrimonial significa que la autoridad que le formula el requerimiento no tiene que probar su sospecha, sino que el funcionario debe probar que es inocente; implicando ello la imperiosa necesidad de que el sospechado 'declare', pues si optara por guardar silencio debería pagar el altísimo costo de quedar automáticamente incurso en el delito que nos ocupa". Ya dijimos arriba que ello no es así, en tanto el delito que estudiamos es de comisión y consiste, no en "no justificar" -como pretende la defensa-, sino en enriquecerse de manera apreciable e injustificada en sus ingresos legítimos como funcionario, y que, por otra parte, al momento de formular el requerimiento corresponde al órgano competente del Estado probar tales extremos de manera específica.').

480 [Unofficial translation] Cámara Nacional de Casación Penal, sala IV, 'Alsogaray', causa n°4787 (2005) (Original text: 'En similar sentido se ha sostenido que el requerimiento de 'justificación', usado por el legislador, sólo puede ser entendido lógicamente como una notificación para que el acusado pueda hacer uso de una oportunidad formal de probar la licitud de su enriquecimiento; que se ha mal interpretado ese concepto, confundiéndoselo con la noción procesal de 'prueba positiva'; y que el tipo es avalorado, neutro y respeta plenamente el derecho de abstención que se deriva, en materia procesal, de la presunción de inocencia. Si el imputado hiciere uso de su derecho a callar, también en este caso serán las instancias judiciales las que tendrán la carga de probar -idéntica a la de otros tipos penales en los casos en que los imputados se abstienen de declarar- (cfr.: C.N.C. y C.C.F., Sala I, voto del doctor Elbert en el precedente 'Cullota', ya citado)').

this case to the Supreme Court[481] and later in the 2017 case of *César Santos Gerardo del Corazón de Jesús Milani*, in which the court also held that '[i]n essence, it is the State that has the burden of proving an appreciable and unjustified increase in the assets of the official or employee'[482] and that rather than reversing the burden of proof, the law gives the targeted person 'the possibility of justifying the origin of his enrichment as well as the power to refuse to testify'.[483]

4.2.2 Can civil illicit enrichment laws infringe on the privilege against self-incrimination?

There is little to no jurisprudence in which the courts have addressed the compatibility of civil illicit enrichment laws with the privilege against self-incrimination.

Some guidance on the issue, however, can be gauged from the High Court case of *National Crime Agency v Zamira Hajiyeva*[484] and the subsequent Court of Appeal case of *Zamira Hajiyeva v National Crime Agency*.[485] These were the first set of cases to deal with the investigative UWO mechanism introduced into the UK's Proceeds of Crime Act.[486]

In this case, the High Court in the UK issued a UWO 'without notice' against Mrs Hajiyeva, requiring her to provide information on the source of funds used to purchase real estate property in London. The property was suspected to be the proceeds of corruption offences committed by Mrs Hajiyeva's husband, the former chairman of the state-owned International Bank of Azerbaijan. She sought to discharge the order on a number of grounds, including that the order infringed on her privilege against self-incrimination – despite the fact that the law specifically states that '[a] statement made by a person in response to a requirement imposed by an unexplained wealth order may not be used in evidence against that person in criminal proceedings.'[487]

Both the Court of Appeal and the High Court dismissed Mrs Hajiyeva's argument, instead

---

481 Corte Suprema de Justicia de la Nación Argentina, 'Alsogaray', Fallos 331:2799 (2008).

482 [Unofficial translation] Poder Judicial de la Nación, Juzgado Criminal y Correccional Federal 3, 'César Santos Gerardo del Corazón de Jesús Milani', CFP 6734/2013 (2017/09) (Original text: 'En definitiva, es el Estado quien tiene a su cargo acreditar el aumento apreciable y no justificado del patrimonio del funcionario o del empleado.').

483 [Unofficial translation] Poder Judicial de la Nación, Juzgado Criminal y Correccional Federal 3, 'César Santos Gerardo del Corazón de Jesús Milani', CFP 6734/2013 (2017/09) (Original text: 'De esta forma, con el llamamiento efectuado, no se invirtió la carga de la prueba ni fue violatorio de la prohibición de declarar en contra de uno mismo, sino que, con dicha convocatoria, se le brindó a Milani la posibilidad de justificar el origen de su enriquecimiento como así también la facultad de negarse a declarar (cfr. C.N.C.P., in re: 'Alsogaray', ya citado)').

484 National Crime Agency v Mrs Zamira Hajiyeva [2018] EWHC 2534 (Admin).

485 Mrs Zamira Hajiyeva v National Crime Agency [2020] EWCA Civ 108.

486 As explained in Section 2.6.1 this mechanism can be distinguished from criminal and civil illicit enrichment laws in that it only grants power to the court to issue a civil order requiring a person to explain the sources of their wealth. The mechanism cannot be used by itself to issue an order for repayment of the unexplained amount, but can only be used to acquire evidence that can then be presented in a subsequent civil recovery proceeding under which it is still necessary for the state to demonstrate that the wealth in question is 'recoverable property' and is connected to criminality in some way.

487 Proceeds of Crime Act 2002 (United Kingdom), Section 362F.

holding the view that parliament had intended that the privilege be 'abrogated' in the context of the UWO procedure.[488] The courts further reasoned that if they were to apply the privilege against self-incrimination to such orders, then this would render the process largely 'nugatory' as the order was created to impose a requirement to provide information.[489] Additionally, both courts also did not envisage a 'real and appreciable risk' that the respondent would face prosecution for a criminal offence in the UK.[490]

It should be noted that some civil illicit enrichment laws also deal with this issue expressly in the statutes themselves by including provisions that prohibit the use of information provided in illicit enrichment proceedings in separate criminal proceedings. For instance, the qualified civil illicit enrichment law of the Bahamas specifically states that any statement made pursuant to an order under this law 'shall not be admissible against the person in any criminal proceeding except a proceeding in respect of the falsity of the statement.'[491] Nonetheless, as with the UK example, such statutory guarantees are still likely to be judicially tested.

---

488 Mrs Zamira Hajiyeva v National Crime Agency [2020] EWCA Civ 108 at [51]; National Crime Agency v Mrs Zamira Hajiyeva [2018] EWHC 2534 (Admin) at [110] - [112].

489 ibid.

490 Mrs Zamira Hajiyeva v National Crime Agency [2020] EWCA Civ 108 at [50]; National Crime Agency v Mrs Zamira Hajiyeva [2018] EWHC 2534 (Admin) at [115]; Both courts also noted that the Mrs Hajiyeva had not actually identified the elements of the requested information that would give rise to the risk (see for instance Mrs Zamira Hajiyeva v National Crime Agency [2020] EWCA Civ 108 at [50]: 'Although the appellant had asserted both privileges in her witness statement, she did not identify what elements of the requested information would give rise to the alleged risk. In short, she had not said which answers to which questions might incriminate her. Mere assertion of the privilege against self-incrimination was not sufficient (see JSC BTA Bank v Ablyasov [2009] EWCA Civ 1125, per Sedley LJ at [39]). Although she said that she had been advised that her responses to the questions posed in Schedule 3 to the UWO and the requirement to produce documents in Schedule 4 to the UWO could be used to incriminate her and/or her husband in criminal proceedings in the United Kingdom, or in Azerbaijan, the court had to be satisfied of the risk of prosecution (see R (CPS) v Bolton Magistrates' Court [2004] 1 WLR 835), which the judge was not.').

491 The Proceeds of Crime Act 2018 (Bahamas), Section 75(3).

4.3 Illicit enrichment laws and the principle against their retroactive application

The principle against retroactive (or 'ex post facto') laws is a widely established legal norm. In a general sense, the principle prohibits the introduction of a law that alters the legal consequences of actions that occurred before the law came into existence. The possession of illicitly acquired wealth, however, is often considered as a continuous action, and consequently such laws can be used to target the continued possession of wealth that was originally acquired before the law came into existence. Courts in several jurisdictions have tackled this issue to assess whether illicit enrichment laws can be applied in this way without unfairly infringing on the traditional norm against retroactive application.

4.3.1 Criminal illicit enrichment laws and retroactivity

In a criminal context, the principle against retroactivity forbids the punishment of a person for an action that was not defined as criminal at the time it was committed. Prohibitions against such laws have been enshrined in both globally and regionally applicable international legal instruments. The UDHR and the ICCPR both state that 'No one shall be held guilty of any penal offence on account of any act or omission which did not constitute a penal offence, under national or international law, at the time when it was committed...'.[492] Similar articles exist in the ECHR,[493] the ACHR,[494] the ACHPR[495] and the Arab Charter on Human Rights.[496] Provisions preventing such laws have also regularly been included in many domestic legal instruments, and are sometimes even specifically prohibited by a country's constitution.

Despite this, prohibitions against retroactive laws are not always strictly applied and such laws are actually quite common in legal systems throughout the world, particularly in the area of tax evasion and avoidance.[497]

This flexibility has often been extended to illicit enrichment laws, and countries have taken significantly different approaches when determining if such laws can be applied in a retroactive sense. For example, while Lithuania and Moldova do not allow their respective

---

492 The Universal Declaration of Human Rights, Article 11; The International Covenant on Civil and Political Rights, Article 15(1).

493 The European Convention on Human Rights, Article 7.

494 The American Convention on Human Rights, Article 9.

495 The African Charter on Human and Peoples' Rights, Article 2.

496 The Arab Charter on Human Rights, Article 15.

497 For example, Australia introduced the Tax Laws Amendment (Countering Tax Avoidance and Multinational Profit Shifting) Act 2013 (Australia - Federal) on 29 June 2013 with retrospective operation (see: Australian Law Reform Commission, *Traditional Rights and Freedoms—Encroachments by Commonwealth Laws*, ALRC Report 129, Tabled 2 March 2016 at [13.107]) while the introduction of retroactive taxation laws in the United States has been described by the Congressional Research Service as 'quite common' (see: M. Mazur, 'Retroactive Tax Provisions, a "Quite Common" Practice', U.S. Department of the Treasury, 2014, https://www.treasury.gov/connect/blog/Pages/Retroactive-Tax-Provisions.aspx, accessed 20 March 2021).

illicit enrichment provisions to apply to property acquisitions that occurred before these laws were enacted, courts in Bolivia, Hong Kong and Uganda have taken the opposite stance and have permitted retroactive applications.

For example, in *Case No 2K-P-93/2014*,[498] the Supreme Court of Lithuania strictly interpreted articles in the ECHR and the Lithuanian Criminal Code that prohibited retroactive legislation, and held that the defendants could not be guilty of illicit enrichment charges concerning the purchase of a house, as the acquisition of this house took place before the act of illicit enrichment had been criminalised.

This interpretation was subsequently reinforced in the 2017 Supreme Court decision, *Case No KT4-N3/2017*, which also held that the illicit enrichment provisions in Lithuania's Criminal Code could not be applied to asset acquisitions that occurred before the enactment of the law. In justifying its position, the court noted that criminal liability for possession of illicitly acquired property arises specifically at the moment in time when the property in question was actually acquired. It reasoned that if this moment in time occured before the illicit enrichment provisions had come into force, then the punishment of this act would require the retroactive application of the law.[499] In addition to this, the court also held that while retroactive application of some criminal offences is permitted in Lithuania for several offences listed under Article 3 of Lithuania's Criminal Code, as the illicit enrichment provision is not specifically included in this list, then the court was not permitted to apply it retroactively.[500]

In *Case no. 60a/2014*,[501] the Moldovan Constitutional Court took a similar interpretation to Lithuania above, and ruled that its illicit enrichment law could also not be applied retroactively, and was thus not in violation of an article in the Moldovan Constitution that prohibited the punishment of actions that did not constitute a crime at the time they were committed.[502]

Other countries have taken the opposite position. In Bolivia, the illicit enrichment provision was challenged in *Sentencia Constitucional Plurinacional 0770/2012*,[503] on the grounds that it could not be applied to wealth acquired before the enactment of the law itself without violating the articles prohibiting retroactive application contained in the Bolivian Constitution, the ICCPR and the ACHR.

In holding that the Bolivian illicit enrichment law could actually be applied to such wealth,

---

498 Criminal case No 2K-P-93/2014, 11 April 2014.

499 Case no. 14/2015-1/2016-2/2016-14/2016-15/2016 - The Constitutional Court of the Republic of Lithuania in the name of the Republic of Lithuania ruling on the compliance of Paragraph 1 of Article 1891 of the Criminal Code of the Republic of Lithuania with the Constitution of the Republic of Lithuania 15 March 2017, no KT4-N3/2017, at [18.1]-[18.4].

500 ibid.

501 Case no. 60a/2014 - The Constitutional Court of the Republic of Moldova, the judgment of 16 April 2015.

502 ibid., at [83].

503 Tribunal Constitucional Plurinacional, Sala Plena, Sentencia Constitucional Plurinacional Núm. 0770/2012 (2012).

the court held that illicit enrichment should be considered as a continuous action that materialises constantly in each moment that passes after the enrichment itself has been observed. Consequently, the court held that even if the initial enrichment took place before the legislation was put in place, the enrichment itself would still be occurring after the legislation was put into force and could thus still be punished under the law.

In *Nestor Machumbi Gasasira v Uganda*,[504] the Ugandan Constitutional Court similarly held that there was no conflict between the illicit enrichment provision contained in Uganda's Anti-Corruption Act and the non-retroactivity article contained in Uganda's Constitution. Even though the applicant in this case had acquired properties before the enactment of the Anti-Corruption Act, the court reasoned that these properties could still legitimately be targeted by the illicit enrichment law on the basis that the applicant was still in 'control or possession' of them after the legislation came into effect.[505]

In Hong Kong, the retroactive application of the illicit enrichment provisions contained in the Prevention of Bribery Ordinance were examined by the Court of Appeal in *Lai Man-Yau v Attorney General*[506] and the Privy Council in *Lai Man-Yau v Attorney General (No.2)*. The appellant in these cases had been employed as a police officer for many years, and his wife had amassed a disproportionate amount of wealth during this time. The appellant argued however that the illicit enrichment provisions could not be applied to him as he had retired from his role two years before these provisions had come into force. Both courts disagreed, and held that as these laws applied to anyone who, 'being, or having been' a public official, had amassed disproportionate wealth, then a clear reading of this phrase would include individuals who had been a public official even before the law had been enacted. In delivering his judgment at the Privy Council, Lord Salmon acknowledged that giving a retrospective effect to a statute is 'normally unjust and should be avoided if it is possible to do so without doing violence to the language of the statute'.[507] Nonetheless, he also reasoned that as the wording of the law itself was clear and unambiguous, and as it was impossible to nullify the retroactive effect of the provision without 'rewriting the whole subsection', then to do so

---

504 Nestor Machumbi Gasasira v Uganda Constitutional Reference No. 17 of 2011.

505 ibid.

506 Lai Man-Yau v Attorney General (No.2) [1978] HKCU 4.

507 Lai Man-Yau v Attorney General (No.2) [1978] HKCU 79 (Lord Salmon referencing Young v Adams [1898] AC 469).

would be both wrong and unfeasible.[508] As a final note, Lord Salmon also acknowledged the severity of the provision, but argued that it could be viewed as an appropriate response to the destructive threat of widespread corruption:

> It has been said that the Ordinance is a draconian measure. No doubt it is. But when bribery and corruption become so rife that they seriously undermine the whole fabric of society, such measures may well be necessary. In any event, it is not for the Courts to decide whether or not an Ordinance ought to have been passed but only what it means once it is passed, and then to enforce it.[509]

4.3.2   Civil illicit enrichment laws and retroactivity

There is very little jurisprudence dealing with the retroactive application of civil illicit enrichment laws. However, it is very likely that such laws can also be applied retroactively in certain jurisdictions.

In general, the issue is not raised and challenged with the same 'vigour' in a civil context, and there are many examples of civil laws around the world that can apply to actions that have occurred before these laws came into force.[510]

This general attitude is reflected in the wording of many civil illicit enrichment laws – which actually specifically permit retroactive application.

For instance, Kenya's illicit enrichment provisions expressly state that the law 'shall apply retroactively' and this characteristic was acknowledged by Kenya's Court of Appeal in *Stanley Mombo Amuti v Kenya Anti-Corruption Commission*.[511]

Moreover, Australia's civil illicit enrichment law at a Federal level specifies that the calculation of a person's total wealth should include an assessment of property that was owned, controlled or disposed of by the person at 'any time'.[512] The Explanatory Memorandum accompanying

---

508   Lai Man-Yau v Attorney General (No.2) [1978] HKCU 79; Lord Salmon also noted that regardless of whether an addition to the wording of the law was permitted, the law would still lead to unusual results no matter what: 'Their Lordships, in spite of the attractive argument by Counsel for the appellant, consider that there is certainly no necessity to make the proposed addition to section 10(1)(b). Indeed, if it were made, the subsection would still operate retrospectively and would also lead to absurd results. Suppose that one police sergeant retired on 15th May 1971, the day after the Ordinance came into effect, and another police sergeant retired on the 13th May, and that neither could give a satisfactory explanation to the Court as to how property which was disproportionate to his past emoluments had come into his control. The first police sergeant would be guilty of an offence, and would, in effect, be punished for bribes he had taken before the Ordinance came into operation. The second police sergeant, however, who was in exactly the same position as the first, except that he had retired two days earlier, would go free. This cannot have been intended when the Ordinance was enacted, and there can be no justification for adding words to the subsection which would produce such a bizarre result. It is impossible not to give section 10(1)(b) retrospective effect without rewriting the whole subsection, which, of course, is not feasible on any view.'.

509   Lai Man-Yau v Attorney General (No.2) [1978] HKCU 79.

510   Australian Law Reform Commission, *Traditional Rights and Freedoms–Encroachments by Commonwealth Laws*, ALRC Report 129, Tabled 2 March 2016 at [13.11]-[13.34].

511   Anti-Corruption and Economic Crimes Act 2003 (Kenya), Section 55(9); Stanley Mombo Amuti v Kenya Anti-Corruption Commission (Civil Appeal No. 184 of 2018); It should be noted however that this issue was not addressed or discussed in great detail.

512   Proceeds of Crime Act 2002 (Australia - Federal), Section 179G.

the bill that introduced these provisions further specifies that at 'any time' is intended to include 'before the time the Commonwealth's unexplained wealth laws commenced', clearly indicating that the law can take into account property acquired by a person before the law was enacted.[513]

This attitude is also unequivocally outlined in the wording of Western Australia's civil illicit enrichment law, which specifically states that it 'applies to a person's unexplained wealth whether any property, service, advantage or benefit that is a constituent of the person's wealth was acquired before or after the commencement of this Act'.[514]

---

513 Explanatory Memorandum, Crimes Legislation Amendment (Unexplained Wealth And Other Measures) Bill 2014 (Australia - Federal).

514 Criminal Property Confiscation Act (Australia - Western Australia), Section 5.

Part 5

Contributions from practitioners

Part 5 Summary

The following part includes contributions from five practitioners.

The first contribution is by **Phillip G. Kagucia**, Assistant Director at the Ethics and Anti-Corruption Commission (Kenya), and provides a summary of the unexplained wealth-related forfeiture provisions in Kenya's Anti-Corruption and Economic Crimes Act. This law – classified as a qualified civil illicit enrichment law within this publication – is a mechanism that has been increasingly used to successfully target and recover proceeds of corruption in Kenya, such as in the judgment of *Ethics and Anti-Corruption Commission v Patrick Ochieno Abachi & 6 Others*[515] handed down on 10 March 2021.[516]

The second contribution is by **Preeya Raghoonundun**, a Senior Integrity Reporting Officer at the Integrity Reporting Services Agency (Mauritius), and outlines the unique unexplained wealth order model contained in the Good Governance and Integrity Reporting Act. Like with the Kenyan example, this mechanism – classified as a civil illicit enrichment law within this publication – is increasingly being used to target proceeds of crime and corruption in Mauritius.

The third contribution is by **Dr. Alcides Chinchay**, a Senior Prosecutor of the Peruvian Public Prosecutor's Office, who discusses the introduction and evolution of the criminal illicit enrichment offence contained in Peru's Código Penal. This contribution covers the 'subsidiary' nature of the Peruvian illicit enrichment offence in the context of other criminal offences, and provides an overview of the key characteristics of this law and the criminal policy objectives behind its introduction.

The fourth contribution is by **Francis H. Cassidy**, National Member for Ireland at Eurojust and former Bureau Legal Officer at Ireland's Criminal Assets Bureau, who discusses the unique forfeiture mechanism contained in Ireland's Proceeds of Crime Act. While this mechanism is not classified as an illicit enrichment law within this publication, this law closely resembles many civil illicit enrichment mechanisms and has proven to be a remarkedly successful tool for Ireland's Criminal Assets Bureau in its efforts to recover proceeds of organised crime.

The final contribution is by **Jonathan Spicer**, Senior Asset Recovery Specialist with the International Centre for Asset Recovery, Barrister and former Specialist Prosecutor and Crown Advocate of the UK's Crown Prosecution Service. This contribution provides an overview of the issue of international cooperation, and

---

515 Ethics and Anti-Corruption Commission v Patrick Ochieno Abachi & 6 Others (ACEC No.15 of 2019), delivered 10th March 2021.

516 An appeal was still an available avenue to the respondents in this case at the time of publication.

specifically mutual legal assistance efforts, within the context of illicit enrichment. It discusses the potential challenges that might arise when illicit enrichment investigations and prosecutions in one country require information and evidence from another country that has not yet enacted an illicit enrichment law.

5.1 Kenya: The Anti-Corruption and Economic Crimes Act and the forfeiture of unexplained assets

Phillip G. Kagucia

Assistant Director at the Ethics and Anti-Corruption Commission and Asset Recovery Attorney

The law

In Kenya, legislation on the forfeiture of unexplained assets is found in Part VI of the Anti-Corruption and Economic Crimes Act 2003 (ACECA) which deals with the Compensation and Recovery of Improper Benefits.

Section 55 of ACECA empowers the Ethics and Anti-Corruption Commission (EACC)[517] to institute civil proceedings in the High Court if:

(a) after an investigation, the Commission is satisfied that the person has unexplained assets; and

(b) the person has, in the course of the exercise by the Commission of its powers of investigation or otherwise, been afforded a reasonable opportunity to explain the disproportion between the assets concerned and his known legitimate sources of income and the Commission is not satisfied that an adequate explanation of that disproportion has been given.

The Court of Appeal in *Stanley Mombo Amuti v Kenya Anti-Corruption Commission* set a precedent by affirming the ingredients for unexplained assets as follows:

i. There must be set time period for the investigation of a person;

ii. The person must be reasonably suspected of corruption or economic crime;

iii. The person must have assets whose value is disproportionate to his known sources of income at or around the period of investigation and

iv. There is no satisfactory explanation for the disproportionate asset.[518]

Application, evidence and thresholds of proof

Before seeking the forfeiture of unexplained assets, the EACC habitually seeks preservation orders under Section 56 of ACECA to prevent the disposal of suspected unexplained assets during investigations, and prior to institution of civil proceedings. An application under this Section can be made ex parte, and the EACC is only required to show that there is a reasonable suspicion that the assets were acquired through corruption.

517 The Ethics and Anti-Corruption Commission (EACC) is an independent commission which draws its mandate from the Constitution of Kenya and other legislation, namely, the Ethics and Anti-Corruption Commission Act 2011 (Kenya), the Anti-Corruption and Economic Crimes Act 2003 (Kenya), the Public Officer Ethics Act of 2003 (Kenya) and the Leadership and Integrity Act of 2012 (Kenya).

518 Kenya Anti-Corruption Commission v Stanley Mombo Amuti (Civil Appeal No.184 of 2018) at [64].

Upon the conclusion of investigations, the EACC may then file an Originating Summons supported by affidavit(s) seeking a declaration that the assets enumerated are unexplained and should, consequently, be forfeited to the state. This is a non-conviction based asset forfeiture proceeding, which is judged on a balance of probabilities.

During proceedings, a shift in the evidentiary burden will occur after the EACC establishes that the Defendant is in possession of assets believed to be proceeds of corruption that cannot be explained. At this juncture, it is incumbent upon the Defendant to discharge that burden by demonstrating that the assets in question were acquired by means other than corruption.

Assets deemed unexplained are consequently surrendered to the Treasury[519] and placed under the stewardship of the Principal Secretary who deposits such assets in the Consolidated Fund. A finding of unexplained assets may be used to corroborate evidence in a criminal trial that the suspect received a benefit and may lend weight to allegations of corruption.[520] It therefore bears significant probative value.

Challenges to enforcement

Comparatively, unexplained assets proceedings are a relatively new area of law in Kenya, and courts are still very much developing an understanding of the issue as a whole. For example, judges of such proceedings have tended to focus purely on the credibility of a respondent's explanation in determining if an asset is 'unexplained' rather than also taking into account wider categories of evidence surrounding the acquisition of the assets themselves.

Moreover, it took years for the judiciary in Kenya to appreciate the nuances of the unexplained wealth provisions, as seen by the very first decision of the High Court in *Kenya Anti-Corruption Commission v Stanley Mombo Amuti*.[521] In this case, the judge felt that there were inconsistencies in the standard of proof when the evidentiary burden shifted from the EACC to the defendant. It appeared, to the judge, that the defendant was required to prove the legitimacy of his assets to a higher standard than that set for the EACC because of the obligation to demonstrate that the assets were acquired other than by corruption – a criminal offence. This misapprehension was resolved by the Court of Appeal in *Ethics and Anti-Corruption Commission (The legal successor of Kenya Anti - Corruption Commission) v Stanley Mombo Amuti*.[522]

In this case and others, defence counsel have taken to challenging the constitutionality of the EACC's mandate citing violation of rights to privacy, property and fair administrative action. Consequently, the process of achieving a final decision that assets are 'unexplained' has the potential to be a long and arduous one.

---

519 Anti-Corruption and Economic Crimes Act 2003 (Kenya), Section 56C.

520 Anti-Corruption and Economic Crimes Act 2003 (Kenya), Section 57.

521 Kenya Anti-Corruption Commission v Stanley Mombo Amuti [2011] eKLR.

522 Ethics and Anti-Corruption Commission (The legal successor of Kenya Anti - Corruption Commission) v Stanley Mombo Amuti [2015] eKLR.

For example, the final determination of the *Amuti* case mentioned above took 13 years, with proceedings running from 2008 up until the exhaustion of all appeal options in 2020.[523]

Nonetheless despite these challenges, and in recognition of the significant role this law can play in combating corruption, the EACC is currently pursuing numerous proceedings targeting unexplained assets.

---

523   Stanley Mombo Amuti v Kenya Anti-Corruption Commission [2020] eKLR.

5.2 Mauritius: Targeting unexplained wealth using the Good Governance and Integrity Reporting Act

Preeya Raghoonundun

Senior Integrity Reporting Officer at the Integrity Reporting Services Agency

The Mauritian context

To help combat illicit enrichment, Mauritius passed the Good Governance and Integrity Reporting Act 2015 ('the GGIR Act') which introduced the concept of 'unexplained wealth' into the canon of Mauritian law.

The GGIR Act represents a unique approach to this issue, and its provisions are currently unmatched by any other legislation.

In Mauritius, criminal convictions and conviction-based asset confiscations can be extremely difficult to obtain. While this is by no means a uniquely Mauritian problem, it can be exacerbated on an island with a small population – where higher-value crimes such as narcotics trafficking and high-level corruption are often accompanied by witness intimidation, cronyism, community pressures and abuses of process, etc.

The GGIR Act aims to address these issues by making it easier to recover criminally acquired assets in a civil context.

Operation of the GGIR

Applications under the GGIR Act are civil proceedings that allow for property confiscation without the need for lengthy and uncertain criminal proceedings.

The GGIR Act is highly effective when deployed in cases in which criminal enrichment is strongly suspected but cannot be proven as it puts the onus on the holder of the property to show, on the balance of probabilities, that it was honestly acquired.

In theory, the GGIR Act's application is very straightforward.

The Act establishes the Integrity Reporting Services Agency ('the Agency') which is empowered to require Mauritian citizens to explain, by way of affidavit, the sources of the funds used to acquire property. The Agency analyses the property holder's explanations and reports its analysis and recommendations to the Integrity Reporting Board ('the Board') which is also established under the Act and empowered to provide oversight.

If the Agency and the Board conclude that the respondent has failed to adequately explain the sources of the funds used to acquire the property, the Agency will seek an Unexplained Wealth Order (UWO). UWOs, however, are only issued by a judge in Chambers who independently assesses both the respondent's explanations and the Agency's evidence. If the Judge issues the UWO, title to the property concerned vests in the Agency and it is realised according to the statute.

The Agency is not obliged to prove anything beyond the ownership or control of property by a citizen of Mauritius (wherever it is located). Once this is established, the onus is then on the owner to show that, on the balance of probabilities, the funds came from legal sources. If the Agency recommends it, and the Board agrees and so directs it, the Agency will apply for a UWO, which may or may not be granted on the basis of affidavit evidence.

The purpose of the GGIR

The key aim of the GGIR Act, although it is not explicitly stated, is to deny criminals the financial benefits of their crimes. Even if convicted, seasoned criminals have no fear of prison, which often provides them with opportunities to extend their criminal networks and plan further crimes. However, if criminals instead lose their home, cars, yachts, Rolexes and the other trappings they enjoy, then criminal enterprises become pointless.

Challenges to enforcement

No matter how finely crafted the statute, the GGIR Act is only useful if it is enforced. And this requires harmony of political will, inter-agency collaboration and the courts. While political will exists abundantly in Mauritius, the Agency has no special investigatory powers and must rely on inter-agency cooperation and the courts to function optimally.

Other law enforcement agencies, public interest agencies and statutory corporations are statutorily obliged to report their reasonable suspicions that someone may have unexplained wealth to the Agency and to give it all reasonable assistance in its investigations. However, there are no sanctions for non-compliance and not all agencies are willing to refer cases to the Agency. 'Turf' issues and silo mentalities are to be found worldwide and they also exist in Mauritius.

Unnecessary delays in court proceedings can also severely hamper the confiscation regime. The Agency has had one application for a UWO before the Court for over a year because the respondent has failed to lodge an affidavit. Instead, she has sought and been granted numerous postponements on often spurious grounds in a clear abuse of process.

An example of success

One simple example shows how the GGIR Act can be simply and effectively deployed. In 2017, a suspected member of a drug trafficking network was interdicted at the airport carrying large sums of undeclared cash in both Rupees and other currencies hidden about his person and in the false bottoms of his luggage. The police searched his home and that of a close relative and found substantially more cash.

Suspecting the cash was an instrumentality of crime, the police arrested him, continued their investigations and reported the case to the Agency. The suspect, in custody, asked the Agency for time to provide documentary evidence of the sources of the funds but ultimately did not submit an affidavit explanation. The Agency subsequently served a disclosure order on him which was ignored – the suspect instead claimed that the funds belonged to someone else.

As he had failed to explain the source of the funds, despite being given ample opportunity to do so, the Agency sought, and was promptly granted, a UWO. The funds were seized and placed in a specially designated bank account for the alleviation of poverty.

A final note

While the GGIR Act certainly has draconian elements, as noted above, it also has inbuilt safeguards to prevent its misuse. With its strong emphasis on independent oversight, the Mauritian GGIR Act outlines a balanced and fair mechanism for the recovery of unexplained wealth.

5.3 Peru: Illicit enrichment as a tool for combating corruption and financial crime

Dr. Alcides Chinchay

Senior Prosecutor of the Public Prosecutor's Office of Peru

Legislative developments

The prohibition of illicit enrichment was originally introduced in Article 62 of the Peruvian Constitution of 1979. However, the constitutional amendment did not introduce a criminal offence but a general constitutional mandate. A criminal provision was finally introduced in the Penal Code by the Legislative Decree No. 121 on 12 June 1981. This Decree introduced the following elements:

- Any public official or public servant who, by reason of his position or functions, unjustly enriches himself, shall be punished with imprisonment of not less than four years and not more than ten years.

- There is a presumption of illicit enrichment when the increase in the assets of the public official, in consideration of his or her sworn declaration(s) of assets and income, is notoriously higher than what he or she would normally have had by virtue of the salaries or emoluments that he or she has received.

As is customary in Peru, the modification of the Penal Code at the time obeyed criminal policy criteria and was carried out through a constitutional mechanism that delegated legislative powers from Congress to the Executive. As this delegation was carried out within the framework of a very precise delegation clause regarding criminal matters, it placed limitations on the use of the illicit enrichment offence in practice. In particular, it required that the new offence be applied in line with the constitutional principles of due process, which implies the respect of constitutional guarantees such as the presumption of innocence and in dubio pro reo among others.

Consequently, a line of jurisprudence based on these constitutional considerations declares that the illicit enrichment offence should have a 'subsidiary' or 'residual' application in relation to other (main) criminal offences. By residual application, it should be understood that the application of this offence is only possible when it has not been possible to identify the underlying criminal conduct that gives rise to the imbalance in the official's assets.

Justification for an illicit enrichment law

The crime of illicit enrichment is important in the fight against corruption for at least two reasons:

i) There is a high percentage of informality in the Peruvian economy (around 70% of economic activities are carried out outside the formal financial system); and

ii) There is little control in state contracting, which means that the use of important public resources is decided without being able to assess the relevance and viability of the public works, which is a fertile ground for fraud.

As a result of the combination of these two factors, Peruvian state contracting has become the main source of the diversion of public funds. Informality makes it possible to receive large sums of cash that can literally be hidden under the mattress and re-injected into the informal economy without major setbacks. In these circumstances, proving that more specific corruption offences such as aggravated collusion, embezzlement, bribery, etc. were committed is particularly difficult. The offence of illicit enrichment is therefore intended to repress crimes against public administration as a last resort and in a residual manner. It is a criminal policy tool that departs from the basic concepts of criminal law and seeks to repress acts of corruption that, in the context of the informality (and other hurdles) mentioned above, are difficult to prosecute.

Legal basis

The legal basis for Peru's illicit enrichment law is contained in the following instruments:

- The Inter-American Convention Against Corruption, Article IX.

- The United Nations Convention Against Corruption, Article 20.

- The Penal Code, Article 401 .

Features

In Peru, the crime of illicit enrichment has a peculiar nature as it does not punish the act or omission of the perpetrator, which are key elements of ordinary criminal prosecutions in civil law countries. Instead, the offence of illicit enrichment punishes a factual situation that corresponds to the possession of assets that cannot be explained.

In other words, the prosecutor does not have to prove a particular conduct but only the illicit enrichment itself. As a result, there is a rupture of the causal link between a conduct and its result (another key element of criminal liability in civil law countries).

It is important to note that the offence of illicit enrichment applies only to public servants. Expressions in the law such as 'by reason of his function', or 'abusing his function' corroborate this situation. Thus, in addition to proving the situation of imbalance, it is necessary to prove the 'public servant' status of the perpetrator and an illegal act of function. However, there could be a petitio principii: proving a specific illegal act of function would lead to incrimination for other crimes. Therefore, the status of a public official should only be proven while the capital increase occurred.

Finally, It is also said that the offence of illicit enrichment operates a reversal of the burden of proof (this is covered in more detail below).

Criminal policy tool

The criminalisation of illicit enrichment makes it possible to prosecute corrupt officials (and their assets) on the basis of an unjustified increase of their wealth. According to jurisprudence, the latter constitutes objective proof of the existence of a crime.

The offence of illicit enrichment is part of a set of legislative measures that implement a state criminal policy against the rise of organised economic crime. The aim of the illicit enrichment provision is to avoid impunity in situations where the prosecution has carried out a thorough investigation into the origin of unjustified wealth but could not identify an underlying offence to the relevant standard of proof. In this sense, the illicit enrichment offence constitutes the last resort (ultima ratio) of the criminal justice system to punish a behaviour that has led to an increase in the official's assets.

Burden of proof

The question of who bears the burden of proof in the offence of illicit enrichment in civil law systems is widely debated in doctrine and jurisprudence. The debated question is whether or not this offence introduces a reversal of the burden of proof.

Some considerations:

- In criminal proceedings, the burden of proof rests with the Public Prosecutor's Office.

- Therefore, there remains a basic duty of the Public Prosecutor's Office to prove the elements of the criminal offence.

- By virtue of the procedural rules relevant to the investigation stage, it is up to the investigating prosecutor to provide the necessary evidence to justify his or her judicial claim.

Against this backdrop, it can be said that there is no full reversal of the burden of proof in illicit enrichment proceedings. The prosecutor must at least prove that there is an imbalance in the assets of the accused official, taking into account his or her declared legal income and his or her recognisable assets. And as noted above, the criminalisation of illicit enrichment makes it possible to prosecute corrupt officials (and their assets) solely on the basis of the increased wealth as it does not require the proof of a specific underlying offence.

If an imbalance is demonstrated by the prosecutor, then a rebuttable presumption arises that illicit enrichment has occurred, and the defendant must demonstrate that this presumption is incorrect, and that there is a legal explanation for the assets in questions.

Causality

Criminal law in civil law countries require that a result (the crime) is the consequence of an unlawful behaviour (causality principle). The approach to illicit enrichment is to circumvent the causal link requirements by focusing the criminal responsibility on the result rather than on the behaviour of the perpetrator: the increase in wealth.

Jurisprudence has determined that in matters of illicit enrichment there is an obligation to prove the causal link between the enrichment and the official position of the perpetrator of the crime, since, as the law states, 'by the nature of the illicit act, the official must have made use of his position to unlawfully increase his wealth'. The enrichment must take place therefore while the perpetrator is in office.

Asset recovery

As a final point, it is important to note that the offence of illicit enrichment does not offer a different regime from other offences with regards to asset recovery. Where proceeds of crime exist, they should be subject to the ordinary regime of criminal confiscation, which under national law is an ancillary consequence of the penalty.

For example, the mansion that the official cannot explain will be confiscated in the context of the criminal proceedings against the corrupt official. As explained above, the reversal of the burden of proof plays an important role in which party bears its burden.

It is worth mentioning that due to its residual or subsidiary nature, illicit enrichment does not make it possible to know exactly the origin of the increase in wealth. Particularly, whether the enrichment originates in private money (as in bribery) or public money (as in embezzlement). As a consequence, the assets involved in the offence cannot be subject to civil reparation or restitution, which presupposes the identification of a specific offence and a victim entitled to restitution or compensation.

5.4 An alternative to illicit enrichment laws: The non-conviction forfeiture remedy contained in Ireland's Proceeds of Crime Act 1996

Francis H. Cassidy

National member for Ireland at Eurojust and former Bureau Legal Officer to the Criminal Assets Bureau

The forfeiture remedy provided for in the Proceeds of Crime Act 1996 ('the POCA') can be difficult to categorise within a legal context. When it was drafted, the POCA was not based on any existing international model, but primarily on the Offences Against the State (Amendment) Act 1985 – a provision designed to target terrorist financing in Ireland.

In brief, it constitutes a statutory remedy, exercised by officers of the State, operating in the following four stages: an interim order, an interlocutory order, receivership and a disposal order.

The key features of the POCA are as follows:

1. It applies to 'specified' property having a value of not less than '5,000 Euros, which directly or indirectly constitutes proceeds of crime, i.e. it operates in rem.

2. Issues of evidence are determined by way of the civil, rather than criminal, evidential test, i.e. 'on the balance of probabilities'.

3. In the first stage of proceedings, the High Court may grant an interim order, ex parte, to freeze property on an application to it by a member of An Garda Síochána not below the rank of Chief Superintendent,[524] once it is satisfied that this property constitutes directly or indirectly the proceeds of crime (Section 2).

4. In the second stage of proceedings, the court may thereafter grant an interlocutory order over such property on application on notice within 21 days, if it appears to the court that the said property constitutes directly or indirectly the proceeds of crime unless the respondent (or any other person) shows to the satisfaction of the court that the particular property does not constitute, directly or indirectly, proceeds of crime (Section 3).

5. During these proceedings, the 'belief' of a member of An Garda Síochána not below the rank of Chief Superintendent shall be 'evidence' (Section 8).

6. Also during proceedings, the court can make an order directing a respondent to furnish details of his earnings over the previous 6 years and to outline his assets (Section 9).

---

524 Or an officer of the Revenue Commissioners (Proceeds of Crime Act 1996 (Ireland), Section 1(1)).

7. It is important to note that any person, including a victim, claiming to have a right to the property can make an application to the court to have this order discharged (Section 3(3)), and that the court is further empowered to vary a Section 2 or 3 order for the purpose of releasing funds for essential legal, business and living expenses (Section 6).

8. Where an interim or interlocutory order is in force, the Act provides for the appointment of a Receiver to either manage the property or, as is more usual, to sell the property and lodge such proceeds to an interest bearing bank account pending a further order of the court (Section 7).

9. Once a Section 3 interlocutory order has been in place for 7 years, the court is empowered to make a disposal order transferring all such property to the benefit of the Central Exchequer (Section 4).

10. The court is also empowered to make an order compensating any respondent should any order made under this Act be shown to have acted unjustly against such respondent (Section 16). It is arguable that this provision obviates the necessity for the Applicant to give an undertaking as to damages, as would ordinarily be required in the case of an application for injunction.

In practice, the courts have been satisfied to determine that a full Section 3 hearing, which may have involved submissions by the respondent challenging the state's case (pursuant to Section 3 (3)), to be a final hearing. Therefore, if the court has concluded in the course of such a hearing that the property in question is the proceeds of crime, it will generally proceed to appoint a receiver to hold, manage and maintain the 'specified' property for the seven-year period before a final disposal order can be made and the property is assigned to the state.[525] The Supreme Court expressed the view that to leave the respondent in possession of the property, which the same court has determined to be the proceeds of crime, for a further seven years would be inconsistent with the purpose of the act.[526]

That being said, such receivership orders tend to take into account the circumstances of the respondent, spouses and needs of dependent children. For instance, spouses have been granted temporary rights of residence and receivership orders have been stayed pending the completion of exams by minors.

It should therefore be noted that it is not the Section 3 order itself, but its combination with a contemporaneous receivership order, that serves to deprive the respondent of the proceeds of his criminal activity in the medium term, and formal title to the property itself does not pass until seven years later when the final disposal order is made. This permits a victim or legitimate owner to lay claim to the property during this time.

---

525 On the application of the Criminal Assets Bureau pursuant to Section 7.

526 Note the judgement of Hardiman J, in CAB v Kelly & Anor [2012] IESC 64.

A unique feature of the POCA: Section 8 belief evidence

While the court may consider the 'belief' of a member of An Garda Síochána as evidence under the POCA, it should be emphasised that it is still up to the court to determine the 'weight' attached to such evidence. The correct procedure regarding the consideration of such evidence, as outlined below by McCracken J in *F. McK v G.W.D*[527] in the seven-step rule, is illustrative:

> It seems to me that the correct procedure for a trial judge in circumstances such as those in the present case is:
>
> 1. He should firstly consider the position under Section 8. He should consider the evidence given by the member or authorised officer of his belief and at the same time consider any other evidence, such as that of the two police officers in the present case, which might point to reasonable grounds for that belief;
>
> 2. If he is satisfied that there are reasonable grounds for the belief, he should then make a specific finding that the belief of the member or authorised officer is evidence;
>
> 3. Only then should he go on to consider the position under Section 3. He should consider the evidence tendered by the plaintiff, which in the present case would be both the evidence of the member or authorised officer under Section 8 and indeed the evidence of the other police officers;
>
> 4. He should make a finding whether this evidence constitutes a prima facie case under Section 3 and, if he does so find, the onus shifts to the defendant or other specified person;
>
> 5. He should then consider the evidence furnished by the defendant or other specified person and determine whether it is satisfied that the onus undertaken by the defendant or other specified person has been fulfilled;
>
> 6. If he is satisfied that the defendant or other specified person has satisfied his onus of proof then the proceedings should be dismissed.
>
> 7. If he is not so satisfied he should then consider whether there would be a serious risk of injustice. If the steps followed in that order, there should be little risk of the type of confusion which arose in the present case.

This has a practical effect that if a respondent decides not to give evidence showing where the property came from lawfully, the court will be able to rely on the evidence of the Chief to make a determination, however jurisprudence suggests that such a determination should not be made without some form of corroborative evidence. For instance, McGuinness J stated in *Gilligan v Criminal Assets Bureau*[528] that such evidence is not 'conclusive' and is 'open to challenge' and that 'a court should be slow to make orders under Section 3 on the basis of such evidence without other corroborating evidence'.[529]

---

527 F.McK v GWD [2004] 2 I.R. 470 at [70].

528 Gilligan v Criminal Assets Bureau [1997] IEHC 106.

529 ibid., at [160].

Section 9 orders requiring respondents to furnish information regarding property

Another controversial section under the POCA empowers a court to order a respondent to provide an affidavit specifying the property that they possess or control and their sources of income.

Jurisprudence and subsequent amendments however have also limited the use of this section in practice. Specifically, due to concern that a Section 9 order could breach a respondent's right against self-incrimination, Justice Moriarty was loath to grant such an order in *M v D*[530] without an indemnity from the Director of Public Prosecutions that such a disclosure would not be used in the course of a criminal trial. A subsequent legislative amendment addressed this concern, decreeing such an affidavit as inadmissible in evidence in any criminal proceedings against that person or his or her spouse.[531] .

Challenges to the POCA regarding its effect on legal rights

In the course of applications made under the POCA, a number of respondents have challenged its compatibility with the legal rights outlined in the Constitution of Ireland (Bunreacht na hÉireann).[532]

Almost all of the relevant points were canvassed in the cases of *Gilligan v Criminal Assets Bureau, Murphy .v. GM PB PC Ltd*[533] and the joint hearing of the appeals for both these cases by the Supreme Court in *Murphy v. M(G)*,[534] delivered on the 18th October 2001.[535] The following are some of the key arguments and determinations that were raised in these proceedings:

Challenge: The mechanism in the POCA is in essence criminal and not civil and subsequently does not ensure the due procedure protections enshrined by Article 38 of the Constitution (i.e. the presumption of innocence, the criminal standard of proof 'beyond reasonable doubt' rather than the civil standard of 'on the balance of possibilities' and a right to a trial by jury).

> **Held:** The proceedings in the POCA are civil, not criminal in nature: 'There is no provision for the arrest or detention of any person, for the admission of persons to bail, for the imprisonment of a person in default of payment of a penalty, for a form of criminal trial initiated by summons or indictment, for the recording of a conviction in any form or for the entering of a nolle prosequi at any stage' - all elements which would indicate that the POCA creates a criminal offence.[536]

---

530   M v. D, IR 175 (unreported judgment).

531   Proceeds of Crime (Amendment) Act 2005 (Ireland), Section 11.

532   Early challenges in this context were made in reference to the constitution rather than the ECtHR as Ireland did not enact implementing legislation regarding this convention until 2001, despite being a signatory in 1951.

533   Murphy .v. GM PB PC Ltd [1999] IEHC 5.

534   Murphy v. M(G), [2001] IESC82.

535   ibid.

536   ibid.

Challenge: The Act constitutes an unfair reversal of the (standard) onus of proof.

> **Held:** The reversal only operates after the establishment to the court's satisfaction of certain issues. Furthermore, there is a right to cross-examine. Finally, there is no 'constitutional infirmity' in the procedure whereby the onus is placed on a person seeking property to negative the inference from evidence adduced that a criminal offence has been committed.[537]

Challenge: The Act infringes a right against self-incrimination.

> **Held:** The court agreed with Moriarty J. in *M.v. D* that before an order is made under Section 9 of the Act there should be a requirement of an indemnity from use by the Director of Public Prosecutions of any evidence given pursuant to such an order.[538]

Challenge: The Act in its operation breaches rights to private property.

> **Held:** The POCA does provide onerous and far reaching penalties and forfeitures but these are directly connected with the establishment to the satisfaction of the court that the property concerned is either directly or indirectly the proceeds of crime.[539] Furthermore, the State has a 'legitimate interest' in the forfeiture of the proceeds of crime,[540] and the 'right to private ownership can not hold a place so high in the hierarchy of rights that it protects the position of assets illegally acquired or held.'[541]

Challenge: The Act is in breach of Article 15(5) of the Constitution in that it is retrospective in its effect.

> **Held:** The acquisition of assets which derive from crime was not an illegal activity before the passing of the POCA and did not become an illegal activity because of the POCA.[542]

Conclusion

The POCA was seen as radical at the time of its introduction, and very much at the forefront of non-conviction based remedies within the European Union. It does not quite reflect the 'unexplained wealth order' legislation existing in other jurisdictions around the world, due to the higher level of 'prosecutor threshold' required in the first four steps of McCracken's

---

537   Gilligan v Criminal Assets Bureau [1997] IEHC 106 at [106].

538   ibid., at [119]; Also note the subsequent introduction contained in the Proceeds of Crime Amendment) Act 2005 (Ireland), which now provides statutory guarantees regarding this issue.

539   ibid., at [132].

540   ibid., at [134].

541   ibid., at [136].

542   ibid., at [140].

judgement and the reservation against a reliance on belief evidence alone expressed in McGuinness's judgement. Instead, it is very much a unique Irish solution to an Irish problem, and one that has contributed enormously to the ability of the Criminal Assets Bureau to address organised crime and recover criminal proceeds.

5.5 Seeking international cooperation in illicit enrichment cases

Jonathan Spicer

Senior Asset Recovery Specialist with the International Centre for Asset Recovery, Barrister and former Specialist Prosecutor and Crown Advocate of the Crown Prosecution Service (UK)

Criminal activity is not confined to national borders and illicit enrichment investigations will often have an international element. Investigators may seek information or evidence from other jurisdictions which relates to the suspected criminal activity that has led to the illicit enrichment or that relates to the possession, concealment or use of illicit assets.

For example, a public official may be suspected of using a foreign corporate structure to hold illicit funds in bank accounts in another jurisdiction. In order to progress the investigation (and potentially freeze the funds), prosecutors will need to use Mutual Legal Assistance (MLA) to obtain evidence from the respective jurisdictions where the foreign company is registered and where the bank account is located.

Alternatively, it may be known that the child of a public official attends a renowned (and expensive) fee paying school overseas. Investigators would be seeking information not only on the amount of fees that have been paid, but also on the source and manner of the payments. The school may voluntarily provide the information on the fees payment but if it does not a court order will be necessary.

Accordingly, insofar as this information is not publicly available, assistance will be required from the authorities in the jurisdictions where intelligence or evidence is held. Whether that jurisdiction is able to assist will usually depend upon its domestic law and also whether it has either illicit enrichment as an offence or civil procedure.

Basis of international cooperation

International cooperation exists at both informal and formal levels. Informal international cooperation is usually seen as cooperation at a law enforcement level or as police to police assistance. Often this will amount to intelligence sharing (for example between financial intelligence units) or it may involve assistance which can be provided without the need for coercive measures (such as obtaining the voluntary assistance of the school in the example above). As these enquiries may be made at an early stage where the investigation is not limited to illicit enrichment but also looking at underlying criminality, there are likely to be fewer difficulties in obtaining assistance.

Formal means of international cooperation, known as MLA, is where a state requests another state to apply its laws to obtain evidence for use in the proceedings being brought by the requesting state. This cooperation usually requires the use of coercive measures by the requested state, for example searches of properties, interviewing of witnesses or production of documents. This formal means of cooperation is usually based on multilateral treaties, bilateral treaties or other forms of state to state agreements. In terms of illicit enrichment proceedings, MLA may be required to obtain evidence during the investigation stage, for example bank statements, or may be required to freeze assets or to enforce a final order for confiscation.

Dual criminality

Under the dual criminality principle, states will only provide MLA in criminal matters if the offence being investigated in the requesting state is also an offence in the State being asked to provide assistance. The application of this principle by states which do not recognise an offence of illicit enrichment can often be an obstacle to international cooperation in illicit enrichment investigations.

The promotion of the criminalisation of illicit enrichment as a measure to tackle corruption is seen within UNCAC[543] as well as other regional treaties such as IACAC[544] or AUCPCC.[545] However the introduction of illicit enrichment offences is not compulsory under these conventions. Under UNCAC and the AUCPCC, non-mandatory language permits states to decide themselves whether to implement illicit enrichment laws, while under the IACAC, states may also refrain from introducing an illicit enrichment offence if they deem that it will contravene existing constitutional rights.

While the IACAC and AUCPCC do not address the issue of dual criminality directly, they both have almost identical provisions on assistance to be provided in illicit enrichment investigations, by States Parties that do not introduce illicit enrichment offences.

Under IACAC at Article IX paragraph 3:

> Any State Party that has not established illicit enrichment as an offense shall, insofar as its laws permit, provide assistance and cooperation with respect to this offense as provided in this Convention.[546]

The United States of America posted a reservation on its signing of the IACAC[547] where it stated that it understood it was not obligated to introduce an offence of illicit enrichment, as this would be inconsistent with the United States constitution and fundamental legal principles due to the burden of proof being placed on the defendant. However, the U.S. does make clear that as far as it is permitted by domestic law, it does intend to assist and cooperate with other States Parties investigating illicit enrichment.

---

543   United Nations Convention Against Corruption, Article 20.

544   Inter-American Convention Against Corruption, Article IX.

545   African Union Convention on Preventing and Combating Corruption, Article 8.

546   Article 8 of the AUCPCC adds the phrase 'to the requesting State'.

547   The excerpt of the text of the reservation is contained in footnote 440.

The provisions of UNCAC emphasise the need for cooperation and address dual criminality directly. Article 43(1) mandates State Parties to cooperate in criminal matters in accordance with Article 44 to 50 of the Convention, before addressing dual criminality in Article 43(2):

> In matters of international cooperation, whenever dual criminality is considered a requirement, it shall be deemed fulfilled irrespective of whether the laws of the requested State Party place the offence within the same category of offence or denominate the offence by the same terminology as the requesting State Party, if the conduct underlying the offence for which assistance is sought is a criminal offence under the laws of both States Parties.

Thus, States Parties receiving MLA requests cannot refuse on the basis of the name of the offence or the category under which it is deemed to fall, but must look at the actual conduct which constitutes the offence and consider whether this would amount to an offence under the domestic law.

However, illicit enrichment offences, and particularly those that include a shifting of the burden of proof on to the defendant, do not compare easily with other types of offending. Nonetheless, Article 46, which addresses mutual legal assistance requires State Parties to 'afford one another the widest measure of mutual legal assistance in investigations, prosecutions and judicial proceedings in relation to the offences covered by [the] Convention'.

Finally, Article 46 (9) of UNCAC makes further provision on MLA and dual criminality:

(a) A requested State Party, in responding to a request for assistance pursuant to this article in the absence of dual criminality, shall take into account the purposes of this Convention, as set forth in article 1;

(b) States Parties may decline to render assistance pursuant to this article on the ground of absence of dual criminality. However, a requested State Party shall, where consistent with the basic concepts of its legal system, render assistance that does not involve coercive action. Such assistance may be refused when requests involve matters of a de minimis nature or matters for which the cooperation or assistance sought is available under other provisions of this Convention;

(c) Each State Party may consider adopting such measures as may be necessary to enable it to provide a wider scope of assistance pursuant to this article in the absence of dual criminality.

It can be said, therefore, that the framers of the Convention sought to encourage the provision of assistance by States Parties which had not criminalised offences under the Convention (including illicit enrichment) to those States Parties which have. Requested states need to consider the purposes of the Convention under Article 1 and to consider whether it is possible to provide assistance falling short of coercive measures under their domestic law.

Despite these provisions, the lack of dual criminality may still prevent jurisdictions from using coercive measures to provide assistance in illicit enrichment investigations / prosecutions. Where this is the case, requesting states may be able to obtain help by outlining the suspected criminal behaviour which is thought to have led to the illicit enrichment. When this behaviour is considered by the requested state, it may consider that it is possible to provide support in the obtaining of evidence using coercive measures. In this respect, requesting states should consider providing a wide explanation of the facts revealed by the investigation and the activities of the suspects, as this will potentially provide grounds for the requested state to assist. There is a caveat that should be highlighted here, which is the rule of specialty. This is that the evidence which is obtained by the requested state should only be used for the investigation or proceedings stated in the request. Therefore, it would not be permitted to apply for evidence on the basis of a corruption investigation and then use it in a hitherto unmentioned prosecution for illicit enrichment. Permission has to be sought from the state which provided the evidence.

Scope for reform?

One of the reasons for the adoption by states of a criminal offence of illicit enrichment is due to the difficulties in investigating the underlying criminality, especially in cases of corruption. However, an offence of illicit enrichment has not been widely adopted in those states where the assets may be held or through which they have been laundered. Notwithstanding this, many of those states encourage the adoption of procedures which tackle corruption and may have some alternative form of addressing illicit wealth, for example non-conviction based forfeiture procedures (incorporating unexplained wealth investigative orders such as the United Kingdom). This does not seem to be enough to overcome the issue of dual criminality for some jurisdictions and the question arises whether further steps should be taken internationally to promote a limited exception to the rule on dual criminality which would apply to MLA requests to obtain evidence in illicit enrichment[548] cases.

---

548 Following the definition given in UNCAC, Article 20.

Index

A

Asset declarations 85, 111, 138

B

Burden of proof 6, 23, 60, 62, 99, 101, 102, 104, 105, 121, 122, 123, 124, 128, 129, 131, 135, 136, 137, 138, 139, 140, 142, 143, 145, 146, 147, 164, 165, 166, 174, 175

C

Calculations 57, 111, 112, 115

Civil recovery 13, 65, 79, 86 (see Non-conviction based confiscation)

Civil restitution 4, 40

Countries 11

Afghanistan 45, 57, 92, 116

Algeria 45, 50, 58

Angola 45, 46

Antigua and Barbuda 45, 52, 68, 75

Argentina 21, 30, 31, 45, 50, 54, 58, 62, 72, 104, 116, 136, 145, 147

Armenia 45, 58

Australia - Australian Capital Territory 24

Australia - Federal Jurisdiction 24, 70, 141, 149, 152, 153

Australia - New South Wales 24, 60, 143

Australia - Northern Territory 24, 56, 77

Australia - Queensland 24, 71

Australia - South Australia 24, 71

Australia - Tasmania 24, 56

Australia - Victoria 24

Australia - Western Australia 23, 32, 60, 66, 72, 77, 93, 103, 140, 153

Bahamas 45, 64, 66, 71, 72, 77, 78, 148

Bangladesh 45, 51

Barbados 79, 87

Benin 45, 53

Bhutan 45, 52, 56, 75

Bolivia 45, 49, 72, 150

Botswana 45, 52, 56, 75

Brazil 45, 46

Brunei Darussalam 22, 45, 52, 63, 74

Burkina Faso 45, 53, 59, 118

Case list

A

- Arrêt n° 07/08/CC/MC du 20 novembre 2008 (Cour Constitutionnelle) (Niger) 64
- Attorney General v Ho Pui-yiu [1981] HKLR 110 (Hong Kong) 127, 128
- Attorney General v Hui Kin-hong [1995] HKCLR 227 (Hong Kong) 117, 125, 126, 127, 128, 130, 131, 133, 134

C

- CA Paris, 14 mars 2018, n° 17/03650 (France) 111
- CAB v Kelly & Anor [2012] IESC 64 (Ireland) 168
- Cámara Nacional de Apelaciones en lo Criminal y Correccional, sala VII, 'L., C. Y otros", Fallos 45793 (2017) (Argentina) 106
- Cámara Nacional de Casación Penal, sala IV, 'Alsogaray', causa n° 4787 (2005) (Argentina) 104, 117, 125, 136, 137, 146
- Case No. 1-135/2018(5846/17), Decision of the Constitutional Court of Ukraine (Ukraine) 138
- Case no. 14/2015-1/2016-2/2016-14/2016-15/2016- The Constitutional Court of the Republic of Lithuania in the name of the Republic of Lithuania ruling on the compliance of Paragraph 1 of Article 1891 of the Criminal Code of the Republic of Lithuania with the Constitution of the Republic of Lithuania 15 March 2017, no KT4-N3/2017 (Lithuania) 100, 115, 119, 124, 136, 146
- Case no. 60a/2014 – The Constitutional Court of the Republic of Moldova, the judgment of 16 April 2015 (Moldova) 150
- Chung Cheong v The Queen CACC001364/1977 (Hong Kong) 114
- Corte Suprema de Justicia de la Nación Argentina, "Alsogaray", Fallos 331:2799 (2008) (Argentina) 104, 136, 147
- Corte Suprema de Justicia de la República, Sala Penal Transitoria Casación, Manuel Enrique Cárdenas Valseca, n° 953-2017 (2018) (Peru) 105, 106
- Criminal case no. 2K-P-93/2014, 11 April 2014 (Lithuania) 150

D

- DB v Commissione Nazionale per le Società e la Borsa (Consob) (Case C-481/19) 2 February 2021 (European Court of Human Rights (ECtHR)) 143
- Director of Public Prosecutions for Western Australia v Gypsy Jokers Motorcycle Club Inc (2005) WASC 61 (Australia) 140
- Director of Public Prosecutions v Morris [No2] [2010] WADC 148 (Australia) 103, 141

L

M

N - P - Q

R

S

T

U - V - W

Visit **illicitenrichment.baselgovernance.org** to view and download the Annexes to this book for free.

Annex I

'A Compilation of Illicit Enrichment Legislation and Other Relevant Legislation', contains excerpts of text from all the illicit enrichment laws that were identified in the research process behind this publication. It also includes excerpts from text of the other asset recovery legislative instruments that are mentioned in this publication for comparative purposes.

Annex II

'Proving Illicit Enrichment Using Financial Investigations and Source and Application of Funds Analysis' is a technical guide for practitioners. It provides an overview of one method that can be used to clearly demonstrate that a person has enjoyed wealth that could not possibly have been derived from lawful sources, namely the Source and Application of Funds Analysis method. It includes a step-by-step guide to the financial investigation that should be used to inform this analysis process.

Printed in Poland
by Amazon Fulfillment
Poland Sp. z o.o., Wrocław

76279236R00112